Data Resource Quality

*Turning Bad Habits
into Good Practices*

Addison-Wesley Information Technology Series

Capers Jones and David S. Linthicum, Consulting Editors

The information technology (IT) industry is in the public eye now more than ever before because of a number of major issues in which software technology and national policies are closely related. As the use of software expands, there is a continuing need for business and software professionals to stay current with the state of the art in software methodologies and technologies. The goal of the Addison-Wesley Information Technology Series is to cover any and all topics that affect the IT community: These books illustrate and explore how information technology can be aligned with business practices to achieve business goals and support business imperatives. Addison-Wesley has created this innovative series to empower you with the benefits of the industry experts' experience.

For more information point your browser to
http://www.awl.com/cseng/series/it/

Sid Adelman, Larissa Terpeluk Moss, *Data Warehouse Project Management*. ISBN: 0201616351

Wayne Applehans, Alden Globe, and Greg Laugero, *Managing Knowledge: A Practical Web-Based Approach*. ISBN: 0-201-43315-X

Michael H. Brackett, Data Resource Quality: Turning Bad Habits into Good Practices. ISBN: 0201713063

Gregory C. Dennis and James R. Rubin, *Mission-Critical Java™ Project Management: Business Strategies, Applications, and Development*. ISBN: 0-201-32573-X

Kevin Dick, *XML: A Manager's Guide*. ISBN: 0-201-43335-4

Jill Dyché, *e-Data: Turning Data into Information with Data Warehousing*. ISBN: 0-201-65780-5

Dr. Nick V. Flor, *Web Business Engineering: Using Offline Activites to Drive Internet Strategies*. ISBN: 020160468X

David Garmus and David Herron, *Function Point Analysis: Measurement Practices for Successful Software Projects*. ISBN: 0201699443

Capers Jones, *Software Assessments, Benchmarks, and Best Practices*. ISBN: 0-201-48542-7

Capers Jones, *The Year 2000 Software Problem: Quantifying the Costs and Assessing the Consequences*. ISBN: 0-201-30964-5

Ravi Kalakota and Marcia Robinson, *e-Business: Roadmap for Success*. ISBN: 0-201-60480-9

David S. Linthicum, *Enterprise Application Integration*. ISBN: 0-201-61583-5

Sergio Lozinsky, *Enterprise-Wide Software Solutions: Integration Strategies and Practices*. ISBN: 0-201-30971-8

Patrick O'Beirne, *Managing the Euro in Information Systems: Strategies for Successful Changeover*. ISBN: 0-201-60482-5

Mai-lan Tomsen, *Killer Content: Strategies for Web Content and E-Commerce*. ISBN: 0-201-65786-4

Bill Wiley, *Essential System Requirements: A Practical Guide to Event-Driven Methods*. ISBN: 0-201-61606-8

Bill Zoellick, *Web Engagement: Connecting to Customers in e-Business*. ISBN: 0-201-65766-X

Data Resource Quality

Turning Bad Habits into Good Practices

Michael H. Brackett

Addison-Wesley

Boston • San Francisco • New York • Toronto • Montreal
London • Munich • Paris • Madrid
Capetown • Sydney • Tokyo • Singapore • Mexico City

The publisher offers discounts on this book when ordered in quantity for special sales. For more information, please contact:

Pearson Education Corporate Sales Division
One Lake Street
Upper Saddle River, NJ 07458
(800) 382-3419
corpsales@pearsontechgroup.com

Visit us on the Web at www.awl.com/cseng/

Library of Congress Cataloging-in-Publication Data

Brackett, Michael H.
    Data resource quality : turning bad habits into good practices /
    Michael H. Brackett
        p.   cm.—(Addison-Wesley information technology series)
    Includes bibliographical references and index.
    ISBN 0-201-71306-3 (alk. paper)
    1. Database management—Quality control. I. Title. II. Series.
    QA76.9.D3 B677 2000
    005.74—dc21   00-060553

ISBN 0-201-71306-3

Text printed on recycled and acid-free paper.
1 2 3 4 5 6 7 8 9 10 — CRS — 04 03 02 01 00
First printing, September 2000

To Chris

Contents

CHAPTER 3 **COMPREHENSIVE DATA DEFINITIONS** 51

CHAPTER 4   PROPER DATA STRUCTURE   73

CHAPTER 8   ACCEPTABLE DATA AVAILABILITY   189

Foreword

As we enter the 21st century, modern life depends upon computerized information systems in the extreme. We exchange goods and services, book travel reservations, and record our investments using our computer systems. The technology we use today is powerful, flexible, and dependable. The decreasing cost of information technology has enabled businesses and government agencies to automate more of their work. Still, organizations around the world face the same barrier to meeting their business objectives with today's rapidly improving information technology—poor data quality.

Poor Data Quality Adds Time and Expense to Data Warehousing

The signs of the data quality problem are everywhere. Data warehousing projects face difficult data access and cleaning issues. Projects put teams of people on detail to find, document, clean up, and integrate legacy data. At one financial services firm, data duplication was so bad that a single data warehouse project had 121 data sources. The work involved in data cleansing and integrating can add millions of dollars in expense to large projects.

A Barrier to E-Commerce Projects

Poor data quality, integration, and accuracy constitute a barrier to rapidly implementing e-commerce systems. Large firms find that locating, documenting, and cleaning legacy data takes longer than building the web-based software that makes e-commerce work. As large, mortar-based companies become more involved in e-commerce, many will find their ability to deploy solutions in the marketplace limited by the quality of their data resources.

Data Quality's Impact on Shareholder Equity

For twenty years I have helped to build information systems and databases in many of the world's largest corporations. Even though we have known the fundamentals of improving data quality, information technology professionals have chosen not to apply these practices consistently. The industry's failure to do so has increased the cost and work burden for thousands of enterprises around the world. Poor data quality doesn't just add time and expense to information systems work, it means extra work for business people as well. One of my favorite examples of this phenomenon is the financial service firm with a "re-work department." The thing the re-work department re-worked was the data it sent to its customers.

As e-commerce becomes the backbone of every modern economy, companies will succeed or fail based upon their ability to deploy and use e-commerce systems. Successful enterprises will be able to mobilize data about their customers, products, and services quickly, beating their competitors into the marketplace. Enterprises that are forced to spend months or years trying to integrate and mobilize their data will see degradation in the value of their equity. Firms that can't manage customer and inventory data well will be left in the dust, replaced by existing competitors or new entrants.

Data Resource Quality: Turning Bad Habits into Good Practices provides insight into a major problem faced by information systems managers around the world: data quality is a barrier to meeting their goals and schedules. As we move into a time of pervasive e-commerce via the Internet, data quality issues will become more than an expense—they will become a barrier to success.

Michael Brackett provides a wake-up call for information technology managers around the world. We can continue with our current practices, slowing down our ability to compete, or we can buckle down and focus on the basics of improving data quality. This book provides a look at the fundamentals of good data management practice. Use it well.

Ron Shelby
Detroit, Michigan

Preface

Why is the data resource failing to adequately support an organization's information needs? What did organizations do to get into their current disparate data situation? What do organizations, public and private, large and small, new and old, do to ruin their data resource quality? What do organizations consistently do, or not do, to mess up one of their most critical resources? Why have people allowed this situation to happen and to continue for so long?

What is it that organizations are doing wrong that results in a low-quality data resource? What bad habits should be avoided? What good practices should be followed? People are asking me these questions with increasing regularity. The underlying theme of most of these questions is, What can organizations do to prevent any further data disparity and develop a high-quality data resource?

I started emphasizing the need to improve data quality in the early 1980s and have continued to emphasize the importance of data quality for the last 15 to 20 years. I have written several books and many articles about the current state of the data resource and how a quality data resource can be developed that truly supports the organization's business information needs. These books and articles explain the concepts, principles, and techniques for designing and building a high-quality data resource within a single, comprehensive, organization-wide common data architecture.

This book is about the ten most prominent ways I have found that organizations destroy their data resource quality or prevent development of a high-quality data resource. It is built around ten sets of bad habits organizations have that build defects into the data resource; bad habits that increase the cost of building, maintaining, and using a data resource; bad habits that waste resources on data; bad habits that use the data resource to cripple an organization; bad habits that compromise business strategies by using data as an internal weapon. If I were to set about slowly, quietly, and subtly ruining the quality of an organization's data resource, these are the things that I would do.

Not all organizations have all of these bad habits, nor are the bad habits done with the same degree of severity on all data in all organizations. An organization's data resource is a blend of the bad habits and the severity of those bad habits governs the current state of the data resource in any organization. These are not all the possible bad habits either; but, overall, they are the most frequent and most severe bad habits that lead to a low-quality data resource.

The material in this book was gained over the last 20 years as I reviewed the state of the data resource in many public and private sector organizations. In 1990[1] I made a statement that I never ceased to be amazed at the ingenious ways that organizations could mess up their data. Since then, I have been literally astounded at the very ingenious, and sometimes quite stupid, ways that organizations ruin a very critical resource.

Understanding the bad habits, however, does not eliminate those bad habits or improve data resource quality. It only raises the awareness about problems that cause a low-quality data resource. A more positive approach is to understand what needs to be done to replace the bad habits with good practices. The main emphasis of this book is what organizations, public or private, large or small, local or multi-national, can do to turn bad habits into good practices that lead to improved data resource quality.

The first chapter explains the current state of the data resource in most public and private sector organizations. The next ten chapters explain each of the ten sets of bad habits that contribute to a low-quality data resource, the impacts of those bad habits, how those bad habits can be turned into good practices, the benefits of the good practices, and the best practices to implement for quick results. The first five of these chapters deal with architectural issues, and the next five chapters deal with non-architectural issues that pertain largely to organizational culture and management of the data resource. The final chapter describes a new direction for improving data resource quality.

---

[1] Brackett, Michael H., *Practical Data Design*, Prentice Hall, 1990.

This is not a technical book and does not contain all the techniques for building and maintaining a high-quality data resource and resolving all existing data disparity. Those topics are covered quite adequately in two previous books.[2] This is a detail book about what can go wrong with data resource quality and what can be done to stop data disparity and improve data resource quality. It contains a summary of the concepts and principles presented in previous books and presents some new concepts and principles about improving data resource quality. It emphasizes what can be done to implement an organization-wide, integrated, subject-oriented data architecture and then build a high-quality data resource within that architecture.

This book is not about the tools or technology currently available to ensure a high-quality data resource. Technology evolves, and what may be current technology when this book was written will be inappropriate or obsolete in the near future.[3] The fundamental problems that result in a low-quality data resource and the basic principles for ensuring a high-quality data resource are, however, relatively static and are independent of the current technology. Therefore, this book concentrates on the basic principles pertaining to data resource quality and not on current technology.

Some people may perceive that this book is academic or esoteric because it does not explain the current tool set that is available for developing a high-quality data resource. These people are looking for readily-available technology that will help them solve their current problems, and anything that does not provide how-to solutions to those problems is perceived to be academic or esoteric. These people are usually looking for quick-fix solutions that resolve current problems with little concern for the future.

Some people may feel that new organizations or organizations involved in Internet and Web-based business do not need to understand what can go wrong with a data resource. These people, however, need to understand what can go wrong so they can prevent the development of a low-quality data resource. Every organization was new at one time and every organization implemented new

---

[2] Brackett, Michael H., *Data Sharing Using a Common Data Architecture*, John Wiley & Sons, 1994, and Brackett, Michael H., *The Data Warehouse Challenge: Taming Data Chaos*, John Wiley & Sons, 1996.

[3] There are very few tools currently available that support the development of a high-quality data resource within a common data architecture.

technology at one time, yet these organizations have low-quality data resources today. There is no reason to believe that new organizations today will be immune to the evolution of a low-quality data resource. It is the case that *those who do not know history are destined to repeat it!* Organizations that know what can go wrong with a data resource are more likely to take steps to avoid those situations than organizations that do not know what can go wrong.

There are two major phases to improving data resource quality. The first phase is a proactive phase to stop any further data disparity; the second is a reactive phase to reduce or eliminate the existing data disparity. This book is about what needs to be done to stop the burgeoning increase in data disparity that is occurring in most organizations today. It does not explain what needs to be done to resolve any existing data disparity. A forthcoming book describes what needs to be done to formally transform existing disparate data within a common data architecture.

This book is intended to raise awareness about the reasons why data resource quality deteriorates and what can be done to prevent those problems. The orientation is toward turning bad habits into good practices that will achieve a high-quality data resource. By understanding what makes the data resource go bad, organizations can learn to recognize the situation and prevent any further data disparity. The material in this book can also be used to evaluate the current state of data resource quality and to lay plans for stopping data disparity and developing a high-quality data resource that produces early results. The material provides hope and encouragement for people who are buried in a data resource mess and perceive that there is no way out.

This book is intended for two audiences. The first audience is executives or managers who need to be aware of the data resource problems, but do not need to be involved with the details about identifying or resolving those problems. The second audience includes people who want to understand what goes wrong with data resource quality and be able to implement solutions to prevent those problems and improve data resource quality.

Chapter 1 explains that the current state of the data resource in most organizations today is one of low quality and that quality is getting lower rather than better. It sets the stage for taking a new direction for improving data resource quality. Chapter 12 is a call to action for organizations to improve their data resource quality, but it is a different type of call for action. It is not the current hype about implementing new technology that can cleanse the data resource in one pass and produce high-quality data. It is a call to action based on what can go wrong with a data resource and what can be done to stop the things that go wrong. These two chapters are useful to both audiences.

Chapters 2 through 11 explain the ten major groups of bad habits that lead to a low-quality data resource and the corresponding good practices that lead to a high-quality data resource. These chapters present the bad habits, the impacts of those bad habits, the good practices that replace the bad habits, the benefits of those good practices, and the best practices that provide early benefits with minimal effort. These chapters are useful to the second audience.

Executives, managers, and others who are interested only in the current state of the data resource and a call to action to improve data resource quality should read Chapter 1 and jump to Chapter 12. They can also refer to Appendix A that summarizes the bad habits and good practices and to Appendix B that summarizes the evaluation criteria for the current state of a data resource. Those who want to understand the specific bad habits and good practices can read the chapters in sequence or can read Chapter 1, jump to Chapter 12, and then return to Chapters 2 through 11.

This book does not explain specific impacts, because the same specific impacts cannot be used for public and private sector organizations. The public sector deals with citizens and the private sector deals with customers. Citizens, in most situations, do not have the same choices that customers have. Unlike customers, they cannot choose to shop elsewhere, wait for sales, or decide not to purchase. They are bound by regulations rather than by choice. Public sector organizations do not face situations like loss of customers, loss of market share, competitive advantage, or bottom-line profits like private sector organizations.

Each organization needs to take the guidelines provided and prepare its own quantitative measures to the impacts of bad habits and benefits of good practices. Organizations are just too varied in their size and orientation to provide general quantitative measures. For example, if a comment was made that a certain bad habit resulted in unnecessary costs of $1,000,000 a year, a large organization might consider this to be *pocket change*. Yet an unnecessary cost of $1,000,000 a year might be double, triple, or quadruple the annual budget of a smaller organization.

The business changes over time, and the information needed to support the business must also change. The data resource must be dynamic enough to provide the data to support those changing information needs. A formal data architecture that is oriented toward the business and integrated across the business is the only way to build a dynamic data resource. If the data architecture is allowed to deviate from this orientation, so will the data resource, the information that is based on the data resource, and the business that is based on the information. If, however, a formal data architecture is properly developed and maintained, a high-quality data resource can be developed and maintained.

You will see in the first chapter that data resource quality is defined as how well the data resource supports the current and future information needs of the organization. Using this definition of data resource quality sidesteps the hype and metrics commonly associated with data resource quality and focuses on what data resource quality really means to the current information needs of an organization. This new focus, however, opens up a broader issue about what data resource quality really means with respect to the future information needs of an organization. Since technology is evolving at an ever-increasing rate, *the ultimate data resource quality is achieving data resource stability across technological change!*

As we enter the new millennium, I believe that progressive organizations will become more interested in data resource quality and in the frameworks and architectures that promote improved quality. As organizations finish resolving their Y2K and Y2K-related problems, the orientation is turning toward data quality and the degree to which the data resource supports the business information needs of an organization. The Y2K problem is only the beginning of many, many more data resource quality issues. It should be the wake-up call to the state of the data resource in many organizations.

Michael H. Brackett
Olympia, Washington
June 2000

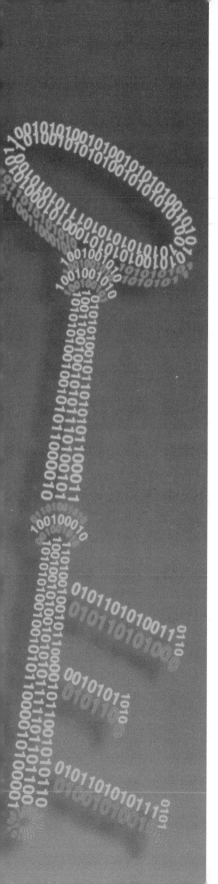

Acknowledgments

I want to thank the many people in both public and private sector organizations who contributed their problems, issues, ideas, experience, and comments about the current state of their data resource and how data resource quality can be improved. Without this tremendous input from professionals and practitioners, this book would not have been possible.

I want to thank David Lotz for his in-depth review of the manuscript, and his comments about the manuscript and data resource quality. Thanks also go to Sandra Hostetter and Cindy Miller who reviewed the manuscript from the firing line perspective. Their comments bring an additional real-world perspective to the data quality issue.

I extend a special thanks to Ron Shelby for his review of the manuscript and for writing the foreword to this book. He has been a professional friend for many years and has always been a strong proponent of formal data resource management and improved data resource quality.

Finally, I want to thank my long-time personal and professional friend John Zachman for his constant interest, encouragement, and support. It was a during a discussion with him at his ZIFA Forum in August 1999 that the spark for this book was created. The discussion was so focused on the problems with data resource quality that I completed the outline on the plane trip home and finished the draft manuscript in November.

About the Author

Mr. Brackett retired from the state of Washington in June 1996, where he was the state's Data Resource Coordinator. He was responsible for developing a common data architecture for the state that spans multiple jurisdictions, such as state agencies, local jurisdictions, Indian tribes, public utilities, and federal agencies, and includes multiple disciplines, such as water resource, growth management, and criminal justice. He is the founder of Data Resource Design and Remodeling and is the consulting data architect specializing in developing integrated data resources for public and private sector organizations.

Mr. Brackett has been in the data processing field for 38 years, during which time he developed many innovative concepts and techniques for designing applications and managing data resources. He is considered the originator of the common data architecture concept, the data resource framework, the data naming taxonomy and data naming vocabulary, the five-schema concept, the three-tier five-schema concept, the expanded five-tier five-schema concept, the data rule concept, and the business intelligence value chain. He has created and defined many new terms to help bring stability to a lexically challenged discipline.

Mr. Brackett has written five books on the topic of application design, data design, and common data architectures. His latest books, *Data Sharing Using a Common Data Architecture* and *The Data Warehouse Challenge: Taming Data Chaos,* explain the concept and uses of a common data architecture for developing an integrated data resource. He is currently writing books on transforming disparate data, data rules as a subset of business rules, and techniques to ensure data resource quality. He has written many articles and given many presentations at local, national, and international conferences. He is a well-known author, speaker, and trainer on data resource design.

Mr. Brackett has a BS in Forestry (forest management), an MS in Forestry (botany) from the University of Washington, and an MS in Soils (geology) from Washington State University. He is a charter member and an active member of the Seattle chapter of DAMA, served as Vice President of Conferences for DAMA International, and is the President of DAMA International for 2000. He taught Data Design and Modeling in the Data Resource Management Certificate Program at the University of Washington, and has been a member of the adjunct faculty at Washington State University and The Evergreen State College. He is listed in Who's Who in the West, Who's Who in Education, and International Who's Who.

CHAPTER 1

State of the Data Resource

> The data resource in most organizations does not adequately meet the dynamic demand for information.

The current state of the data resource in most public and private sector organizations is not good and it is getting worse. In some organizations it is totally chaotic and disruptive to the business. Simply put, the data resource in most organizations is not providing the desired level of support for the current and future information needs of that organization. It may not even be providing an acceptable level of support for the current needs.

Organizations should routinely review the state of their data resource, much the same as the President reviews the state of the union, a governor reviews the state of the state, a county executive reviews the state of the county, or a mayor reviews the state of the city. A state of the data resource report would show its current state and how it could be improved over the next year or biennium, much the same as an annual report summarizes the fiscal well-being of an organization. If, however, a state of the data resource report that reflected the true state of the data resource were prepared, it probably would not be presented to the stockholders or the citizens because their confidence in the organization would be shaken.

Most organizations are routinely, methodically, systematically, consistently ruining the quality of their data resource. They are compromising nearly every effort to maintain or improve their data resource quality. They may be doing it intentionally or unintentionally, knowingly or unknowingly, wittingly or unwittingly, but they are doing it.

I am literally astounded at the millions of hours of productivity that are wasted each year in both public and private sector organizations by the impacts of a low-quality data resource. The dollar amount of lost productivity alone is staggering, to say nothing of the lost customers in the private sector or the irate citizens in the public sector. This lost productivity could be easily turned to more productive tasks if there were only a high-quality data resource supporting the organization.

What is the reason for the current state of the data resource in most organizations? How did the data resource get into its current state of dis-repair? Why do organizations allow the quality of a critical resource to deteriorate to the point that it impacts the business? These questions are often difficult to answer on an individual basis within an organization. They are, however, relatively easy to answer as one looks across many organizations over a long period of time to determine the basic problems.

Disparate Data Resource

The data resource in most public and private sector organizations today is in a state of disarray. The data are not integrated within any type of a uniform or consistent organization-wide data architecture and are seldom designed or maintained by any formal, consistent, detailed set of techniques. The data resource is seldom managed with the same intensity as other critical organizational resources.

In this book the term *data* represents the facts that are contained in a data resource. In this context, the term is considered plural the same as the term *facts* would be plural. For example, *the data are disparate* is synonymous with *the facts are disparate*. The term *data resource* represents a collection of data, or facts, within a specific scope. In this context it is singular, such as the *customer data resource*, the *environmental data resource*, or the *enterprise data resource*.

Business Information Demand

Data quality is often viewed as the quality, or accuracy, of the data values. This is only one small part of the overall data resource quality. As we began looking in depth at data resource quality, it became obvious that something more than a few simple metrics were needed to evaluate data resource quality. The real need was a basic understanding of what data resource quality really represented.

> Data resource quality is a measure of how well the business information demand is supported.

The ***business information demand*** is an organization's continuously increasing, constantly changing need for current, accurate, integrated information, often on short notice or very short notice, to support its business activities. It is a very dynamic demand for information to support the business that can change on very short notice. ***Data resource quality*** is a measure of how well the organization's data resource supports the current and future business information demand of the organization. Ideally, the data resource should fully support all the current and future information needs of the organization to be considered a high-quality data resource. The degree to which it actually supports those information needs is the level of data resource quality.

Disparate Data

The term *disparate data* was coined in the late 1980s.[1] ***Disparate*** means fundamentally distinct or different in kind; entirely dissimilar. ***Disparate data*** are data that are essentially not alike, or are distinctly different in kind, quality, or character. They are unequal and cannot be readily integrated. They are low-quality, defective, discordant, ambiguous, heterogeneous data. A ***disparate data resource*** is a data resource that is substantially composed of disparate data that are dis-integrated and not subject oriented. It is in a state of disarray where the low quality does not, and cannot, adequately support the business information demand.

> Disparate data are just plain crummy data.

---

[1] I coined the term *disparate data,* and subsequently *massively disparate data,* after working with very large quantities of data across a wide varietey of public sector agencies.

I was explaining the meaning of disparate data and a disparate data resource to one organization when an employee commented "You mean that disparate data are just plain crummy data." I replied, "In a nutshell, yes!" This statement got the message across to the audience better than any formal definition.

Disparate data reign supreme in many organizations today. In some large private organizations and major public sector organizations the state of the data resource is massively disparate. ***Massively disparate data*** is the existence of large quantities of disparate data within a large organization or across many organizations involved in similar business activities. There are many specific conditions that identify disparate data and a disparate data resource, such as poorly named data, undefined data, physically structured data, and so on. The list is quite long and very boring to review. This list, however, can be condensed to four basic problems with disparate data.

Lack of Awareness

The organization at large is not aware of all the data within the organization or from outside the organization that are at their disposal. There is seldom a complete inventory of all data within the organization, and even less likelihood of an inventory of data available from outside the organization. Individuals often know the data that exist in their organizational unit or that support their specific business activities, but they are not aware of all the data that are available to the organization.

> There is a general lack of awareness of the data available
> to an organization.

Generally, about 15% of an organization's data are inventoried.[2] Generally only the automated data are inventoried; non-electronic data are seldom inventoried. Usually only the business critical data are inventoried; departmental and personal data are seldom inventoried. The data available to the organization from outside the organization are very seldom inventoried.

---

[2] I have not conducted a formal statistical analysis of the portion of an organization's total data resource that has been inventoried, but the formal inventorying of disparate data in preparation for cross-referencing indicates that about 15% of an organization's data resource are inventoried.

This lack of awareness about data availability results in a huge hidden data resource. The ***hidden data resource*** is the large quantities of data that are maintained by the organization that are largely unknown, unavailable, and unused because people either are not aware that the data exist or do not understand the data. Even though the data are disparate, there is still a tremendous wealth of information about the business buried in those data. This information could be readily available to the business if people were only aware that the data existed.

Lack of Understanding

There is a general lack of thorough understanding of all the data in an organization's data resource. Even if there was a complete, current, detailed inventory of all the data within and available to the organization, there is still a profound lack of understanding of those data. The real content and meaning of the data are seldom thoroughly understood. A limited number of individuals may thoroughly understand a small subset of data, but there is no widespread, common understanding of the total data resource by people in the organization.

> People do not understand the content and meaning
> of disparate data.

Generally, less than 10% of an organization's total data resource is thoroughly understood by the business clients at large.[3] Usually, the best understood data are the business critical data. Departmental data are less understood by the organization at large and personal data are the least understood. There are always some data in the data resource that nobody understands. This lack of understanding creates an uncertainty about the data. People often avoid using existing data because of this uncertainty, and create new data that they understand.

Some people may claim that it is not necessary for everyone in the organization to understand all the data in the organization. This statement is probably true; but, there are two important situations involved in understanding data.

---

[3] I have not done a formal analysis of the portion of the data resource that is generally understood by business clients in the organization, but the formal cross-referencing of disparate data indicates that only a small percentage of the data is thoroughly understood by the business clients.

First, people need to understand the data well enough so that they will not create additional redundant data. Second, the data need to be documented to the extent that people can readily understand those data when the need arises. In most organizations, neither of these situations is true.

The data resource in most organizations is seldom completely documented and, if documented at all, that documentation is seldom consolidated in one place, readily available to anyone interested in the data resource, or kept current with a dynamic data resource. Most of the real understanding about the data resource is vested in people, and many of these people are leaving the organization. The lack of good documentation about the data resource severely limits both the understanding and utilization of the data resource, and contributes to the hidden data resource.

High Redundancy

The data in most organizations is highly redundant. The same fact has been independently captured and stored in multiple locations without any coordination or synchronization. This situation is not the same as the formal replication of a fact from a primary database to different data sites for ready access. Data redundancy represents the unknown and unmanaged duplication of data, while data replication represents known and managed duplication of data.

> Data redundancy in the typical data resource
> is exceptionally high.

Generally, for organizations that have been in existence for a number of years and have developed a substantial data resource, each fact exists ten times in that organization's data resource.[4] These redundant data values are often inconsistent and out of synch with each other. It is often unclear which of the redundant data values is the most current or most accurately reflects the real world. Many times the most current value is not the most accurate. It is often extremely difficult to determine which redundant data value should be used as the pre-

---

[4] I have not done any formal survey of the redundancy in a data resource, but the formal cross-referencing of disparate data in a variety of different organizations indicates a ten-fold redundancy of individual facts.

ferred data source. Not having a preferred source for each fact is confusing and frustrating for people, and is disruptive to the business.

High Variability

The data resource in most organizations is also highly variable. Generally, there are 10 or more different variations in format, content, or meaning of a fact across reports, screens, documents, and databases. For example, an employee's name may be normal or inverted, complete or abbreviated, or a variety of lengths across the organization. Measurements can be in a variety of different units and monetary values can be in different currency types. The format frequently changes from one data file to the next and may change from one record to the next in the same data file.

> Disparate data are highly variable across the organization.

The high variability of disparate data makes those data extremely difficult to interpret and use. The use of highly variable data often lead to erroneous, and often disastrous, results. At the very least, productivity is lost either finding the correct data or correcting mistakes made with the wrong data. The impacts of these problems are explained in more detail in the following chapters.

Disparate Data Cycle

A disparate data resource perpetuates itself by encouraging the continued creation of disparate data, as shown in Figure 1.1. The *disparate data cycle* is a self-perpetuating cycle where disparate data continue to be produced at an ever-increasing rate because people either do not know about existing data or do not want to use existing data. Typically, people do not know that the data already exist. They may know that the data exist but do not thoroughly understand the data or do not trust the data, or the data are in such poor form that excessive time is required for them to be of use, or they are not readily available.

Whatever the reason, people create new data that add to the disparity. Sometimes, people just want control of their own data and do what they want to do with minimal concern for the business as a whole. The ready availability of client-friendly products encourages people to create their own data. These new data are not prop-

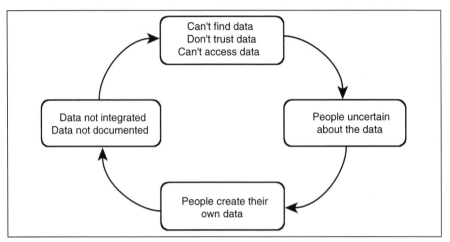

Figure 1.1   Disparate data cycle.

erly designed or thoroughly documented because people understand the data, at least momentarily. In many situations there are no procedures for proper design and thorough documentation, or there is no time to follow those procedures.

> The disparate data cycle perpetuates data disparity.

The improper design and limited documentation of data cause additional data disparity, which decreases understanding and increases the uncertainty, which causes additional data to be created, which are not properly designed or documented, which creates the additional data disparity. The cycle just keeps going because people are not aware that they are contributing to that cycle.

Disparate Data Spiral

There are many individual scenarios that contribute to the disparate data cycle. These scenarios are not really important; but what is important is that the disparate data cycle continues to produce disparate data. I stated in an earlier book that the disparate data situation would get worse before we gained control of the disparate data cycle and stopped producing disparate data.[5] My vision was

---

[5] Brackett, Michael H., *Practical Data Design*, Prentice Hall, 1990.

that organizations would become aware of the creation of disparate data and take action to slow, and ultimately stop, disparate data creation. Data disparity would be limited to current operational systems.

> The disparate data spiral results from disparity moving into new technology.

To my surprise, this has not happened in most organizations. Disparate data are being created at least as fast as they have ever been created. There is a burgeoning disparity of operational data in most organizations. To my utter amazement, this disparity is moving into newer technology, such as enterprise resource planning (ERP) applications and data warehouses. It appears likely that it will move into e-commerce applications through XML tags and even into universal databases, complex data types, and other new technologies.

XML (extensible markup language) offers a wonderful technology to formally tag the data that are being transferred from one person to another, or one organization to another. That technology could, if used properly, resolve a substantial portion of the existing data disparity, That technology could, however, cause a rapid increase in data disparity if the tags are developed in an informal manner. Refer to the next chapter on Formal Data Names for a better understanding of how to prepare XML tags.

The movement of data disparity into new technology creates a situation where the disparate data cycle is spiraling out of sight. The ***disparate data spiral*** is the spiraling increase in data disparity from existing technologies into new technologies. Both the volume of disparate data and the complexity of that disparity are increasing. This spiraling data disparity will certainly impact the business activities of any organization that is moving into new technologies.

Data Resource Drift

There is a natural drift of a data resource toward low quality, as shown in Figure 1.2. ***Data resource drift*** is the natural, steady drift of a data resource toward disparity if its development is not properly managed and controlled. This data resource drift is continuing unchecked in many public and private sector organizations today, and will continue to drift until people make a conscious

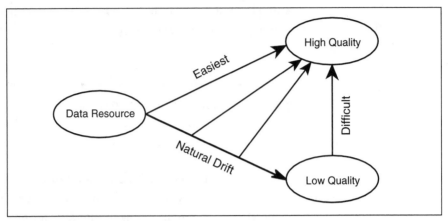

Figure 1.2   Data resource drift.

effort to alter that drift by recognizing the existence of the disparate data cycle and disparate data spiral.

> The data resource will naturally drift toward disparity
> unless controlled.

The sooner that people make a conscious effort to alter the natural drift toward disparity, the easier it will be to achieve a high-quality data resource. The longer that people wait to alter the natural drift, the more difficult it will be to achieve a high-quality data resource. The surprising thing is that most people will not fight altering the natural drift of the data resource. Most people really want a higher quality data resource. Most people are enthused about improving data resource quality. The problem is that they just do not know how to go about improving data resource quality without impacting business operations. They do not want to impact the current situation in order to make something better.

Impact on Information Quality

Many people still confuse data and information. Data, as explained above, are the individual raw facts that are out of context, have no meaning, and are difficult to understand. **Data in context** are facts that have meaning and can be readily understood. They are more than raw facts, but they are not yet information. *Information* is a set of data in context with relevance to one or more people at a point in time or for a period of time. Information is more than just data in context; it must have relevance and a time frame.

Many people also confuse data resource quality and information quality. Data resource quality, as defined above, is a measure of how well the data resource supports the current and future business information demand. *Information quality* is a measure of the ability to get the right data to the right people, in the right place, at the right time, in the right form, at the right cost, so they can make the right decisions and take the right actions.

> Information quality can be no better than the supporting data resource quality.

Information quality can be no better than the quality of the data resource used to produce that information. The impact of disparate data on information quality is substantial and the impact of low-quality information on the business is often incalculable. Indications are that when reasonable data edits—not tight data edits—are applied to disparate data, up to 50% of the data records fail to pass the edit because of one or more errors.[6] In many situations, the data edits can be tightened so that nearly all of the records will fail to pass because of one or more errors. This does not mean that all the data values contained in a data record fail to pass the data edit; it means that at least one of the data value in a data record failed to pass the edit. The chapter on Precise Data Integrity Rules explains more about defining the rules for data editing.

High-Quality Data Resource

How do you stop the creation of disparate data and develop a high-quality data resource? How do you break the disparate data cycle and prevent the disparate

---

[6] I have not conducted a formal survey of the disparate data that fail data edits, but I have been involved in many situations where disparate data that are passed through very rigid data rules can result in up to 90% of the data records failing because one or more data values in that record do not pass the data rules.

data spiral? How do you alter the natural drift of the data resource toward disparity? How do you start building a data resource that supports the current and future business information demand of an organization? These are the questions that I am repeatedly asked.

Disparate Data Shock

The answer begins with realizing that the disparate data situation exists, that the disparity is growing rapidly, and that the situation is creating an increased impact on the business. *Disparate data shock* is the sudden realization that a data dilemma exists in the organization and that it is severely impacting an organization's ability to be responsive to changes in the business environment. It is the panic that an organization has about the poor state of its data resource.

> Disparate data shock is the first step to resolving data disparity.

The *data dilemma* is the situation where the ability to meet the business information demand is being compromised by the continued development of large quantities of disparate data. The dilemma arises from the conflict between building a high-quality data resource within a formal data architecture for long-term stability and striving for early deliverables, inexpensive implementations, and quick fixes to current business problems. Most organizations have repeatedly chosen the latter option and are paying the price for that choice.

I am convinced after looking at many public and private sector organizations for many years that the problem is not the availability of good techniques. The techniques to stop the development of disparate data and to resolve existing disparate data exist today. The problem is not an awareness of the disparate data situation. Many people in an organization, including executives, are aware that data disparity exists and most of these people are aware that the techniques exist to prevent this disparity. The basic problem is the attitude about managing the data resource.

Data Are a Resource

The next step is to view data as a critical resource of the organization, the same as people, finances, and real property. Data are managed by the same basic principles by which any other resource is managed. There is really nothing different about data, except that they are a little less tangible than other critical resources. Most organizations would not allow their people, finances, or real property to be managed like their data are being managed. If they did, the chances are very good that there would be employee terminations and possibly civil or criminal actions. Yet management of the data resource continues to be a free-for-all in most organizations.

I am often asked why data are not considered an asset of the organization. I have also been asked to convince management that data are really an asset of the organization. Many data administrators and data resource managers are promoting the concept, and even demanding, that data be treated as an asset of the organization.

I had two memorable encounters with referring to data as an asset. The first was with a private sector financial officer who claimed, rather vehemently as he threw a pencil across the table at me, that nothing in the organization was an asset until it was listed on the general ledger or chart of accounts, and data were not there. The second was a public sector line manager who stated, rather quietly, that in his daily work he dealt with many assets and liabilities. At the present time, data was one huge liability to the performance of his responsibilities. Both of these situations point out that data are not yet an asset to many organizations, and are seldom a good resource.

> Data should earn the right to be called an asset.

The best approach is to view data as a very critical resource of the organization. Every effort should be made to ensure that the data resource is high-quality and fully supports the current and future business information demand. Then, through a proof-positive approach, the data resource should earn the right to be viewed as a true asset of the organization. We all too often get caught in the trap of demanding that the data resource be considered an asset rather than earning the right for them to be recognized as an asset.

Compare Data Resource

When data are viewed as a critical resource of the organization, the development of a high-quality data resource can begin. *Comparate* is the opposite of disparate. *Comparate data* are data that are alike in kind, quality, and character, and are without defect. They are concordant, homogeneous, nearly flawless, nearly perfect, high-quality data. A ***compare data resource*** is a data resource that is composed of comparate data that adequately support the current and future business information demand. The data are easily identified and understood, readily accessed and shared, and utilized to their fullest potential. A comparate data resource is the ideal, high-quality, official record of reference for the organization. It contains certified data that consistently meet the quality required to support the business information demand.

The two basic benefits of a comparate data resource are high-quality data that are readily shared across the business. Many people talk about breaking down the barriers to sharing data. They believe that if you find the organizational and cultural barriers to data sharing, and break down those barriers, that the data will be readily shared. I have not found this approach to be valid, because you cannot force people to share data. You can only make data good enough that people want to share those data. *You can only achieve data sharing by making it the easiest route for people to follow.*

A comparate data resource is integrated and subject oriented.

A comparate data resource is essentially an enterprise data resource that is developed within a common data architecture. It is not developed independent of the common data architecture like the traditional enterprise data resource. Specific data models are developed from the comparate data resource and any new data are first defined within the common data resource and then added to specific data models.

The comparate data resource contains all the detail for developing any specific data model, but not all of that detail is used on any specific data model. The situation is similar to the building codes. The building codes encompass all buildings, but not all of the codes apply to any single building. People build different types of buildings based on their individual needs, and only a part of building codes apply to those buildings. Similarly, people build different types of data models based on their individual needs, and only part of the detail from the comparate data resource applies to those data models.

A fully comparate data resource is the ideal state for any organization, but an organization may never reach the ideal state. A comparate data resource only needs to be good enough for people to make business decisions within their comfort level. It only needs to be good enough to adequately support the current and future business information demand to the organization's satisfaction. It may have defects, but those defects are known and are within the tolerance level for managing the business.

The two basic principles of a comparate data resource are integration within a common data architecture and orientation toward business subjects. In an earlier book I referred to a comparate data resource as being synonymous with an integrated data resource; but it is more than just the integration of data. Following the definitions for data warehouse data and operational data stores promoted by Bill Inmon, the phrase *integrated, subject oriented data resource* is more appropriate.

Integrated Data Resource

An ***integrated data resource*** means that the data are integrated within a single, organization-wide, common data architecture. A ***data architecture*** is the science and method of designing and constructing an integrated data resource that is business driven, based on real-world objects and events as perceived by the organization, and implemented into appropriate operating environments. It is the overall structure of a data resource that provides a consistent foundation across organizational boundaries to provide easily identifiable, readily available, high-quality data to support the business information demand.

> A common data architecture transcends all data
> in the data resource.

The ***common data architecture*** is a formal, comprehensive data architecture that provides a common context within which all data are understood and integrated. It includes primitive and derived data; elemental and combined data; tabular and non-tabular data; automated and non-automated data; and current and historical data. It includes data in purchased software, custom-built application databases, programs, screens, reports, and documents. It includes all data used by traditional information systems, expert systems, executive information systems, geographic information systems, data warehouses, and object oriented systems. It includes centralized and decentralized data regardless of where they reside, who uses them, or how they are used. A common data architecture encompasses both disparate and comparate data.

Albert Einstein gave us the basic principle that a problem cannot be resolved with the same technology that was used to create the problem. The resolution requires a higher level of technology. This statement provided a new direction for creating a higher level of technology to solve the disparate data problem. The common data architecture is a principle-based concept based on sound theory; it is not hypothetical, esoteric, or academic. It is a practical and proven way to develop a high quality data resource that supports the current and future business information demand. *The common data architecture is that higher level of technology for both preventing and resolving disparate data.*

Subject-Oriented Data Resource

A **subject-oriented data resource** means that the data resource is built from data subjects that represent a business object or business event in the real world where most public and private sector organizations operate. A **business object** is a person, place, thing, or concept in the real world, such as a customer, river, city, or account. A **business event** is a happening in the real world, such as a sale, purchase, fire, or flood.

> Business objects and events are the basis for a
> subject-oriented data resource.

A **data subject** is a person, place, thing, concept, or event that is of interest to the organization and about which data are captured and maintained. Data subjects are defined from business objects and business events, and a comparate data resource is built on data subjects. *A comparate data resource is a subject-oriented data resource that is about the business, by the business, and for the business.*

Terminology

Information technology is a lexically challenged discipline—a very lexically challenged discipline. Many of the terms used in information technology are borrowed from other disciplines and other ages. For example, people continue to emphasize that we are in a new information age that is the next age beyond the industrial age, the agricultural age, and the hunter-gatherer age. However, they use terms like hunting, mining, farming, cleansing, refining, warehousing, harvesting, and so on that are definitely industrial and agricultural age terms.

> The information technology discipline is lexically challenged.

This lexical challenge is an open door for anyone who wants to create and maintain hype about the information technology discipline. Many terms are coined, used, misused, and abused, and terms are often used interchangeably. Many people bring in new terms, define them differently, use them inappropriately, and cast them aside when their usefulness is over. This situation is not helping the information technology discipline gain recognition.

I continue to create a vocabulary of terms specific to data resource management and use them consistently throughout the books and articles I write. This approach resolves at least some of the lexical challenge related to managing a quality data resource. Many of the terms I define and use are new terms that have no counterpart in use today; they are new terms with new meanings. Some of the terms do have counterparts in use today, but they are so misused and abused that any precise definition would be overlooked because of existing perceptions.

Traditionally, the terms *data entities* and *data attributes* are used when logically designing a data resource. Database technicians typically use the terms *tables* or *files* and *fields* or *columns* when developing and maintaining a database. Business people are oriented toward the business world and use terms like *business objects* and *business events,* as explained above. The result is a confusion of terms and difficult communication between the business clients, data analysts, and database technicians.

> Consistent, meaningful terminology supports
> data resource management.

The terms shown in the Figure 1.3 are very useful when referring to the data resource. People can talk to a variety of audiences from executives to database technicians by using the appropriate, audience-specific terms, and promote a better understanding of the data resource.

Real World	Common Data Architecture	Logical Data Model	Physical Data Model
Business Object Business Event	Data Subject	Data Entity	Data File (Table)
Business Feature	Data Characteristic		
	Data Characteristic Variation	Data Attribute	Data Item (Column)
Object Existence Event Happening	Data Occurrence		
	Data Instance	Data Instance	Data Record (Row)

Figure 1.3   Consistent terminology for data resource management.

In the business world there are business objects and business events, as explained above. A ***business feature*** is a trait or characteristic of a business event or business object, such as name, size, color, or date. A ***business object existence*** is the actual existence of a business object, such as a specific person, river, vehicle, or account. A ***business event happening*** is the actual happening of a business event, such as a specific sale, purchase, fire, or flood.

In the common data architecture, a data subject represents business objects and business events, as explained above. A ***data characteristic*** is an individual characteristic that describes a data subject. It represents a single or combined fact about a data subject. Each data subject is described by a set of data characteristics. A ***data characteristic variation*** is a variation in the content or meaning of a data characteristic. It represents a variant of a fact about a data subject. Each data characteristic usually has multiple data characteristic variations in a disparate data resource. A ***data occurrence*** is a logical record that represents the existence of a business object or the happening of a business event in the real world. A ***data instance*** is a set of data values for the facts in a data occurrence that are valid at a point in time or for a period of time. There are usually many data instances for each data occurrence, particularly when historical data are maintained.

In a logical data model, a ***data entity*** is a person, place, thing, event, or concept about which an organization collects and manages data. It represents a data subject in a logical data model. A ***data attribute*** represents the variant of a fact about a data entity. It represents a data characteristic variation in a logical data structure. A data entity is described by a set of data attributes. Even in a logical data model, a data attribute usually has specific content or format, such as measurement units or a normal or abbreviated sequence. A data instance in a logical data model is the same as a data instance in the common data architecture. There is no equivalent for a data characteristic or a data occurrence in a logical data model.

In a physical data model or database, a ***data file*** is a physical file of data that exists in a database management system, such as a computer file, or outside a database management system, such as a manual file. It is referred to as a data table or a table in a relational database. A data file generally represents a data entity including any adjustments made during data denormalization. A ***data item*** is an individual field in a data record and is referred to as a data column or a column in a relational database. A data item represents a data attribute including any adjustments made during data denormalization. A ***data record*** is a physical grouping of data items that are stored in or retrieved from a data file. It is referred to as a data row or a row in a relational database. A data record represents a data instance. There is no equivalent for a data characteristic or a data occurrence in a database.

Compare Data Cycle

Building an integrated data resource based on data subjects starts a compare data cycle that begins altering the natural drift of a data resource away from disparity. The ***compare data cycle*** is a self-perpetuating cycle where the use of compare data is continually reinforced because people understand and trust the data. The compare data cycle changes the mindset that is inherent in the disparate data cycle. It builds on understanding, improvement, and increased use of high-quality data. It prevents the continued creation of disparate data and an increased hidden data resource. It alters the natural drift of the data resource from disparity to business support. It sets the foundation for adding value to the business.

People can easily identify the data they need, they trust those data, and they can readily access those data. The increased use of existing data fosters a shared data resource. When new data need to be created, they are created within the common data architecture and are thoroughly documented so they can be easily identified. They readily become part of the shared data resource. *A shared data resource is a high quality data resource because, as the use of data increases, so does the quality of those data!*

When the data are easily recognized, thoroughly understood, and trusted, people will readily use those data rather than creating new data, as shown in Figure 1.4. As those data are used, they will be improved and enhanced to meet changing business needs. This improvement results in a higher-quality data resource which is easier to use, and the cycle keeps going.

> A comparate data cycle starts a cycle of improvement
> and increased use.

Business Intelligence Value Chain

John Zachman often comments about the dis-integration of organizations when explaining his Framework. One of the major contributors, though not the only contributor, to the dis-integration of an organization is dis-integration of the data resource. Whenever a critical resource dis-integrates, anything depending upon that resource is one step closer to dis-integration.

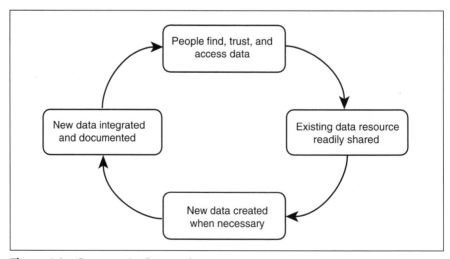

Figure 1.4   Comparate data cycle.

A disparate data resource results in dis-integration of the business.

I wrote an article on the *Business Intelligence Value Chain*[7] explaining that the data resource is the foundation for an intelligent, learning organization (the i-organization), as shown in Figure 1.5. The **business intelligence value chain** is a chain where value is added from the data resource, through each step, to the support of business goals. The data resource supports the development of information through the information engineering process. Information, in turn, supports the knowledge worker in a knowledge environment, and the knowledge worker supports business intelligence in the intelligent, learning organization. Business intelligence supports the business strategies that support the business goals of the organization.

Any level in the business intelligence value chain has no better quality than its supporting level. Since the data resource is the foundation of the business intelligence value chain, the quality of any level can be no better than the quality of the data resource. The degree to which the business goals are met can be no better than the quality of the data resource.

The data resource is like the foundation of a house. If the foundation is not square or level, the carpenter will fight that error clear to the last shingle on the peak of the roof. If, however, the foundation is level and square, the house remains level and square. If the data resource is low-quality, it will impact the business intelligence value chain clear to the business goals; but if the data

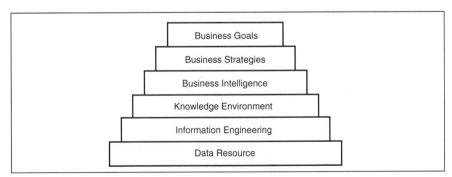

Figure 1.5   The business intelligence value chain.

---

[7] DM Review, March 1999 cover story.

resource is high-quality, it will adequately support the business intelligence value chain. A comparate data resource is a foundation that is level and square. It adds the initial quality to the business intelligence value chain.

> A comparate data resource contributes to the
> Business Intelligence Value Chain.

The bottom two levels in the business intelligence value chain are in the information technology realm, the middle two levels are in the human resource realm, and the top two levels are in the business realm. The information technology function should be responsible for managing the information technology realm and supporting the human resource realm, but they should not be responsible for managing the human resource realm. One of the current hypes is to develop knowledge bases and knowledge management systems for the human resource realm. Information technology would do better to get the data resource foundation in place that supports the knowledge workers in an intelligent learning organization.

Data Risk and Hazard

A disparate data resource poses a hazard that could become a risk to the business intelligence value chain. A *hazard* is a possible source of danger or a circumstance that creates a dangerous situation. For example, a large quantity of dry fuel and hot, dry winds create a fire hazard. The larger the quantity of fuel, the drier the fuel, and the stronger the wind, the greater the hazard. A *risk* is the possibility of suffering harm or loss from some event; a chance that something will happen. For example, the chance that a spark or flame will start a fire in the hazardous fuel is a risk.

A disparate data resource poses both a hazard and a risk to the organization. The *data resource hazard* is the existence of low-quality data just sitting in the data resource. The greater the volume of disparate data and the lower the quality of those data, and the greater the hazard. The *data resource risk* is the chance that the disparate data will be used and adversely impact the business. If the disparate data just sit there and are never used, there is no impact to the business. Unlike the fuel example above, the impact may not be spectacular or apparent for some time. The impact, in many situations, is more like radioactive and hazardous waste that gets into the wind and groundwater; it may not be immediately obvious.

> Both the hazard and risk are reduced with a
> comparate data resource.

A comparate data resource reduces both the data resource hazard posed by disparate data and the corresponding risk that use of the data resource will adversely impact the business. It also reduces a secondary risk that the data will not be recognized or understood and the hidden data resource will not be used to the organization's advantage.

The Ten Sets of Habits and Practices

What is the best way to avoid creating disparate data and begin building a comparate data resource? I am asked this question more times than I care to count. The best place to start is by understanding the bad habits that create disparate data. Once these bad habits are understood, they can be turned into good practices to prevent the creation of disparate data. This does not correct the existing disparate data; that is another topic unto itself.[8] It does, however, stop the continued production of disparate data.

> Understanding the ten worst practices is the best way
> to prevent those practices.

A *habit* is a recurrent, often unconscious pattern of behavior that is acquired through frequent repetition. It can be something that is routinely done that

---

[8] Current techniques for resolving disparate data are presented in Brackett, Michael H., *Data Sharing Using a Common Data Architecture,* John Wiley & Sons, 1994, and Brackett, Michael H., *The Data Warehouse Challenge: Taming Data Chaos,* John Wiley & Sons, 1996. A companion to this book explaining the best ways to resolve existing disparate data through formal data transformation is under development.

shouldn't be done, or something that is routinely not done that should be done. **Bad habits** are the things that are being done to ruin data resource quality. A **practice** is to perform something habitually, customarily, or repeatedly. **Good practices** are the things that should be done to achieve a high-quality data resource. **Best practices** are the best of the good practices that lead to early benefits and successes.

The ten ways to achieve data resource quality are listed below. The following chapters go into each of those ten ways in more detail, including the bad habits leading to low data resource quality, the impacts of those bad habits, the good practices leading to improved data resource quality, the benefits of the good practices, and the best practices that bring early results. The basic orientation of each chapter is to identify the bad habits that cause disparate data and change those bad habits into good practices that create a high quality data resource.

The first five ways to achieve data resource quality pertain to the architecture of the data resource. They include formal data names, comprehensive data definitions, proper data structure, precise data integrity rules, and robust data documentation. The last five ways are non-architectural and pertain to the availability and management of the data resource. They include a reasonable data orientation, acceptable data availability, adequate data responsibility, expanded data vision, and appropriate data recognition.

Architectural
    Formal data names
    Comprehensive data definitions
    Proper data structure
    Precise data integrity rules
    Robust data documentation

Non-Architectural
    Reasonable data orientation
    Acceptable data availability
    Adequate data responsibility
    Expanded data vision
    Appropriate data recognition

Each chapter summary contains a list of all the bad habits, their impacts, the good practices, their benefits, and the best practices contained in that chapter. A complete list from all of the chapters is shown in Appendix A. You are encouraged to refer to Appendix A throughout this book to maintain an overall perspective of the ten ways to achieve data resource quality. You are cautioned, however, not to become overwhelmed at the total list of bad habits and good practices. Take one set at a time and understand the bad habits and good practices in that set.

Each chapter summary also contains a matrix of the bad habits, good practices, and best practices. A complete matrix from all the chapters is shown in Appendix B. You are encouraged to use these matrices to evaluate the current status of your data resource and the progress you are making toward improving data resource quality.

Chapter 12 on the Data Resource Quality Direction summarizes the bad habits, the good practices, and the best practices. It sets a new direction for developing a high-quality data resource based on the good practices. You may want to jump to that chapter if you have an interest in an overview and a call to action about data resource quality, or want to avoid the detail of the bad habits and good practices. You can return to Chapters 2 through 11 for more detail at any time. Alternatively, you can proceed through the ten sets of bad habits and good practices in the next ten chapters and end with the summary and new direction presented in Chapter 12. Appendices A and B may be referenced at any time for a listing of the bad habits, good practices, and evaluation criteria.

Summary

A disparate data resource does not support the current and future business information demand because people are not aware the data exist, people do not thoroughly understand the data, the data are highly redundant, and the data are highly variable. The disparate data resource is perpetuated through a disparate data cycle that becomes a disparate data spiral as it encompasses new technology. The impact of a disparate data resource on the business can be severe and often cannot be calculated.

An organization needs to go through the shock of discovering the impact of a disparate data resource on the business, recognize data as a critical resource of the organization, and resolve to build a comparate data resource. The shock is usually a financial impact, or some other severe pain (such as a political or cultural impact) that could ultimately result in a financial impact. The comparate data resource must be integrated within a common data architecture and be oriented toward business subjects. This approach starts a comparate data cycle that supports the business intelligence value chain in an organization. The hazard presented by disparate data is reduced and the corresponding risk of business impact is substantially reduced.

The ten ways to achieve data resource quality were identified from looking at the disparate data in many organizations over several years. Most public and private sector organizations are continuing one or more of the bad habits that ruin the quality of their data resource quality. Unless these bad habits are recognized and turned into good practices for developing a comparate data resource, the data resource will continue to deteriorate at an ever-increasing rate and the impact on the business will increase proportionally.

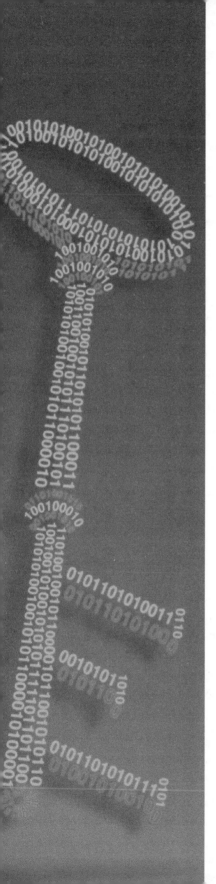

CHAPTER 2

Formal Data Names

Formal data names are mandatory for the
identification and recognition of data.

The first way to achieve data resource quality is
through the development of formal data names. One
of the most prominent problems with a data resource
today is the lack of formal, consistent, readily understandable data names. When any person, whether a business client, citizen, customer, data architect, or database
technician, encounters the data resource they need to
readily identify the data. If the data cannot be readily identified with a formal data name, they cannot be
used appropriately to support the business information
demand.

Data names are labels for facts or sets of facts contained
in the data resource or displayed on screens, reports, or other
documents. Like a person's name or a part name, a data
name must readily identify the data. The lack of formal data
names severely limits the identification of data the same as
the lack of a formal name limits identification of any object.
A person just cannot readily recognize facts or sets of facts
without a formal data name. If the data cannot be readily
identified, people will create their own data and will continue to perpetuate the disparate data cycle.

Organizations must begin developing formal data names if they want to create a comparate data resource. No more random data names or numbers, no more random abbreviations, no more poorly structured names, no more meaningless names, and no more synonymous or homonymous data names. Formal data names must be developed to readily identify each fact or set of facts contained in the data resource.

Informal Data Names

Informal means casual, not in accord with prescribed form, unofficial, or inappropriate for the use intended. **Informal data names** are data names that are casual and inappropriate for their intended use to readily and uniquely identify each fact or set of facts in the data resource. There is no formality, no structure, no nomenclature, and no taxonomy to informal data names.

How do you recognize an informal data name? What do you look for? How do you know you have them in your data resource? These are the questions that I am frequently asked. The flip side of these questions is why do you consider these names to be informal? After all, we readily understand them and the business clients are using the data every day. Why do formal data names need to be developed? What benefit could they possibly provide?

> Most organizations have informal data names
> in their data resource.

Generally, any organization that has developed and maintained a data resource has informal data names. Informal data names are quite prevalent throughout most data resources. People were not concerned about creating formal data names when they began building their data resources because they were more concerned about meeting business objectives. Once started on the path of developing a data resource with informal data names, people just keep going and make little effort to change either the existing or new data names.

The prominent bad habits leading to informal data names are explained below. You should understand these bad habits to determine if informal data names exist in your data resource.

Meaningless Data Names

Informal data names are often meaningless or less than fully meaningful. Data names like Name in a customer file could mean the organization name, a person's name, a contact person within the organization, the name of the building where the customer does business, or any of several other possible names. Similarly, Date in a shipping file could mean shipped date, delivery date, invoiced date, and so on. Even a data name like Ship Date could mean the sales person's estimated ship date, the factory planned ship date, or the actual ship date.

> Many disparate data names are meaningless on first sight.

Another problem is determining what a general data name, such as Code, represents. For example, Employee Code could be a management level code, an education level code, an ethnicity or race code, or any of a variety of other codes. Worse data names are Field 1, Field 2, and Field 3. It is certainly not obvious what these data names represent. Many commercial applications have generic data names, like Date 1, Date 2, and Date 3, or Name 1, Name 2, and Name 3. These data names are totally meaningless without any further explanation.

Non-Unique Data Names

Many data names, abbreviated and unabbreviated, are not unique across the organization's data resource and are often not unique within a database. Can you imagine not having unique names for the employees in an organization, unique names for chemicals, or unique names for prescription medications? Would you have any confidence in prescription medications if each doctor and each pharmacist used their own names?

> Most data names are not unique across the data resource.

A disparate data resource contains many ***data name synonyms;*** the same fact that is labeled with more than one data name in different parts of the data resource. For example, an employee's birth date could be named Empl_bd, Employee Birth Dt, Emp_Bth_Dt, or a variety of other data names.

I am frequently asked if data name synonyms are really bad. The answer is that data name synonyms are not ideal in the data resource; but if the synonyms are thoroughly understood within the common data architecture, there are usually minimal problems. If, however, the synonyms are not readily understood within a common context, there can be significant problems identifying, understanding, and using the proper data. The basic principle is that the synonyms must be readily understood within a common context.

A disparate data resource can also contain many *data name homonyms;* different facts in the data resource that are labeled with the same data name. For example, Empl_Dt might be the employee's hire date in one data file and the employee's birth date in another data file. Homonyms are worse than synonyms, even if they are readily understood in a common context, because people tend to apply a connotative meaning to the data resulting in inappropriate use of the data.

> Many of the data name synonyms and homonyms originate from business terms.

The more I look at the business terms in an organization, the more I realize that the widespread use of synonyms and homonyms is not limited to data names. In fact, there is good evidence that many of the synonyms and homonyms that appear in data names are a result of the synonyms and homonyms that exist in the business. The fact that databases were developed for small segments of the business often explains why those business terms appear in the data names.

The existence of synonyms and homonyms in the business creates two levels of synonyms and homonyms in data names. The first level is the use of business synonyms and homonyms in data names. The second level is the use of synonyms and homonyms for data names in spite of the business terms. People just created data names regardless of the business terms that were in use. Both of these levels of synonyms and homonyms combine to create considerable confusion about the fact that a data name actually represents.

Structureless Data Names

Most disparate data names have no formal structure. Generally a few words are just put together to get a label for the data. There is no structure of data entity name followed by data attribute name, or even data file name followed by data item name. There is seldom any sequence or pattern to the words in a data name, such as general to specific. Many data names are simply a collection of words and many of those words are abbreviated.

> Most disparate data names have no formal structure.

The use of data naming conventions, such as the Of Language, the role—type—class convention, or the prime word—modifier—class word convention, added some structure to data names. However, many of these data naming conventions were not applied consistently across all the databases in the data resource. Most people just picked a few words that sounded okay and used that as the data name. Many disparate data names are quite long, others are quite short, and some have imbedded prepositions and special characters. The general approach was to do it quick and get it done.

Incorrect Data Names

In some situations the data name is flat wrong. It does not match the data definition, or the data structure, or the data values. There could be several reasons for this situation. A person may have had the wrong perception to begin with, the data definition could have changed, a person may have guessed at a previous physical data name, the original intent may have been abandoned and the data field used for another fact without a name change, or there were no data edits enforcing correct data values. Whatever the reason, the data name is incorrect.

> Many disparate data names are just plain incorrect.

Another bad habit is to concatenate multiple facts into one data attribute or one data item. For example, the first three characters are the customer's status code, the second six characters are the customer's first order date, the next five characters are the customer's credit rating, and so on. An even worse example is where the sequence of multiple facts varies by the record type. The data name may be Comment or Explanation, but the contents are far from a comment or explanation; they are a sequence of individual facts. The chapter on Reasonable Data Orientation will explain more about multiple facts in a single data attribute.

I have also encountered data file names that do not correctly represent the contents of the data file. For example, an affirmative action table contained all the training classes taken by an employee. Maybe the training data appear on an affirmative action report, but one would not reasonably expect to find training data in an affirmative action file. Incidentally, the name of this data file was Action. Would anyone reasonably expect to find training data in this data file?

Informal Data Name Abbreviations

Many applications and database management systems have length limitations on data names. Although I totally disagree with any name length limitations, the fact remains that many applications still limit the length of data names. I remember working with FORTRAN many years ago when the data name was limited to 6 alphanumeric characters. We were forced to use combinations of characters and letters that were largely meaningless as data names. SuperNatural, a prominent ad hoc reporting feature with ADABAS, was limited to 19 characters. COBOL was limited to 32 characters, and DOS was limited to 8 characters with a 3-character extension. People were forced into using abbreviated data names by these limitations. Many of these abbreviated data names still persist in the data resource today.

> Most disparate data names have length limitations.

I remember turning a database application I developed that used fully spelled-out data names over to a production programmer. The first thing he said after looking at the database was that he sure needed to shorten the data names to save typing. There was no mention about the design, performance, or anything else, just the data name length and the volume of typing involved. He set about randomly shortening the data names and has been suffering the consequences ever since.

Many design tools and repositories today still have length limitations on data names. They attempt to circumvent the problem by providing an additional description field for the complete data name. In most situations this description field is never used, or it is used as a definition of the data name. Refer to the next chapter on Comprehensive Data Definitions for bad habits related to data definitions.

Physical name length limitations forced people into using abbreviations for data names. Many of the abbreviations that appear in disparate data are informal or random abbreviations. There is seldom any consistency to the way data names were abbreviated. In some situations, there may be consistency within a database, but there is no consistency across the data resource.

Once people were forced into limiting the length of data names, they started using a variety of abbreviation schemes. Most abbreviations were done on a personal basis with little or no coordination between individuals. Many of these personal abbreviation schemes were random, with little or no consistency from one file or database to another. The randomness across many individuals caused the current situation of totally rampant abbreviations. This situation is referred to as *informal data name abbreviations*, meaning that there had been no formality to the abbreviations.

> Data name abbreviations are not applied consistently.

In a few situations, there was some consistency to data name abbreviations, but it was usually at the personal level, not the data resource level. Individuals adopted some consistency in the way they abbreviated data names, but seldom any consistency across the data resource. When abbreviation standards did appear, they were physically oriented formal abbreviations of informal data names. In many situations all manifestations of a root word were abbreviated the same. There was seldom a formal abbreviation of a formal data name.

Many people appear to work quite well with abbreviated data names, as noted in the comment above where people understand informal data names and business clients are using them, so why create formal data names? First, business clients seldom have a choice if those are the only data names they have available.

They just learn to live with the data names. Second, people are actually surviving on short-term memory for understanding abbreviated data names by memorizing the meaning of the short name. When these people go on a vacation for two weeks or take a training class for a week, they return and have great difficulty with the abbreviated data names until they are re-memorized.

Unnamed Data Resource Components

Some components of the data resource, such as data sites and data versions, are not formally named. This usually occurs when the core components of the data resource, such as data files and data items, are not being formally named. It is difficult to formally name subsets, groupings, and versions of things that themselves are not formally named. It may also result from a lack of concern over naming what are considered the less important aspects of a data resource.

> Many components of the data resource have no data name.

Most coded data values are not named, even if the data files and data items are named. There is usually a coded data value and a very short phrase that may be a name or a brief definition. The next chapter on Comprehensive Data Definitions explains the confusion between data names and data definitions for coded data values in more detail.

Informal Data Name Impacts

Informal data names impact the organization in several ways. Some of the impacts are more immediate and obvious than others, but the impacts are still there. *Informal data names, along with the vague data definitions described in the next chapter, are the single largest cause of disparate data in most organizations!* Together, they have the largest short-term and long-term impact on the organization.

Limited Data Identification

Informal data names severely limit the rapid identification of data. The more informal the data name, such as very short data names or abbreviated data names, the more severe the limit on identification. One of the major functions of a data name is to provide an index to the facts in an organization's data resource.

An informal data name does not provide a good index, and people cannot readily identify the facts they need.

> Informal data names limit the ready identification
> and location of data.

Informal data names might be fast to type when creating application code or in a query statement, but the time spent finding the right fact far exceeds any time saved in fast typing. In addition, the time spent interpreting code that contains informal data names often exceeds the time spent finding the right fact to code in the first place. Informal data names also delay people who are trying to find a data definition that further explains the data.

Perpetuated Data Disparity

Informal data names perpetuate the disparate data cycle. When the data cannot be readily identified, people are not aware that the data exist, and additional redundant data are created. If people cannot readily find the data they need, regardless of how good those may be, they will create their own data. The prevalent attitude that I encounter in many organizations is "If I cannot readily find the data, I'll create my own." Informal data names are the leading cause of the continued creation of disparate data.

> Informal data names perpetuate the disparate data cycle.

The increase in disparate data leads to incomplete use of the data resource and an increase in the hidden data resource. Like any other resource of the organization, the data resource should be utilized to the fullest extent possible. The hidden data resource often contains an abundance of facts that could be useful to the business; but if these facts cannot be readily identified, they remain hidden in the disparity. The phrase "If we only knew what we know!" is so appropriate to the real resource hidden in disparate data. A huge hidden data resource is laying untapped in many public and private sector organizations because the data cannot be readily identified.

Lost Productivity

The combination of limited data identification and the increase in data disparity result in a tremendous loss of productivity. Productivity is lost trying to locate the proper data, trying to remember the meaning of informal data names, and trying to gain an initial understanding of the facts represented by the data. Productivity is lost creating the redundant data and again trying to determine which redundant version is the most current or correct. Memorizing informal and abbreviated data names takes time, both to learn them initially and to stay refreshed.

> Informal data names result in an unnecessary loss of productivity.

The dollar amount of lost productivity from informal data names is very difficult to determine because there are both tangible and intangible aspects of lost productivity. It is very difficult to determine exactly how much time a person loses through informal data names. In addition, the lost productivity could result from the combination of any of the bad habits explained in this chapter and subsequent chapters. The dollar amount also varies from one organization to another depending on their size, the size of the data resource, the degree of disparity, and so on.

This lost productivity, however large, could be better spent on more productive value-added tasks. Very few public or private sector organizations have the time to spend on non-productive, cost-incurred tasks. Most organizations are faced with increased demand and limited resources to meet those demands. Turning the productivity lost from informal data names to meet the increased demands would contribute to the organization's success.

Formal Data Names

Formal data names are the cure for the impacts resulting from informal data names. *Formal* means having an outward form or structure, being in accord with accepted conventions, consistent and methodical, or being done in a regular form. A *formal data name* readily and uniquely identifies a fact or group of facts in the data resource. It is developed within a formal data naming taxonomy and is abbreviated, when necessary, with a formal set of abbreviations and an abbreviation algorithm.

The prominent good practices for developing formal data names are explained below. You should learn these good practices and use them to replace the bad habits described above.

Data Naming Taxonomy

There are numerous data naming conventions in use today, such as the role—type—class and prime word—modifier—class word conventions. I reviewed about a dozen of these conventions for use with the common data architecture. Many of these conventions have good features, but I could not find one that was robust enough to formally name all components in the data resource and to uniquely identify all the existing disparate data.

> Existing data naming conventions did not meet the need
> to formally name data.

A new, more robust method was needed to meet these two objectives and support the formal naming of data within the common data architecture. A method was needed that would make the naming of data equivalent to the naming of animals, plants, minerals, and chemicals. A method was needed to formally and consistently name every component of the data resource, including data subjects, data characteristics, data characteristic variations, data codes, data sites, data versions, and even data rules.

A formal *data naming taxonomy* was developed to provide a primary name for all existing and new data, and all components in the data resource. The data naming taxonomy also provides a way to uniquely designate other features in the data resource, such as data characteristic substitutions and data values. Some of these features are beyond the scope of this book, but are shown here to illustrate the robustness of the data naming taxonomy.

> A formal data naming taxonomy provides consistent data names.

The components of the data naming taxonomy are shown in Figure 2.1. Each component has a special character to identify that component and I strongly urge people to use the special characters when using the data naming taxonomy. Initially, people chose to ignore the special characters because they seemed unnecessary. After several thousand formal data names are developed, however, the special characters add clarity to the data names.

Data subject, data characteristic, and data characteristic variation were defined in the last chapter. A *data site* is any location where data are stored, such as a database, a server, or a filing cabinet. A *data occurrence role* is a role that could be played by a specific data occurrence, such as a maintenance vendor or a lease vendor. A *data occurrence group* is a set of data occurrences that were selected based on some criteria, such as all employees that are certified as pilots. A *data characteristic substitution* indicates that any data characteristic variation can be used for a data characteristic, such as (Date) can mean any form of a date. A *data code set* is a specific set of data codes for a general topic, such as the different sets of management level codes in different organizations. A *data value* is any data value, such as a date, a name, or a description. A *data version* identifies the specific version of data, such as a date or time frame. A *data hierarchy aggregation* identifies the level of aggregation of a hierarchy, such as the product hierarchy in a data warehouse. A data rule is explained in the chapter on Precise Data Integrity.

```
Data Site:
Data Subject.
"Data Occurrence Role"
[Data Occurrence Group]
Data Characteristic,
Data Characteristic Variation-
(Data Characteristic Substitution)
Data Code Set;
'Data Value'
<Data Version>
Data Hierarchy Aggregation^
Data Rule!
```

Figure 2.1   Data naming taxonomy components.

The data naming taxonomy applies to all the terms shown in Figure 1.4. Business objects, business events, data entities, and data files use the data subject name component. Business features and coded data values use the data characteristic component. Data attributes, and data items use the data characteristic variation component. The existence of business objects, the happening of business events, data occurrences, data instances, and data records, are not named according to the data naming taxonomy.[1] Selected sets of these occurrences use the data occurrence set component.

A few examples of formal data names that might appear in the data resource are shown in Figure 2.2. Not all the components of the taxonomy are used in

Data names with special characters	Data names without special characters
Boston:	Boston
Employee.	Employee
Boston: Employee.	Boston Employee
"Maintenance" Vendor	Maintenance Vendor
[Pilot Certified] Employee.	Pilot Certified Employee
Boston: [Pilot Certified] Employee.	Boston Pilot Certified Employee
Employee. Birth Date,	Employee Birth Date
Employee. Birth Date, CYMD-	Employee Birth Date CYMD
Management Level. University:	Management Level University
Management Level. University: Code,	Management Level University Code
Employee. Birth (Date)	Employee Birth Date
Gender. Code 'M'	Gender Code M
Boston: Employee <1st Quarter 1997>	Boston Employee 1st Quarter 1997
Boston: Employee <1st Quarter 1997, Set 2>	Boston Employee 1st Quarter 1997 Set 2
Customer. Inactive Retention!	Customer Inactive Retention
Customer. Age, Change!	Customer Age Change
Customer. Age, Change! Payroll-	Customer Age Change Payroll
Product Class. Level 2^	Product Class Level 2

Figure 2.2   Data name examples.

---

[1] Unique identification of data occurrences, data instances, and data records is explained in the chapter on Proper Data Structure.

every data name. The components are used as needed to formally name any component or feature in the data resource. The data names on the left contain the special characters and the data names on the right do not have the special characters. Notice how difficult it is to determine what the data name represents, even with this limited set of examples. Therefore, it is highly beneficial to use the special characters with the data names.

Data Naming Vocabulary

The class word is a prominent feature of many data naming conventions. The *class word* is a word that has a common meaning wherever it is used in a data attribute name. Some organizations use a very restricted set of class words that are closely aligned with the data types available in a database management system, such as Date, Timestamp, and Text. Other organizations use a less restricted set of class words, such as Quantity, Description, Name, and so on.

The class word concept was adopted for the data naming taxonomy, with one enhancement. If a set of class words brought common meaning to data attribute names and helped people understand data attributes, then a set of class words for each component of the data naming taxonomy would be even more helpful. Therefore, a set of common words is developed for each component of the data naming taxonomy.

> A formal vocabulary of common words supports
> the data naming taxonomy.

A *common word* is a word that has consistent meaning whenever it is used in a data name. The collection of all these sets of common words forms a *data naming vocabulary* that supports the data naming taxonomy by providing consistency to the words used in data names. Some of the common words are organization-dependent and other common words are consistent across organizations.

For example, Activity, History, and Suspense might be common words for data subject names meaning transaction data, historical data, and data pending some type of action, respectively. When these common words are applied to Employee, Customer, and Vehicle, they provide the data subject names Employee Activity, Employee History, Employee Suspense, and so on. The result is ready identification of data subjects.

Similarly, the common words Number, Amount, Count, and Quantity mean an identifying number, a monetary amount, a count of items, and a capacity or size, respectively. When these common words are applied to data attributes, they provide names like Package Number, Sales Amount, Container Count, and Trailer Cubic Foot Quantity.

Common words like Estimated, Measured, Normal, and Inverted can be applied to data characteristic variation names to provide Name Normal and Name Inverted, or Depth Estimated and Depth Measured. Similarly, measurement units can be used as data characteristic variation names, such as Depth Inches and Depth Feet.

Each organization must establish a data naming taxonomy and develop their own data naming vocabulary. Although this takes a little effort initially, it provides big benefits as formal data names become prominent.

Primary Data Name

The *primary data name* is the formal data name that is the fully spelled out, real world, unabbreviated, untruncated, business name of the data that has no special characters or length limitations. All other data names are considered aliases of the primary data name. An *alias data name* is any data name, other than the primary data name, for a fact or group of facts in the data resource. It may be formal or informal, abbreviated or unabbreviated, long or short, or meaningful or meaningless.

> Formal data names must be developed according to the
> data naming taxonomy and supporting vocabulary.

Every fact or set of facts in the data resource must have a primary data name based on the data naming taxonomy and data naming vocabulary. One or more components of the data naming taxonomy are used for each primary data name, but not every component of the data naming taxonomy is used in every primary data name. This primary data name provides a unique identification of each fact or set of facts. People encountering the data resource can use the primary data name to readily identify the data they need.

Primary data names must be meaningful to the business! The data naming taxonomy and supporting vocabulary are only useful if they are used with meaningful business names for the data. Well-structured, unique, consistent data names that do not reflect the business perception of the real world are little better than informal data names.

> Formal data names must be meaningful to the business.

There are many synonyms and homonyms in the business terms in most organizations, as mentioned earlier. For example, the prominent term for the geographically distinct sales areas within which the sales people operate is Sales Area. Synonymous terms might be Sales Territory, Sales Region, Market Area, Market Region, and so on. Since Sales Area is the prominent term, it is used as the primary data subject name. The other names become aliases for that data subject name. Market Area is also a homonym that refers to areas where promotional campaigns are conducted. Other terms might be Promotional Area, Advertising Region, and so on. Let's say that Promotional Area is the prominent term and becomes the primary data subject name. The other terms, including Market Area, are synonyms of Promotional Area.

Business clients can help provide the most prominent and readily acceptable business term for the primary data name. I was in one organization where the business clients found out that I was formally naming the data so the data could be readily identified. Several business clients contributed extra time during breaks and evenings to provide the most meaningful business terms so that the best possible data names could be formed. They were sorting through the business synonyms and homonyms to provide the most prominent business terms in the organization. There was not a single hint of concern or anxiety about what I was doing, only a tremendous willingness to help.

Standard Data Names

I am often asked about the data names being proposed by various standards organizations. In the great majority of cases, the data names in these standards are not developed within any formal data naming taxonomy, and there is seldom any consistency across the data standards. Some of these data names are developed within a less formal data naming convention, and others are not developed within any data naming convention. The result is a mixture of data names that usually cause more confusion than understanding. The people developing data standards are encouraged to develop those standards within a formal data naming taxonomy.[2]

> Data standards and data registries need formal data names.

I am also asked about the data name registries that are being developed. The concept of data name registries is good because it allows people to register their data names and definitions so that others can pick up those names and definitions without creating their own. The problem, however, is that the data names being placed in these registries are usually not formal data names that were developed within a data naming taxonomy and there is seldom any control over the data names. The result is the perpetuation of data disparity. People entering their data into data registries are strongly encouraged to develop formal data names within the data naming taxonomy and comprehensive data definitions (described in the next chapter) before placing their data into the data registries.

The extensible markup language (XML) provides tags that contain a data name for the data being transferred or stored. The technology is excellent and could provide a solution to much of the existing data disparity, but the technology will only be as good as the data name used in that tag. If people continue to use informal data names in the XML tags, there will be another wave of data name synonyms and homonyms that causes confusion and will eventually need to be resolved. If, however, the XML tags contain formal data names, or the formal abbreviation of data names as described below, they will provide a tremendous benefit to people using the data. People developing XML applications are strongly encouraged to develop formal data names for the XML tags.

Data Name Word Abbreviation

If the primary data name needs to be abbreviated to meet a length restriction, it must be formally abbreviated. A ***formal data name abbreviation*** is the formal shortening of a primary data name to meet a length restriction according

---

[2] Refer to the chapter on Appropriate Data Recognition for a more detailed explanation of data standards.

to formal data name word abbreviations and a formal data name abbreviation algorithm. A ***data name word abbreviation*** is a formal abbreviation for each word used in a data name. The abbreviation must be unique for the root word and for all manifestations of that root word, and it must not create another word.

> Data name abbreviations provide consistent shortening
> for data names.

The procedure for developing data name word abbreviations is to find the root word and all manifestations of that root word. A unique abbreviation is then formed for each of these words. For example, a person may request an abbreviation for the word Management. The root word is Manage, and the manifestations of the root word are Manager, Managers, Management, Managing, Managed, Managerial, and so on. The respective abbreviations would be Mng, Mngr, Mngrs, Mngt, Mngg, Mngd, Mngrl, and so on. Note the consistent use of suffixes to the abbreviation of the root word.

The same abbreviation should not be used for the root word and all of its manifestations because the automated abbreviation and unabbreviation of data names would not produce consistent results. Future capability should not be compromised by today's actions. People seem to be very good at doing just that in the information technology discipline.

Data Name Abbreviation Algorithm

An algorithm must be developed to formally apply the data name word abbreviations to the data name. A ***data name abbreviation algorithm*** is a formal procedure for abbreviating the primary data name using an established set of data name word abbreviations. There are a variety of different algorithms for applying data name word abbreviations. One approach is to always abbreviate every word in the data name. Another approach is to abbreviate the words from the left until the length restriction is met. A third approach is to abbreviate some components different than other components, such as data subject names and data characteristic names.[3]

---

[3] Brackett, Michael H., *Data Sharing Using a Common Data Architecture*, 1994 provides examples of different data name abbreviation algorithms.

> A formal data name abbreviation algorithm must be developed.

An organization may develop multiple sets of data name word abbreviations and abbreviation algorithms for different length limitations. These multiple abbreviation schemes can be applied to the same primary data name depending on the situation. *It is not the number of abbreviation schemes that is important; it is the formality of those abbreviation schemes that is important for achieving a high quality data resource!*

Formal Data Name Benefits

The primary benefit of formal data names is avoiding the impacts of informal data names from this point forward. It still does not resolve the problem of existing informal data names. That is another issue that needs to be addressed, but is beyond the scope of this book. The major benefits of formal data names are that people can readily identify the data, the disparate data cycle begins to be limited, and productivity begins improving.

Readily Identified Data

One important benefit of formal data names is that the facts contained in the data resource can be readily identified. A unique, understandable data name meaningful to the business helps people find the data they need to perform their business activities. Primary data names that are developed within a formal data naming taxonomy and supporting vocabulary are a ready index to the data resource.

> Data are readily identified and located with formal data names.

Formal data name abbreviations help meet the length restrictions of products, yet still provide a meaningful data name. Data name abbreviations developed with a formal set of word abbreviations and a formal abbreviation algorithm provide a consistency that does not exist with disparate data. Business terms, alias data names, informal data names, and data name abbreviations can be placed in a thesaurus that helps people find the primary data name. The chapter on Robust Data Documentation explains the use of a data name thesaurus.

Limited Data Disparity

Another important benefit of formal data names is that it starts slowing the disparate data cycle. Developing formal data names and data name abbreviations does not stop the disparate data cycle, but it begins putting the brakes on the growing volume of disparate data. It allows people to readily identify existing data, gain confidence in those data, and begin using the data without creating additional data. Each successive good practice that is implemented further slows the disparate data cycle until it is stopped completely.

> Formal data names begin slowing the disparate data cycle.

Limiting the disparate data cycle also begins the comparate data cycle. It begins solving the four basic problems with disparate data by raising the awareness of the data that exist in the data resource and by providing an initial understanding of those data. It also begins to surface the hidden data resource, which further limits data redundancy. It is the turning point for stopping the burgeoning data disparity; because if you cannot readily identify the data, not much else really counts.

Improved Productivity

The most important benefit of formal data names is the beginning of productivity improvement for both business clients and information technology staff. The time that was lost sorting through informal data names to find the right data can be spent on more productive activities. The time that was lost remembering or memorizing the informal data names can be spent on more important tasks. The time that was spent tracking down and correcting wrong business actions can be better used preventing those situations from happening.

> Productivity is substantially improved with formal data names.

Staff morale and enthusiasm are usually higher when the data can be readily identified with a formal data name, which boosts productivity. Business clients are often very willing to help develop formal data names. When they see something beneficial happening, they usually contribute as much time and energy as necessary to provide the most meaningful data names. I have seen a tremendous increase in morale and enthusiasm in both information technology staff and business clients in organizations that can readily identify their data and spend the time saved on more value-added business activities.

Best Practices

The good practices for formal data names emphasize developing primary data names and creating formal data name abbreviations for all components in the data resource. Developing and abbreviating primary data names for all components in the data resource is a monumental task, particularly for organizations with a large quantity of disparate data. It requires building a whole vocabulary for the data resource and using that vocabulary to consistently develop data names.

Formal data names can be leveraged for success.

That task could take years to complete even in the most productive organizations. The task, however, can be simplified to produce early successes that increase the motivation to continue formally naming and abbreviating data. The best practices to achieve early successes with a minimum effort are explained below.

Business Critical Data

The best practices for formally naming and abbreviating data begin with the identification of business critical data. The data that support the core business activities should be formally named and abbreviated first. If the set of business critical data is too large to manage, then a subset of those data that are causing the biggest problems should be identified. Then the data that are causing less impact or are less critical to the business can be formally named and abbreviated. This approach provides the maximum benefit to the business with a minimum effort and produces early successes that motivate people to continue formally naming data.

Core Component Names

Providing formal data subject names, data characteristic names, and coded data value names for the business critical data is a tremendous step in the right direction. It begins the process of improving the identification of data that support the core business functions. Business clients become involved very quickly and contribute to data names that are meaningful to the business. When these basic data resource components are formally named, the formal naming of the other data resource components falls into place relatively easy.

Core Component Abbreviations

Providing formal abbreviations for data subject names and data characteristic names is also a big step in the right direction. Formal data name abbreviations begin the process of formally and consistently abbreviating data names so they can be readily understood with a minimum of effort. The database staff become involved very quickly because it helps them understand the physical data names and maintain the physical database. When these formal data name abbreviations are developed, the formal abbreviation of other data names will happen in due time.

Summary

The bad habits leading to informal data names, the impacts of those bad habits, the good practices for formal data names, the benefits of those good practices, and the best practices for success motivation are summarized below. This list is also contained in Appendix A.

Bad habits leading to informal data names:
Meaningless data names—difficult to identify and initially understand the data.
Non-unique data names—many synonyms and homonyms across the data resource.
Structureless data names—no formal structure or sequence to the words in the name.
Incorrect data names—no match to the definition or the structure.
Informal data name abbreviations—random, informal, and inconsistent.
Unnamed data resource components.

Impacts of informal data names:
The data cannot be readily identified.
The disparate data cycle is reinforced and disparate data increase.
Lost productivity finding data, remembering abbreviations, and creating additional data.

Good practices for formal data names:
Data naming taxonomy must be established.
Supporting data name vocabulary must be established.
Primary data names must be developed based on acceptable business terms.
Standard data names can be useful if developed within the data naming taxonomy.
Data name word abbreviations must be developed.
Data name abbreviation algorithm must be developed.

Benefits of formal data names:
    The data are readily identified.
    The disparate data cycle begins to be limited.
    Productivity begins to improve for business clients and information technology staff.

Best practices for success motivation:
    Identify business critical data that cause major problems.
    Formally name data subjects, data characteristics, and coded data values.
    Formally abbreviate data subject and data characteristic names.

The bad habits, good practices, and best practices for data names can be used to evaluate the status of an organization's data resource. Fill in the horizontal bar (below) to show the degree to which the bad habits exist and the degree to which the good practices and the best practices have been implemented. You can provide definitions for the Poor, Fair, Moderate, Good, and Excellent headings to suit your organization, or you can use a numeric scale if it is more appropriate. You can also select the items that are important for your organization, but don't be too hasty at excluding items, because they may be valuable later. This list is also contained in Appendix B.

	P	F	M	G	E
Bad Habits					
Meaningless data names	☐	☐	☐	☐	☐
Non-unique data names	☐	☐	☐	☐	☐
Structureless data names	☐	☐	☐	☐	☐
Incorrect data names	☐	☐	☐	☐	☐
Informal data name abbreviations	☐	☐	☐	☐	☐
Unnamed data resource components	☐	☐	☐	☐	☐
Good Practices					
Data naming taxonomy	☐	☐	☐	☐	☐
Data naming vocabulary	☐	☐	☐	☐	☐
Primary data name	☐	☐	☐	☐	☐
Standard data names	☐	☐	☐	☐	☐
Data name word abbreviations	☐	☐	☐	☐	☐
Data name abbreviation algorithm	☐	☐	☐	☐	☐
Best Practices					
Business critical data identified	☐	☐	☐	☐	☐
Data subjects named	☐	☐	☐	☐	☐
Data characteristics named	☐	☐	☐	☐	☐
Data codes named	☐	☐	☐	☐	☐
Data subject names abbreviated	☐	☐	☐	☐	☐
Data characteristic names abbreviated	☐	☐	☐	☐	☐

CHAPTER 3

Comprehensive Data Definitions

> Comprehensive data definitions are needed
> to thoroughly understand the data.

After formal data names, the second way to achieve
data resource quality is through the development of
comprehensive data definitions. A prominent problem
with the data resource in many organizations is the lack
of comprehensive data definitions that fully explain the
content and meaning of the data in business terms. Next
to informal data names that limit a person's ability to
quickly identify data, the lack of comprehensive data definitions severely inhibits a person's ability to thoroughly
understand the data. A person not only cannot readily
identify the data, they cannot thoroughly understand
those data when they are identified.

A person who cannot identify the data is in trouble. A
person who can identify the data, but does not thoroughly
understand those data, is still in trouble. But a person who
cannot readily identify or understand the data is in deep
trouble as well. No matter what a person does, that person
cannot fully utilize the data resource to support business
activities.

People need to thoroughly understand the data in order
to use those data to support business activities. Inhibiting

data understanding in any way results in an inhibited understanding of the business. A person who does not understand the data or the business cannot adequately perform his or her business activities. The development of comprehensive data definitions is the only way to thoroughly understand the data resource and fully utilize it to support the business.

Vague Data Definitions

A *vague data definition* is any data definition that does not thoroughly explain, in simple understandable terms, the real content and meaning of the data with respect to the business. Vague data definitions can be anything from a non-existent data definition to meaningless data definitions. I am frequently asked how to identify the existence of vague data definitions in the data resource. The basic indicator of vague data definitions is that if you read a data definition and do not thoroughly understand the data, it is a vague data definition. An even better basic indicator is that if a newcomer to the organization reads the data definition and does not thoroughly understand the data, it is a vague data definition.

> Vague data definitions inhibit data understanding
> that inhibits business understanding.

The prominent bad habits leading to vague data definitions are explained below. They are not listed in any particular order of importance, but they all exist in one form or another in most data resources. You should understand these bad habits to determine if vague data definitions exist in your data resource.

Non-Existent Data Definitions

Data definitions in many organizations are non-existent. They may never have been developed, or were developed at one time and have since been misplaced or lost. Whatever the reason, there is often considerable data in the data resource for which there is no data definition.

> Non-existent data definitions provide no data understanding.

The lack of data definitions severely inhibits a person's understanding of the data resource. There is absolutely nothing for a person to reference that gives a clue to the real content and meaning of the data, other than a data name that may not provide any identification let alone an understanding. If people do not understand the data they will not use the data, and the disparate data cycle continues unchecked.

Many coded data values exist in most data resources. *Coded data values* are data values that have been encoded or shortened in some manner. They began in the days of the 80-column card, which some of you may remember all too well. Space was limited on the 80-column card and it was difficult to have a data record span multiple cards, so data values were often encoded to conserve space. Data items that were ten or twenty characters long were reduced to one or two characters, resulting in a tremendous savings of space. Many of these initial coded data values still exist today, and the practice of encoding data still continues even though there are no limitations like the 80-column card.

> Most data codes have no corresponding data definition.

The question often arises as to whether coded data values are still needed. With the capability of current database management systems, the answer is "no," but people still continue to develop coded data values. I have tried to get people in a number of different organizations to stop using coded data values and use a word or phrase, but it seems an impossible task. People just want to encode data for some reason. In addition, many of the initial coded data values still exist, so they will need to be managed until they can be eliminated.

Coded data values seldom have a formal data name, and many coded data values have no data definition of any kind. At best they have a short data description that could be a name or a definition. Many documentation applications today provide a short description and a long description. The short description may be an abbreviated name and the long description may be the full name of the coded data value; the short description may be the full name of coded data value and the long description may be a short data definition; or there may be only a short description with no long description. These situations are very confusing for many people using the data resource.

I encountered codes for undergraduate student, graduate student, and post-graduate student in a major university. I asked a person in the registrar's office what those codes really meant, since I was familiar with only undergraduate and graduate student codes. She replied that she didn't know; she just entered the data. I asked where she got the data, and she replied that she got it from the student. What did you ask the student to get the data? She replied that she asked if they were undergraduate, graduate, or post-graduate, and entered whatever they told her. Did the students know what you were asking them? She replied that she didn't know, she just asked the question and entered the response. After some investigation, I found that the terms were really undergraduate student, graduate student, and post-doctoral student. That made more sense, but it only meant that the codes that were already entered were probably in error.

At best, only the data entities or data files, data attributes or data items, and coded data values are defined in most organizations. The other components of the data resource, such as data sites and data versions, are seldom formally named, let alone defined. Usually, only automated data are defined; the manual data seldom have data definitions. Overall, the great majority of the total data resource at an organization's disposal is undefined.

Unavailable Data Definitions

Data definitions that are not readily available have essentially the same impact as data definitions that are non-existent. They do not exist in the eyes of the person needing those definitions to understand the data supporting the business. Data definitions may exist, and they may be the most comprehensive, thorough definition ever written, but if they are not readily available to the person needing that definition, it is the same as being non-existent. It is much like a policy or a mission statement that is not readily visible to employees; it essentially does not exist. A person's understanding of the data resource, and corresponding use of the data, are compromised.

> Unavailable definitions inhibit understanding the same as non-existent definitions.

The only difference between unavailable and non-existent data definitions is that by making unavailable data definitions readily available, they can become useful for understanding the data. It is a far easier task to make data definitions that exist readily available than it is to create good data definitions where none exist. The availability of data definitions will be further explained in the chapter on Robust Data Documentation.

Short Data Definitions

Many data definitions are short, truncated phrases, or incomplete sentences that provide little meaning. This practice began many years ago when very short physical data file and data item names were common. A short definition provided some meaning to a very short physical data name. For example, CST_NM may be difficult to understand, particularly when there were literally thousands of data items with these short names. Even a short phrase like The name of the customer provided some insight into the content and meaning of the data. Many of these short data definitions were essentially a longer data name.

> Short truncated phrases provide some data understanding.

By far the most classic short data definition that I have ever encountered is No information available. It is similar to a page in a workbook with the note This page is intentionally left blank. Maybe a lengthy explanation of why there is no information available would help; then again maybe it wouldn't. I ran across this numerous times in one client's database. It may be nice to know that no information is available, but it would be interesting to know the source of that statement. Perhaps someone was just filling in definitions after the fact and could not find any information on what the data attributes meant. Perhaps it is a default value when there is no definition provided to a data dictionary.

Very seldom do you see short, abbreviated, informal data names with a comprehensive data definition. Short data names and short data definitions usually appear together. If people do not have the time to develop formal data names, they usually do not have the time to develop comprehensive data definitions. You do, however, frequently see comprehensive data definitions with formal data names because people have made the time available to do a good job with both.

Meaningless Data Definitions

I often encounter many data definitions that are meaningless. The English and grammar were acceptable, but the explanation of the content and meaning of the data was useless. For example, Ship Date was defined as A column used to store the shipping date, and Acct_Num was defined as A field containing the customer's account number. These definitions provide no insight into the real content or meaning of the shipping date or the customer's account number.

> Meaningless data definitions are just plain useless, or worse.

Another example is a meaningless definition with poor grammar. The data item Override Flag is defined as The flag contains a 'Y' when the value are overridded. First, it is very poor grammar, which casts doubt on the integrity of the data. The data value could be very accurate, but the perception of the quality of the data value is poor based on poor grammar. Second, it is not clear what value was being overridden or why that value is being overridden. There were several values in the table and any of those values could be overridden, yet there was no definition for any of those values that alluded to a possible override. The result is confusion about the meaning of the data.

Meaningless data definitions allow people to provide a connotative meaning to the data that may not be correct. They perceive a meaning based on their experience and knowledge in the organization. That experience and knowledge may be valid, but the connotative meaning applied to the data may not be correct. Further, the connotative meanings provided by different people for the same data characteristic frequently conflict, resulting in misunderstanding and misuse of the data.

Outdated Data Definitions

The business activities of most organizations constantly change over time, and the data values supporting those business activities must also change to reflect and support those business changes. The data values slowly evolve, but the data definitions are not kept current with that evolution. The data definitions slowly become out of synch with the data values being stored. This situation occurs both with the data values and with the data items contained in a data file.

> Data definitions that are not routinely enhanced
> become meaningless.

Many data design approaches concentrate on developing an initial data definition—maybe even a very good data definition—documenting it, and then forgetting about it. The data definition is perceived to be valid forever. One bad habit that people have is to believe that once a data definition is completed it is valid for the life of the organization.

Incorrect Data Definitions

Some data definitions are just plain incorrect or inaccurate. They are not in synch with the data name, the data structure, or the data integrity rules. This causes uncertainty and confusion because people are not sure which is correct. One very confusing situation that is encountered is a mismatch between the data name and the data definition. When the data name and data definition are not matched, it leaves people in a quandary as to whether the name or the definition is correct.

Incorrect data definitions cause considerable uncertainty.

I ran across a physical data name prd_ht that was defined as The height of the product in ounces. Now considering that weight is abbreviated as wt and height is abbreviated as ht, there is only one letter difference between height and weight, and there is little difference in spelling between inches and ounces, it is difficult to determine if the data values represented the height in inches or the weight in ounces. There was no other data characteristic that referred to the product weight. It took two people a little over an hour reviewing the actual data to determine that the data values were the height in inches. We had no idea how much confusion this mismatch had caused over the last several years, or how many wrong operational decisions were made as a result of this mismatch.

Unrelated Definitions

Many times a definition is unrelated to an understanding of the real content and meaning of the data. The definition may be useful in another context, but it is not useful to understanding the content and meaning of the data. In many situations these unrelated definitions were prepared to meet the documentation requirement, and this was the only information that was readily available.

Data Entry Instructions

I often encounter data definitions that are nothing more than data entry instructions. They explain, sometime in very good detail, how the data are to be entered into an information system. Although the definition is useful to the people who capture and enter the data, it provides very little understanding about what the data represent in business terms. Data entry instructions are not the same as a definition of the content and meaning of the data.

Data entry instructions are not data definitions.

Data entry instructions really belong with the process associated with the data entry. Data entry instructions are usually specific to a business activity and may vary from one business activity to another, even though they use the same data item for storing the value that is entered. Since the process of data capture and storage varies with business activities, the data entry instructions should be documented with the business activity, not with the data definitions.

Data Use Explanation

Many definitions describe, often in great detail, how the data are used. There is minimal definition about what the data represent in business terms. An extensive definition of the data uses will never be completed. All of the current and possible uses of the data cannot be described in an organization with evolving business information needs. This approach requires considerable ongoing effort and will never be completed.

Describing data use limits identifying other uses for the data.

When a person is looking for data to meet his or her business needs, an extensive explanation of the data use does not help identify the data needed. An extensive definition of all the possible uses of the data actually blocks a person's ability to perceive how the data might be used for that person's business activities. Those who cannot perceive how the data might suit their business needs are likely to create their own data. An explanation of the use of data is more appropriate to the process that manipulates the data than with the data definition.

I was asked to attend a session where the team was having difficulty developing data definitions. When I entered, they were discussing the definition of Employee Name. The team had already defined that the employee's name was used for pay checks, attendance at training classes, and affirmative action. The discussion was continuing with uses for project assignment, time tracking, and so on. This process will never go to end-of-job. My suggestion was that they define the employee's name as the legal name of the employee as shown on a legal document, such as a birth certificate, social security card, driver's license, court document, or other government document. Then let that employee's name be used wherever necessary to meet business needs. The team was greatly relieved, discarded many of the data definitions they had already prepared, and moved on to developing meaningful data definitions.

An example of the data is not considered a description of the data use. It is often quite helpful to include an example of the data for a better understanding of the content and meaning. For example, am employee might be defined as Any person who works for the organization whose time is tracked in the payroll system and who is paid through the payroll system, such as full-time employees, part-time employees, and volunteer workers, but excluding contractors. Note that the examples and exclusion qualify the content and meaning of the data but do not describe how the data are used.

Data Source Explanation

A lengthy definition of the data source is no more appropriate than data entry instructions or a definition of the data use. It may be nice to know the source of the data, how they were captured, where they are stored, and how they were processed. Such a definition may be interesting and informative, but it does not contribute to an understanding of the real content and meaning of the data.

> Describing the data source contributes little
> to understanding the meaning.

The data source, method of capture, storage location, movement between data sites, and processing can be defined and maintained as part of a ***data tracking*** initiative. I often work with both public and private sector organizations to track the movement of data from initial capture, through a variety of locations and alterations, to their present location. The source of data and its original meaning at the time of data capture is referred to as the **data heritage**, and the pathway from the data origin to its current location and the alterations made to the data along that pathway is referred to as **data lineage**. These definitions, however, are part of the data tracking process and do not belong in the data definitions about the content and meaning of the data.

Vague Data Definition Impacts

Vague data definitions can impact an organization by severely inhibiting data understanding, inappropriate use of the data, incomplete use of the data resource, and lost productivity. These impacts are in addition to the impacts resulting from informal data names mentioned in the last chapter. *The combination of impacts from informal data names and vague data definitions is the largest single cause of the burgeoning disparate data!*

Inhibited Data Understanding

One prominent impact of vague data definitions is a severely inhibited understanding of the data contained in the data resource. Many of the other data-related problems in an organization originate from people not thoroughly understanding the real content and meaning of all data in the data resource. If they do not readily understand the data, they cannot use those data to support their business needs.

> Inhibited data understanding is the primary impact
> of vague data definitions.

The same situation applies to business terms. There are many synonyms, homonyms, and acronyms in business terms within an organization, as mentioned in the last chapter. In addition, many business terms are misused and abused because they are not thoroughly understood due to vague definitions. No wonder many of the data in an organization's data resource are vaguely defined when they are based on business terms that are vaguely defined.

Inappropriate Data Use

Another prominent impact of vague data definitions and inhibited data understanding results in inappropriate use of the data resource. Organizations often take the wrong business actions or miss business opportunities because people do not thoroughly understand the data. The impact of wrong actions and missed opportunities can be minor or major, it can be short term or long term, and it can be a narrow scope or far reaching.

Inappropriate business decisions can be minor or disastrous.

The more an organization deals with situations involving human life and property damage, the more severe the impact of inappropriate data use. It is one thing if the shirt you ordered is not delivered on time or is the wrong color, or your credit card has a double charge. It is a totally different thing if a loved one dies because someone did not thoroughly understand or properly interpret the data.

Perpetuated Data Disparity

Vague data definitions, like informal data names, perpetuate the disparate data cycle. Through misinterpretation, misunderstanding, and individual connotations, vague data definitions keep the cycle going that keeps impacting the business. When the real content and meaning of data cannot be readily understood, the data usually cannot be trusted, people have no confidence in the data, the data are not used, and redundant data are created. As mentioned in the last chapter, the prevalent attitude in many organizations is if people cannot readily understand the data, they will create their own. This attitude just keeps the disparate data cycle going.

Vague data definitions perpetuate the disparate data cycle.

The increase in data disparity leads to incomplete use of the data resource and an increase in the hidden data resource. The data resource, like any other organizational resource, should be utilized to the fullest extent possible. Hiding a potential wealth of information about the business in data disparity does not benefit the organization and may be detrimental to its survival. Most organizations cannot afford to take this risk.

Lost Productivity

The most serious impact on the organization is the lost productivity resulting from an inhibited understanding of the data resource. Vague data definitions result in a substantial loss of productivity through inappropriate use of the data, incomplete use of the data resource, and perpetuation of the disparate data cycle. There are many specific ways that the productivity is lost, but the bottom line is that when the data understanding is inhibited, productivity is lost.

> Few organizations can afford to waste productivity
> on vague definitions.

Take the simple example of the height or weight confusion described previously. If there are 5,000 data items in that organization's data resource, and only two people a year took an hour to figure out the meaning of those 5,000 data items, that's 10,000 staff hours lost per year just understanding the data. That's five staff years lost in one year! Worse yet, this estimate may be low, based on situations I have encountered in some organizations.

This is only the ***primary productivity loss*** related just to understanding and use of a disparate data resource. There is a ***secondary productivity loss*** that includes unnecessary business activities, such as legal appeals, suits, returned merchandise, protests, vandalism, and other actions against the organization that take resources to resolve. It is far better to prevent these situations than to resolve these situations. There is also a ***tertiary productivity loss*** that is the lost customers and sales in the private sector and the avoidance of regulations in the public sector. It takes resources to find new customers, regain old customers, and find violators.

How many organizations, public or private, can afford this degree of wasted productivity? In this time of decreasing resources and increasing demand, most public and private sector organizations cannot afford any loss of productivity. Every effort should be spent on constructive, value-added business activities.

Comprehensive Data Definitions

Comprehensive data definitions are the cure for vague data definitions. A *comprehensive data definition* is a formal data definition that provides a complete, meaningful, easily read, readily understood definition that thoroughly explains the content and meaning of the data. It helps people thoroughly understand the data and use the data resource efficiently and effectively to meet the business information demand. Along with formal data names, comprehensive data definitions help start the comparate data cycle.

> Comprehensive data definitions directly support the business.

The prominent good practices for developing comprehensive data definitions are explained below. You should learn these good practices and use them to replace the bad habits described above.

Meaningful Data Definitions

A comprehensive data definition describes the real content and meaning of the data with respect to the business. It is not based on the use of the data, how or where the data are used, how they were captured or processed, or where the data are stored. There is a place for these definitions with processes, but not in a comprehensive definition of the content and meaning of the data.

> The primary orientation is toward the content
> and meaning of data.

I frequently present vague data definitions to a group of people knowledgeable about the business. These are both business clients and information technology staff that know the business. I ask that each person provide, in writing or orally, a more comprehensive data definition, one that they would like to see to thoroughly understand the data.

If the responses are written, there is often a tremendous discrepancy in the definitions among the participants. This is one way to get a comprehensive data definition and to surface the differences that may indicate that there are multiple facts included in one data definition. If the responses are oral, we seldom get beyond the second or third person before there is an open, and sometimes quite vocal, discussion of the real meaning of the data. If the synergy of this discussion can be focused, the result is very comprehensive data definitions.

One excellent way to develop data definitions that are meaningful to the business is to include business clients in the preparation of those data definitions. At a client several years ago, many tables of coded data values were defined that contained codes, a short description, and long description. In order to obtain comprehensive definitions of the data codes, the existing codes and descriptions were made readily available on the network for review and update by the business clients. The only thing I asked was that each person put in their comment along with their initials and date. This was a no-blame, no-whitewash approach to reaching a comprehensive data definition of all coded data values.

I must admit that this was done hesitantly, but I was pleasantly surprised. I reviewed the definitions on a daily basis and saw comments being entered that alluded to different perceptions and to different uses of the coded data values. As I was thinking about ways to resolve this situation, a manager entered the scene and was making constructive decisions about what the coded data values meant. That manager had already discovered that the coded data values were not being applied consistently across the business because their meaning was not clear. He was taking steps to ensure that they were being used consistently.

The result was a set of coded data values that were comprehensively defined and consistently applied across the business. Since this was a public sector organization, the benefit to the business was substantially reduced appeals and a resulting reduction in non-productive work resolving those appeals. The time saved was spent on more constructive tasks.

I now use this approach with many clients and expand it beyond coded data values to include all data definitions. One key factor to making this process work, however, is to supply initial definitions, a straw definition to get people started. Providing no definition and asking people to start from scratch does not work well. Providing an initial definition that is relatively accurate draws people into the process and results in more input and a better definition.

Thorough Data Definitions

A comprehensive data definition must be thorough to be meaningful to the business. There must be no length limitation or restriction on the data definition and it must use appropriate business terminology. A comprehensive data definition must have a strong denotative meaning to limit the variability and confusion caused with multiple connotative meanings, as explained in the example above.

A comprehensive data definition must be long enough to fully explain the data. A general guideline is one or two paragraphs of two or three sentences each. The definition may be shorter for some data attributes and it may be longer for some data entities. I have encountered data characteristic definitions that are quite complete with two sentences and data subject definitions that take a full typewritten page. Data subject definitions frequently exceed half a typewritten page.

> There is no length limitation to a comprehensive data definition.

Many software products still provide 255 characters or less for a data definition. It is extremely difficult to get a comprehensive data definition in 255 characters. These applications should be avoided in favor of applications that allow a comprehensive definition without a length limitation.

The terms *description*, *data description*, and *explanation* should be avoided when referring to data definitions. These terms have been quite abused over the years and continue to be abused in many methods and applications today. A description can be a short name or a long name, or a short description or a long description depending on a particular person's perspective. In some situations a description is a name and an explanation is a definition. In other situations a description is a short name and an explanation is a long name.

Some methods and software products are still stuck in yesteryear with a short description and a long description. These could be used for a short name and a long name, or a name and a definition, or a physical name and a business name. Seldom is there a comprehensive definition. The discipline has moved far beyond the days of the 80-column card and the 255-character string that limit the length of data names and definitions. The capabilities are there to support primary data names and comprehensive data definitions without length restrictions. People need to actively use that capability.

Correct Data Definitions

In addition to being thorough, comprehensive data definitions must be kept current with the business. Data definitions that are not continuously enhanced are soon out of date in today's rapidly evolving business world. One bad habit, as mentioned above, is that data definitions are often considered good for the life of the data once they are completed.

> Data definitions must be continually enhanced
> to remain current and correct.

Data definitions must be routinely reviewed and enhanced to ensure that they remain current and correctly represent the data they contain. As the business evolves, the data evolve to support the business. The data definitions must evolve so that people can adequately understand the data. The development of data definitions is not a one-time task; it is an ongoing process to keep the data definitions current.

Fundamental Data Definitions

Comprehensive data definitions can be enhanced with the use of fundamental data definitions. *Fundamental data* are data that are not stored in databases and are not used in applications, but support the definition of specific data. *Fundamental data definitions* are the comprehensive data definitions for fundamental data. *Specific data* are data that are stored in databases and are used in applications. The comprehensive definitions of specific data may inherit fundamental data definitions.

> Fundamental data definitions can be inherited
> by specific data definitions.

For example, latitude and longitude data characteristics may be defined as fundamental data. Specific data, such as wellhead latitude and longitude or an intersection latitude and longitude can inherit the fundamental definitions of latitude and longitude. The result is maximum meaning and consistency in data definitions with minimum wording.

Comprehensive Data Definition Benefits

The primary benefits of comprehensive data definitions are an improved understanding of the data, increased use of data, more appropriate business actions, less redundant data, and improved productivity. Each of these benefits is explained below.

Improved Data Understanding

Comprehensive data definitions help people better understand both the data and the business supported by the data. This improved understanding increases the use of the data resource and taps the hidden data resource that exists in most organizations. Keeping the data definition current also helps people understand the current state of the business.

> Comprehensive data definitions improve
> data understanding and use.

Improved data understanding ensures that the data are used to take appropriate business actions. Inappropriate business actions are avoided, and the effort required to correct those actions are avoided. The use and success of new technology, such as data warehouses, data mining, and extensible markup language (XML), are supported with improved data understanding.

Limited Data Disparity

Comprehensive data definitions further limit the disparate data cycle. Formal data names begin to slow the disparate data cycle and comprehensive data definitions continue to put the brakes on that cycle. Together they make substantial progress toward substantially slowing, and ultimately stopping, the disparate data cycle.

> Comprehensive data definitions further slow
> the disparate data cycle.

Comprehensive data definitions also support the compare data cycle. Increased data understanding draws people into the process of preparing data definitions that support the business, which further increases the understanding, which draws in more people. Once comprehensive data definitions are started, the process catches on and is self-perpetuating. The result is comprehensive data definitions that are routinely enhanced to meet changing business needs.

Increased Productivity

The result of improved data understanding and further limitation of the disparate data cycle is an increase in productivity for both business clients and the information technology staff. The time spent understanding the data and determining how to properly use those data is saved and applied to more appropriate tasks. Taking the appropriate action initially and avoiding missed opportunities eliminates that loss of productivity. It prevents a cost-incurred approach and allows people to take a more value-added approach to business actions.

> Comprehensive data definitions substantially increase productivity.

The best criteria for a comprehensive data definition is what you would like to see if you were encountering the data for the first time. What would you like to have available to help you fully understand the data and use it appropriately to support business activities? Better yet, what would newcomers to the organization or the business unit like to see to help them thoroughly understand the data?

When the good practices described above are used to develop data definitions that you think are comprehensive, ask someone new to the organization or in another business unit if they can thoroughly understand the content and meaning of the data from those definitions. If they can readily understand the data, you did an excellent job. If they cannot, then you need to identify the weakness in the definitions and correct those weaknesses.

One of the best ways to enhance data definitions is to continually seek the opinion of people new to the organization or new to the business unit and respond to any criticism they have about the data definitions. This is value-added enhancement of the data definition.

Best Practices

The good practices for developing comprehensive data definitions emphasize the thorough understanding of the content and meaning of the data. *Along with formal data names, comprehensive data definitions are the most critical step in developing comparate data and stopping the creation of disparate data!*

> Comprehensive data definitions can be leveraged for success.

The task of developing data definitions for the entire data resource is formidable; it is larger than the task of developing formal data names. This task, like the development of formal data names, can be reduced to produce early success and increase motivation to continue the process.

Core Component Definitions

Developing comprehensive data definitions for data subjects, data characteristics, and coded data values is the initial effort that gains the maximum benefit. Adding comprehensive data definitions to the data that have been formally named provides early successes and gains wider interest in the process. These successes motivate people to continue developing comprehensive data definitions. Combining the preparation of formal data names and comprehensive data definitions provides a one-two punch that substantially limits further development of disparate data and promotes the development of comparate data.

Business Client Involvement

Business clients must be involved in the development of comprehensive data definitions. They know the business better than most information technology staff and can contribute that knowledge to the development of comprehensive data definitions. Their involvement also helps resolve the synonyms and homonyms involved in the business terms and definitions. The bottom line is that their involvement helps align knowledge about business with a thorough understanding of the data resource.

Summary

The bad habits leading to vague data definitions, the impacts of those bad habits, the good practices for comprehensive data definitions, the benefits of the good practices, and the most beneficial best practices are summarized below. This list is also contained in Appendix A.

Bad habits leading to vague data definitions:

    Non-existent data definitions—never existed, lost, or misplaced.

    Unavailable data definitions—exist but are not readily available.

    Short data definitions—short, truncated phrases.

    Meaningless data definitions—useless for understanding the data.

    Outdated data definitions—never enhanced after development.

    Incorrect data definitions—do not correctly represent the business.

    Unrelated data definitions—not related to the content and meaning of the data.

Impacts of vague data definitions:

    Inhibited data understanding.

    Inappropriate use of the data.

    Perpetuation of the disparate data cycle and hidden data.

    Continued loss of productivity.

Good practices for comprehensive data definitions:

    Meaningful data definitions prepared based on business meaning.

    Thorough data definitions prepared with no length limitations.

    Enhanced data definitions that remain current with the business.

    Fundamental data definitions created to be inherited by specific data definitions.

Benefits of comprehensive data definition:

    Improved data understanding.

    Continued slowing of the disparate data cycle.

    Improved productivity of business clients and information technology staff.

Best practices for success motivation:

    Data subjects, data characteristics, and coded data values are defined first.

    Business clients must be directly involved in data definitions.

The bad habits, good practices, and best practices for data definitions can be used to evaluate the status of an organization's data resource. Fill in the horizontal bar (below) to show the degree to which the bad habits exist and the degree to which the good practices and the best practices have been implemented. You can provide definitions for the Poor, Fair, Moderate, Good, and Excellent headings to suit your organization, or you can use a numeric scale if it is more appropriate. You can also select the items that are important for your organization, but don't be too hasty at excluding items, because they may be valuable later. This list is also contained in Appendix B.

	P	F	M	G	E
Bad Habits					
Non-existent data definitions	☐	☐	☐	☐	☐
Unavailable data definitions	☐	☐	☐	☐	☐
Short data definitions	☐	☐	☐	☐	☐
Meaningless data definitions	☐	☐	☐	☐	☐
Outdated data definitions	☐	☐	☐	☐	☐
Incorrect data definitions	☐	☐	☐	☐	☐
Unrelated data definitions	☐	☐	☐	☐	☐
Good Practices					
Meaningful data definitions	☐	☐	☐	☐	☐
Thorough data definitions	☐	☐	☐	☐	☐
Current data definitions	☐	☐	☐	☐	☐
Fundamental data definitions	☐	☐	☐	☐	☐
Best Practices					
Data subject definitions	☐	☐	☐	☐	☐
Data characteristic definitions	☐	☐	☐	☐	☐
Data code definitions	☐	☐	☐	☐	☐
Business client involvement	☐	☐	☐	☐	☐

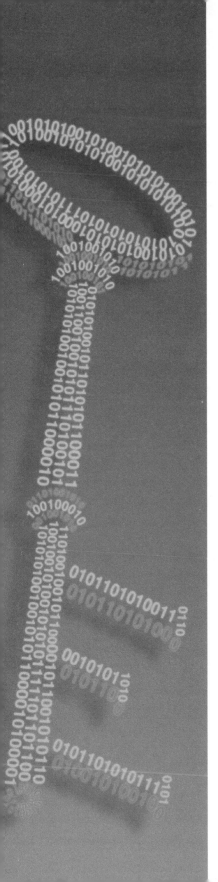

CHAPTER 4

Proper Data Structure

> A proper data structure adequately
> represents the business.

After comprehensive data definitions, the third way to achieve data resource quality is through the development of proper data structures. As the business becomes more complex, the data resource that supports the business becomes more complex. As more people have increased access to the data resource and the data are used to support more business activities, the representation of the business through the data structure becomes more important. When the data resource was accessed by relatively few people that thoroughly understood the business, an improper data structure would have little impact. As business becomes increasingly dynamic and interactive and the data resource supporting the business becomes more complex, the data structure becomes more important.

The proper structuring of data is a very involved and far-reaching topic. There are many different concepts and techniques for representing the data supporting a business through a data structure, and these concepts and techniques are continually evolving. This chapter provides an overview of the bad habits involved in developing data structures and how those bad habits can be turned into good practices. It does not provide an in-depth presentation of all the details for structuring data.[1]

This chapter does not include issues related to orientation of the data resource toward supporting business activities. Although the orientation is related to data structure, it is more related to management of the data resource. It is more cultural than structural and is explained in greater detail in the chapter on Reasonable Data Orientation.

Improper Data Structures

A *data structure* is a representation of the arrangement, relationship, and contents of data subjects, data entities, and data files in the common data architecture. The term is often used in a physical sense meaning the physical structure of data within a database or application. Although this is one aspect of a data structure, it is not the only aspect. A data structure also represents the logical structure of data independent of the database where the data are stored or the application where the data are used. Both the logical and the physical data structures are developed within the common data architecture.

Improper means not suited to the circumstances or needs. An *improper data structure* is a data structure that does not provide an adequate representation of the data supporting the business for the intended audience. It is a sure way to misrepresent the business and a person's understanding of that business.

> An improper data structure does not adequately
> represent the business.

There are many different things that contribute to an improper data structure. All of these things, however, boil down to the four basic bad habits explained below. You should understand these bad habits to determine if improper data structures exist in your data resource.

---

[1] Techniques for structuring data are presented in Brackett, Michael H., *Data Sharing Using a Common Data Architecture,* John Wiley & Sons, 1994, and Brackett, Michael H., *The Data Warehouse Challenge: Taming Data Chaos,* John Wiley & Sons, 1996.

Detail Overload

The typical data structure is shown with an entity-relation diagram. In most situations there is just too much detail on these diagrams. In an attempt to get all the detail in one place and represent all audiences, there is an excess of detail that is very confusing to most people. The diagram may even be confusing to the people who developed it after they have been away from it for a period of time. The situation is much like the abbreviated data names mentioned above; the developers have literally memorized the entity-relation diagram.

> Traditional diagrams contain too much detail
> causing overload and confusion.

The prominent things that overload an entity-relation diagram are useless semantics, data cardinalities, data attributes, and primary and foreign key notations. Each of these overloads is explained below.

Useless Semantics

Useless or less than useful semantics can easily overload an entity-relation diagram. Semantic data modeling was prominent before diagramming became an easy task on the computer. Some of us remember those days all too well. **Semantic statements** verbally describe the relationship between data entities, such as A Customer can place many Orders or A Stream is composed of many Stream Segments. The reciprocal semantics were often stated, such as An Order is placed by only one Customer or A Stream Segment contributes to only one Stream.

> Semantic statements often add nothing to an entity-relation diagram.

When diagramming became easier, these semantic statements were placed on the lines representing the relationship between data entities, as shown in Figure 4.1. The rule is to read the semantic statements clockwise to understand the reciprocal semantics. Note that a data entity is represented by a box with bulging sides and a data relation is represented by a dashed line.

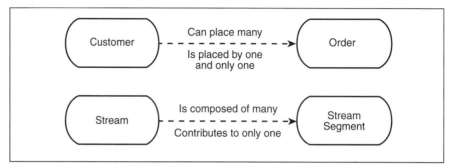

Figure 4.1   Example of semantic statements on data relations.

Semantic statements can be useful if done properly. Sometimes, however, the semantic statements are meaningless. Rather than a meaningful statement like those above, statements such as has many, is one of, belongs to, and so on, are often used. These statements add very little understanding to the diagram and increase the overload. Some diagrams even contain semantic statements that are not correct when read in a clockwise manner. This causes even greater confusion about the meaning of the relation.

Data Cardinalities

Data cardinality is the number of data occurrences allowed on either side of a data relation. Semantic statements provide a **general data cardinality** for the relationship between data entities, such as one Customer and many Orders or one Stream and many Stream Segments. The data relations in Figure 4.1 show the general data cardinalities. A line with no arrowhead represents a one-to-one relation, a line with one arrowhead on one end represents a one-to-many relation in the direction of the arrowhead, and a line with an arrowhead on both ends represents a many-to-many relation. Many entity-relation diagrams contain the general data cardinality in a semantic statement that does not match the cardinality of the data relation. This situation can be both confusing and frustrating.

> Data cardinalities can often be confusing on an entity-relation diagram.

Specific data cardinalities are a specific cardinality shown on the data relation. A 0,1 or 1,1 is often shown on the parent side of the data relation and a 1,m or 0,m is often shown on the child side of the data relation, although there are a variety of other notations. There are three problems with the specific data cardinality notations.

First, these notations are redundant, with the line representing the data relation and with the semantic statements. This redundancy adds to the overload. Second, the redundant notations can be conflicting, as mentioned above, between the data relation and the semantic statement. This conflict is confusing and frustrating because people are uncertain as to what the data relation represents. Third, the specific data cardinality is not always important to all audiences, such as managers and business clients.

Data Attributes

The data attributes contained in a data entity are often shown on the entity-relation diagram. There are several different notations for showing the data attributes, including listing them within the symbol representing the data entity and adding an additional symbol for each data attribute around the data entity symbol. The problem with showing the data attributes on the entity-relation diagram is an overload of detail that is quite confusing to many people. It is very difficult to understand the relations between the data entities when those relations are confused with all the data attributes.

This approach may be acceptable for training classes where there are only a few data attributes in a data entity. When data entities contain 20 or 30 data attributes, it becomes very confusing. When data entities contain over 50 data attributes, which is possible with some major data entities, the diagram becomes incomprehensible.

> Data attributes on an entity-relation diagram often cause confusion.

Another bad habit is that data attributes may not be shown at all. I have seen many data structures with only an entity-relation diagram and have been told that, if you get the data entities and data relations right, that the data attributes will fall into place. Who really needs to worry about the data attributes anyway? This is like saying that if you get the correct foundation and framing on a house that the wiring, plumbing, and so on, will all fall into place. Why include them on the building plans?

Primary Key Notation

Primary keys and foreign keys[2] are often placed on the entity-relation diagrams. Like the semantic statements, cardinalities, and data attributes mentioned above, the inclusion of primary keys and foreign key notation on the entity-relation diagram leads to an overload of detail that causes confusion. Even with one single attribute primary key and a few single attribute foreign keys and the notations PK and FK, the detail is often too much to comprehend.

> Primary key notation is often very confusing
> and difficult to interpret.

When the primary keys contain multiple data attributes, and the same data attribute appears in more than one foreign key, it is nearly impossible to readily comprehend the roles that data attributes play in primary and foreign keys. The notations PK1, PK2, FK1, FK2, (FK1, FK2), and (PK1, FK1, FK2) become very confusing. A person cannot readily identify the components of the primary and foreign keys and have difficulty verifying the relationships with these notations.

A third problem occurs when there are alternate primary keys, and corresponding alternate foreign keys. This situation is becoming more prominent today with the designation of business and physical keys and the designation of candidate keys from disparate data. It is quite difficult to interpret the primary and foreign keys, even with notations like APK, AFK, APK1, AFK1, and (APK1, AFK2). It is not readily obvious what is a primary key, a foreign key, an alternate key, and so on.

Detail Overload Recap

Entity-relation diagrams often contain data entities, data relations, semantic statements, cardinalities, primary keys and foreign keys, and the data attributes. All of this detail overloads the diagram and makes the data structure very difficult to

---

[2] Primary keys and foreign keys are defined later in this chapter.

interpret. People often take a precursory look at the diagram, do not want to admit they are overwhelmed, and say that it looks good to them. This response should immediately alert you to a problem. *When people do not understand the diagrams, they are not intimately involved in the data that supports their business!*

> Excess detail limits the involvement of business clients.

We do not put this much detail on the drawings in other disciplines. Can you imagine just one drawing of a residence that has all the foundation, structure, roofing, siding, plumbing, wiring, windows, doors, kitchen and bathroom appliances, light fixtures, carpets, drapes, and so on? Can you imagine just one diagram of a commercial airplane that shows the structure and all the detail for mechanics, electrical, and occupancy? It would be impossible to interpret.

Putting all of the detail on one entity-relation diagram makes that diagram impossible to comprehend. It is just too confusing considering the level of complexity involved in developing a high-quality data resource. Yet many people still try to do just that.

There is no principle that I know of requiring all of the data structure detail to be placed on one entity-relation diagram. I often ask people where this concept originated. The answer I most often receive is that it is the way the design software does it. If that is really the problem, then we need to actively change the design software. The other most prominent answer is that it was the way they were taught in class. If this is the problem, then the classes need to be changed.

Wrong Audience Focus

The excessive detail on an entity-relation diagram often results in the wrong focus for a particular audience. There are three basic bad habits associated with a wrong audience focus: there is the wrong detail for the audiences, there is a poor presentation format, and all the necessary audiences are not covered. Each of these bad habits is explained below.

Wrong Detail for Audience

A single entity-relation diagram with excessive detail is often presented to a wide variety of audiences from executives, to managers, to business clients, to knowledge workers, to data analysts, and to database technicians. A portion of the detail is relevant to one audience, but is not relevant to another audience. For example, a manager is probably not interested in specific data cardinalities or physical data names. A database technician is probably not interested in many-to-many data relations and semantic statements.

Many data structures are developed by database technicians or technical analysts, whose basic objective is getting enough detail to construct and implement a database. This level of detail is certainly necessary for constructing and implementing a database. However, it is not necessary for presenting the design to line managers, middle managers, or executives in order to show how the data resource supports the business.

All too often, technical people go to management with the wrong set of details. Many executives and managers look at some of the entity-relation diagrams that are presented to them, roll their eyes back, and tune out the presentation. Their interest is in how the data structure represents the business, not how the database will be constructed and implemented. The detail presented to them is not relevant to their perception of the business world. No wonder we do not have executive awareness of the data resource problems; we all too often turn off executives with a technical perception of their business world.

> The wrong detail is often presented to an audience.

Similarly, database technicians are turned off by diagrams prepared for managers that include many-to-many data relations, extensive business definitions, lack of detailed data and file specifications, and so on. The detail on the diagram, though relevant to a business manager, is not relevant to the construction, implementation, and maintenance of the database. No wonder database technicians go off and do their own thing.

In the middle are the logical modelers and data architects, trying to cater to both audiences. Yet they are adding their own spin to the data structure by playing with the notations, being too academic or esoteric in their approach, and so on. No wonder the database does not match the business needs and many data architects have a bad reputation. *There is a major disconnect between the business and the physical database!*

I was in a design session with a group of business people discussing one aspect of their business. I was putting a diagram on the board to represent their view of the business world and had an assistant taking notes. I noticed another data modeler taking prolific notes and wondered what he was doing. During a break I reviewed his notes to see if I was missing something. He was actually documenting the same data structure that was on the board, but was doing it in several different notations.

Poor Presentation Format

The format for presentation of the data structure can be very difficult to interpret. In addition to the excessive detail and the wrong audience focus, the entity-relation diagram can be presented in a format that is too difficult to understand. Even the correct detail for the audience, when presented in a poor format, can be difficult to interpret and understand, which results in people missing the message.

> The presentation format often makes the data structure difficult to interpret.

I have seen diagrams that run the full length of a conference room wall with data relations that run most of the way across the diagram. The data relations run only in cardinal directions and make numerous direction changes across the diagram. Some data relations disappear behind data entities and a person is not sure where they reappear, particularly when there are several data relations that disappear behind the same data entity. Many data relations cross, and it is difficult to follow the route of one data relation. Adding the semantic statements and cardinalities to these diagrams makes them impossible to readily interpret.

These diagrams are referred to as **butcher paper diagrams** because it is like unrolling a roll of butcher paper around the room. As one business client commented, "It looks like the wiring diagram of the space shuttle." If we made diagrams like this for boats, airplanes, buildings, bridges, hydro-electric dams, and so on, and presented them to people for review, we would not be in business very long.

Audiences Not Covered

A third bad habit is that all the possible audiences are not adequately covered. Many times an entity-relation diagram is very physically oriented; it is essentially a ***file-relation diagram*** that shows the data files and the data relations between them as they are to be implemented. These diagrams are usually not presented to business clients, managers, or executives for the reasons explained above. I have often heard comments from technical people that there is no need to present an entity-relation diagram or a file-relation diagram to a manager or executive. After all, it is none of their business how the database is built.

> All audiences are not adequately involved in reviewing the data structure.

After careful consideration, however, it is their business how the data resource supports the business activities of the organization. It is their business that the funds spent on building the data resource are used appropriately. It is their business that the data resource is going the same direction that the business is going.

The problem is that the physical data structures with excessive detail that are presented in the wrong format are alienating some people whose review comments are critical. The typical response is to just not include them in any more reviews. After all, they do not appear to be interested. Technical people, and to some degree data analysts and data architects, have not learned how to represent the complexity of the business and the structure of a data resource that supports that complexity to managers in terms that are relevant to them and their perception of the business.

Recently the term *information model* has been used to represent an entity-relation diagram. The hope was that calling a traditional entity-relation diagram an information model would make it more important to the business people and they would become more involved. The problem, however, is that the same problems arise because the same bad habits are used to develop the model.

Inadequate Business Representation

The excessive level of detail in a data structure and the wrong audience focus usually result in an inadequate representation of the business. A data resource is not developed to fully support the business activities as desired. The three bad habits associated with an inadequate business representation are incomplete business detail, incomplete business coverage, and redundant business coverage. Each of these bad habits is explained below.

Incomplete Business Detail

The business detail is seldom completely represented in a data structure. One approach to the excess detail contained on an entity-relation diagram is to eliminate some of the detail. Rather than not including the audience as mentioned above, some of the technical detail is dropped from the data structure. The problem is that the appropriate business detail is not added to the data structure so that it is relevant to the audience. Although this is a step in the right direction, it does not resolve the problem.

> The data structure may not contain the relevant business detail.

One cause is that the design tools today will not readily support different sets of detail for different audiences. Although products continue to improve, they are relatively weak for filtering out the detail that is not relevant for a particular audience and displaying only the detail that is relevant for a specific audience. Most design tools are primarily oriented toward the physical design and construction of a database. They are relatively weak on presenting subsets of detail relevant to a specific audience and the automatic transformation from one level of detail to another.

Incomplete Business Coverage

The second problem with inadequate business representation is that the data structure seldom represents all the data that support the business. The operational data structure usually encompasses the core business activities and maybe some of the ancillary business activities, but seldom does it cover all the ancillary activities. In many organizations the departmental and personal data are not included. In some organizations all of the core business activities may not be completely covered. Generally, only the less intricate parts of the business are included in a data structure; the real intricate parts are seldom included. Depending on the size of the organization, its length of time in business, and whether it is a public or private sector organization, less than a third of the business is included in a data structure of any kind.[3]

---

[3] Searching for data structures representing disparate data in a variety of organizations indicate that this is the level of formal data structure development in those organizations.

> The entire business is seldom adequately represented
> with a data structure.

In most cases, only the operational data needed for the day-to-day business activities are included in a data structure. Seldom are the historical data or audit trails included. Very few of the cross-system reporting databases, data marts, and data warehouses that are currently being developed have a formal logical data structure. They may have a physical data structure that bears some resemblance to the physical operational data structure, but they seldom have a logical data structure oriented toward the business. This makes the percent coverage of the business even lower.

When the non-automated data are included, the percentage goes yet lower. Overall, less than 15% of the total data resource of an organization is included in any kind of a data structure.[4] That means that, at best, only 15% of the business is represented by a data structure. How can any organization ever hope to fully meet their business objectives with a data resource that has this level of understanding? How can any organization realize its full potential if there is this low level of understanding of their data resource? The answer is that if the organization does meet its objectives and realize its potential with this level of formal understanding, it is done by sheer physical work that does not maximize employee productivity.

Redundant Business Coverage

The third bad habit with inadequate business coverage is that multiple data structures exist for the same segment of the business. As mentioned above, less than 15% of the total data resource in an organization has any kind of a data structure. Worse yet, some segments of the business have five or six different data structures, developed by different people, using different notations, and stored in different design tools. Many of these data structures simply relate to issues of your technique versus my technique, or your tool versus my tool, or your perception of the business versus my perception of the business.

---

[4] The inventorying and cross-referencing of disparate data in many organizations provides a good indication that this is the level at which data structures have been developed.

There is often an intense competition over the technique, tool, or perception that is to the detriment of the organization. I have witnessed many discussions, sometimes quite heated, about a data structure that is nothing more than the notation used or the features of a design support tool. It is not oriented toward a more thorough understanding or representation of the business.

> Disparate data structures may be redundant and inconsistent.

These redundant data structures are seldom identical or consistent, resulting in disparate data structures. Whether the disparity is due to different art forms of design, different perceptions of the business, different notations, different levels of detail, or poor design techniques, is not really important. What is important is that multiple data structures that are redundant and inconsistent cause considerable confusion about how well the data resource actually represents the business. People do not know which version is the correct version, or if any of the versions are the correct version.

Poor Data Structure Techniques

There are many things that constitute poor data structure design techniques. Many of these technical bad habits are beyond the scope of this book, but the most prominent bad habits are related to the normalization and denormalization of data, the designation of primary keys, the location of data definitions, and incorrect data structures. Each of these bad habits is described below.

Data Normalization and Denormalization

The techniques of data normalization and data denormalization have been around for many years. **Data normalization** is the process that brings data into a normal form that minimizes redundancies and keeps anomalies from entering the data resource. It provides a subject-oriented data resource that is based on business objects and events. Many entity-relation diagrams are not properly normalized and are not truly subject-oriented from a business perspective. People took a physical approach and did not start with the business objects and events. The chapter on Reasonable Data Orientation describes the situation in more detail.

> The data structure is seldom normalized or denormalized properly.

Data denormalization is the process that adjusts the normalized data structure for optimum performance in a specific operating environment without compromising the normalized data structure. Many data structures were not properly denormalized because they were not properly normalized in the first place. A typical approach is to develop a physical data structure oriented toward database construction and implementation. It is what we call a *brute-force physical approach.*

In some situations, people claim they have developed a logical data structure that is normalized and a separate physical data structure that is denormalized. On close examination, however, these data structures are simply variations of a physical data structure which are referred to as *physical-logical data structures* and *physical-physical data structures.* Most design tools do not support automated transformation from a normalized data structure to a denormalized data structure.

An even worse situation is the development and implementation of a normalized data structure without any denormalization. The data structure represents the business but has extremely poor performance. I worked with a public sector organization that developed one of the best normalized data structures I have seen and implemented it without any denormalization because it represented the business so well. The result was disastrous performance where the only reasonable solution that did not impact the business was the acquisition of additional hardware.

Primary Key Designations

A second bad habit with data structure design is the proper designation of primary keys. A *primary key* is one or more data attributes that uniquely identify each data occurrence in a data subject. Remember from the chapter on Formal Data Names that a data occurrence is not formally named. Each data occurrence is identified with a primary key that functions as a unique label for each data occurrence. For example, an employee may be uniquely identified with their social security number and a stream may be uniquely identified with the U.S. Geological Survey (USGS) river reach number.

Primary keys are an important component of the data normalization process. Ideally, the primary key should consist of one or more business related data attributes that ensure the data are properly normalized with respect to the business. One of the recent developments in database management systems is the use of system-assigned primary keys. The database management system assigns consecutive numbers to uniquely identify each data occurrence. They are useful because they optimize the performance of a database.

> The use of business and physical primary keys is often confused.

The problem is that these system-assigned primary keys have no business meaning. As a result, the data structures are poorly designed. For example, a person may design a data file that contains data about trees, rivers, and vehicles. A system-assigned primary key is used, and the data normalization process verifies that each data occurrence—whether it represents a tree, river, or vehicle—is uniquely identified with that system-assigned primary key.

When business clients are asked what uniquely identifies trees, rivers, and vehicles, they reply scientific name, USGS river reach number, and vehicle identification number, respectively. When these facts are provided, the data normalization process indicates there should be three separate data entities for trees, rivers, and vehicles. This puts a whole different business perspective on the data structure.

Data Definition Inclusion

The data definitions are often included with the data structure. In the last chapter on Comprehensive Data Definitions, it was mentioned that there are often redundant data definitions. One of the major reasons for this situation is that data definitions are included with the data structure. For example, wherever a data attribute name appears, the data definition is included with that data attribute. If the data attribute happens to be part of a primary key or foreign key and appears in several different data entities, the data definition is replicated for each of these appearances. These redundant data definitions soon get out of synch and become confusing. The result is that maintenance of any data definitions is abandoned.

> Data definitions are frequently stored with the data structure.

Design tools frequently require that a data definition appear with each data attribute. This requirement forces people to write the same data definition several times. The chance of consistent definitions initially is unlikely, but the chance of consistent enhancements to those data definitions over time is poor.

Incorrect Data Structure

Poor data structure design techniques lead to an incorrect data structure. The data structure is wrong and people often have no idea where the data structure originated. It may have been a normalized design that was abandoned, or a purely physical approach, or physical changes that were made and not documented, or simply people hurrying to get the database implemented.

I frequently encounter people randomly inserting foreign keys after data normalization so they can get to the data quicker, or replicating data to other tables for faster access. I have encountered a mismatch between architectural components where the structure does not match the data names, the data definitions, or the data integrity rules. I could literally write a book on the poor data structure design techniques I have encountered.

> The data structure may not match the names,
> definitions, or integrity rules.

The basic cause of incorrect data structures is a lack of formal training. I often ask people where they learned their data resource design techniques. The most common answer is that they had a class on developing databases that was taught by a database management system vendor, or that they once read a database management system manual. When pressed about formal training on developing a normalized data structure oriented to the business followed by a denormalized data structure for implementation, most people said that they had no such training. We certainly would not let this situation occur with financial or human resource management, or with the design of airplanes, automobiles, or bridges.

Improper Data Structure Impacts

The bad habits described above lead to improper data structures that can profoundly impact the data resource. The data may be formally named and comprehensively defined, but an improper data structure can ruin it all. When any of the bad habits leading to improper data structures are encountered, it should be apparent that the data resource is in real trouble.

Poor Business Understanding

One major impact of an improper data structure is that it does not contribute to business understanding or to a data resource that supports the business information demand. Many business clients and managers ceased to be involved in the development of data structures because they were constantly confronted with data structures that they did not understand and were not relevant to the business. The technical people moved ahead with a data structure that they believed is correct, only to have a data resource that does not support the business.

> An improper data structure results in poor business understanding.

The author was told by the director of a public sector organization that they did not want to see another (expletives deleted) entity-relation diagram. There had been too many entity-relation diagrams developed in their organization, they were relatively uninterpretable by the business clients, they provided no benefit for understanding the business or defining the data resource, and they were too costly. The truth of this situation is not the issue. The issue is that a prominent director perceived that entity-relation diagrams were not providing any benefit to the business.

Poor Performance

Another major impact of improper data structures is poor hardware and software performance. There are two aspects to poor performance: one is related to an improper data structure and the other is related to a true limitation of hardware and software resources. It is the first performance aspect that is of concern. People may have intended good performance with their data structure, but the performance was actually worse than they intended due to an improper data structure. The data structure may have been a logical data structure that was not properly denormalized or a physical data structure that was not developed with the implementation platform in mind. In either situation, the performance was less than expected.

> An improper data structure often results in poor performance.

I was in an organization that had an extremely poor data structure as a result of poor design techniques. I could not even begin to understand the business and I saw many reasons for poor performance. This situation was mentioned to the designers and they replied that there was, in fact, very poor performance. They had even shut off all the data edits, real-time logs and audit trails, and some of the real-time reporting with no substantial improvement in performance. The reasons for performance were pointed out and there was utter amazement that their data structure could have caused that degree of poor performance.

Continued Data Disparity

An improper data structure, like informal data names and vague data definitions, contribute to the disparate data cycle. In most situations, when people do not understand the data structure or there are performance problems with the data structure, a new data structure is developed. Seldom is there any attempt to correct or enhance the existing data structure. The problem is often blamed on the design method and notation rather than on the design techniques.

> An improper data structure enforces the disparate data cycle.

The typical approach is that if this data structuring method did not produce the right results, then another method might be better. This approach, along with a variety of egos involved in different design methods, produces more improper data structures that are redundant and inconsistent, which increases the disparity and reduces the understanding.

Lower Productivity

Poor business understanding, poor performance, and continued data disparity all result in a loss of productivity. Productivity is lost building improper data structures, implementing improper data structures, and correcting improper data structures. Productivity is lost understanding what the data represent and how to best use those data to support business activities. The business activities, themselves, are performed at a lower level of effectiveness and efficiency.

An improper data structure results in lower productivity.

Both business clients and information technology staff lose productivity because they are developing and redeveloping a data resource in order to understand the business, support the business, and achieve good performance. This is a waste of good resources that could be put to far more productive tasks. There are no basic statistics about loss of productivity that apply to all organizations. If the bad habits mentioned above are reviewed and applied to the data resource that supports the critical business function, people can get a good idea of the lost productivity in their organization.

Proper Data Structure

The bad habits that lead to improper data structures can be turned into good practices that support the development of a proper data structure. A ***proper data structure*** is a data structure that provides a suitable representation of the business, and the data resource supporting that business, that is relevant to the intended audience. The good practices include the basic components of a proper data structure, the data structure appropriate for different audiences, the formal data structure design techniques, and the development of a comprehensive data structure.

Proper data structures adequately represent the data
supporting the business.

This section is not about formal data modeling or developing a formal data architecture. The author has other books that present these techniques in detail. This section only provides the basic good practices for developing proper data structures and preventing the impacts of improper data structures. It provides an overview of the things to look for in a proper data structure. If you do not see these things in your data structures, you should be worried because there is a problem and the business is at risk from a low-quality data resource.

Data Structure Components

A proper data structure consists of two major components; an entity-relation diagram and a data attribute structure. These two components, collectively, contain all the detail necessary to understand the data structure and allow the detail to be filtered so that it is relevant to a specific audience. These two components also integrate quite well with other components of a data architecture, such as data names, data definitions, and data integrity rules.

> A proper data structure consists of an entity-relation diagram and an attribute structure.

Entity-Relation Diagram

An **entity-relation diagram** contains only the data entities and the data relations between those data entities. It does not contain any of the data attributes in those data entities, nor does it show any roles played by those data attributes. It may contain semantic statements, if those statements are meaningful and useful to an understanding of the data structure. It may also contain specific data cardinalities, if those cardinalities are meaningful and useful to the intended audience and do not conflict with the semantic statements.

The entity-relation diagram is laid out in a manner that is easily interpreted and readily understandable by the intended audience. The data relations are generally straight lines that can run at any angle between data entities and never cross or disappear behind a data entity. The data entities may be grouped into separate diagrams for core data structures and ancillary data structures for better understanding. A single butcher-paper diagram must be avoided at all cost. In other words, there should be many small diagrams that cover a particular subject area. It is a concept that we call *technically correct and culturally acceptable*.

The entity-relation diagram can be used at the business understanding level, at a logical design level, or at a physical implementation level. At the physical implementation level, it becomes a file-relation diagram that represents the physical implementation of the data. Appendix C shows examples of entity-relation diagrams.

Data Attribute Structure

A **data attribute structure** is a list that shows the data attributes contained within a data entity and the roles played by those data attributes. It shows all the primary keys, including business keys and physical keys. It shows the foreign keys for the relations to parent data entities, and may show semantic statements with those foreign keys. It shows all the data attributes in that data entity and serves as an index to the data available to the organization.

The data attribute structure, like the entity-relation diagram, can be used at a business understanding level, at a logical design level, or at a physical implementation level. At the physical level, it becomes a **data item structure,** a list that represents the physical implementation of the data attributes. Appendix C has examples of data attribute structures. It is the physical version of a data attribute structure for implementation.

Proper Detail for the Audience

The entity-relation diagrams and data attribute structure must have the appropriate detail for the intended audience. This approach allows a wide variety of audiences to be involved with developing a data resource that supports the business information demand. Executives, managers, business clients, data architects, and database technicians can all be involved in developing and maintaining the data resource when the relevant detail is provided to them.

> A proper data structure provides the relevant detail
> for the intended audience.

The common data architecture contains all the detail necessary for all audiences. The basic principle is to select the relevant detail for the intended audience and present that detail in understandable segments. In other words, the details are filtered for presentation to a specific audience. Understanding of the business and the data resource supporting the business comes in bite-sized chunks rather than in one huge diagram that fills a conference room wall. The five-schema concept and the three-tier concept provide the foundation to meet these objectives.

Five-Schema Concept

A *schema* is simply a data structure. The *two-schema concept* for data structure began many years ago. There was an *internal schema* representing the way data were stored and an *external schema* representing the way data were used by applications. This concept created a problem when applications needed data in a structure different from the structure used to store the data. The resolution was to create additional internal schema through extracting, sorting, and merging existing data. This was the origin of the data redundancy problem that we face today.

The two-schema concept was resolved with the addition of a *conceptual schema* that was the common denominator between the internal schema and the external schema. It was the beginning of modern-day database management systems and logical data modeling. The problem was that these three schemas were still oriented toward building a database with one structure that met the multiple structure requirements of applications. There was no consideration of how the data were used by the business.

> The five-schema concept added business understanding.

This situation became apparent when we began to include business clients in the data modeling and data normalization process many years ago. We were repeatedly asked what data were actually being normalized. The final answer, after some grueling discussions, was that the business transactions were being normalized. The data used in reports, screens, documents, transactions, and so on, were normalized. This led to creation of the *business schema* that represented the structure of business transactions.

The only thing that was missing, which became apparent as client/servers began to evolve, was a schema that represented the distribution of data over a network. This issue led to development of a *deployment schema* showing the distribution of data on a network. The deployment schema proved most useful as the whole concept of networks evolved.

These five schema are shown in Figure 4.2. The business schema is the structure of the data as used by the business, such as in business transactions. The *data view schema* is the structure of the data as normalized into data entities, and was the original external schema. The *logical schema* is the structure of the data by data entities as optimized from the individual data views, and was the original conceptual schema. The deployment schema is the structure of the data as deoptimized and deployed to various sites in the organization. The *physical schema* is the structure of the data as denormalized and physically implemented, and was the original internal schema.

Three-Tier Data Structure

The *three-tier concept* for data structures addresses the level of detail that is presented to specific audiences. The development of conceptual data structures began with definition of the conceptual schema that typically represented logical data structures at a detail level. It became obvious that some higher level of data structure was needed to represent the business. The logical data structure began to represent the detail level and a conceptual data structure began to represent the business level.

> The three-tier concept provides views for multiple audiences.

There were two problems with this new conceptual data structure. First, it looked like a detailed logical data structure that was just renamed for the business people. Second, the term *conceptual* was viewed as esoteric or academic by many people and was not readily accepted. In the infinite wisdom of information technology, we kept pushing the idea hoping that it would take.

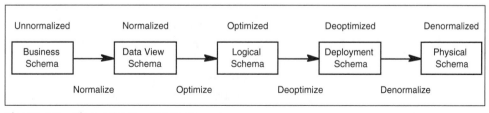

Figure 4.2   Five-schema concept.

After talking with many managers and executives, it became obvious that these two problems had to be solved if we were to make any progress at all with involving business people in developing the data structure. We now use the terms *strategic data structure* and *tactical data structure,* rather than *conceptual data structure,* to represent the business. These two tiers are stacked on top of the detail data structure to provide the three-tier concept shown in Figure 4.3.

The term *conceptual data structure* has now evolved into a strategic view, a tactical view, and a detail view of the data resource that is useful for specific audiences. The **strategic tier** is appropriate for executives and managers. The **tactical tier** is appropriate for line managers and business clients. The **detail tier** is appropriate for data analysts and database technicians. Appendix C shows entity-relation diagrams for these three levels.

Combined Three-Tier and Five-Schema

The three-tier concept and the five-schema concept can be combined into a single concept that addresses multiple audiences, as shown in Figure 4.4. The arrows represent the progression for developing the various schema. Generally, a data structure is developed from the strategic tier through the tactical tier to the detail tier. The business schema lead to the data view schema, which provides detail to the logical schema. The logical schema are used to develop the deployment schema, which are used to develop the physical schema.

Notice that the arrows also flow upward from the logical schema to the tactical tier to the strategic tier. This approach is used when the detail is already

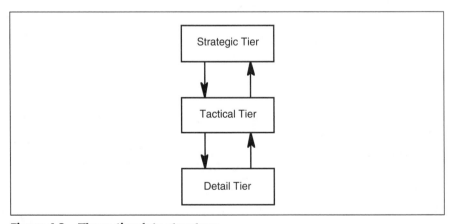

Figure 4.3   Three-tier data structure.

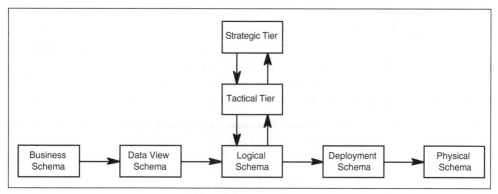

Figure 4.4   Combined three-tier five-schema concepts.

available and can be filtered to provide only the detail necessary for the tactical tier and the strategic tier. Not shown on this diagram are arrows moving from the physical schema to the deployment schema to the logical schema. This approach represents the documentation and understanding of disparate data and is beyond the scope of this book.[5]

Some people ask if the strategic and tactical tiers fit over the data view schema or the business schema. The answer is "no" with respect to the data structure. There is no tactical or strategic equivalent to either of these schema. People also ask if there is a strategic and tactical tier over the deployment schema or the physical schema. There could be strategic and tactical views of these schema, but they are usually oriented toward the physical platform or operating environment rather than to the data structure. They are not shown in the three-tier five-schema concept.

The term *information model* is becoming popular, as mentioned earlier. With respect to the three-tier five-schema concept, the information model is represented by the business schema. The business schema show the sets of data as they are presented to the business to support business activities. If developed properly, these schema contain data in context that are relevant to one or more people for a period of time and become information. The business schema are the bridge from the data resource tier to the information tier in the business intelligence value chain. These business schema could be combined to produce a model of the information presented to the business.

---

[5] A book covering the understanding and formal transformation of disparate data is currently being prepared.

Formal Design Techniques

One prominent trend today is to get through the logical design quickly, then get on with the "physicalization" of the data the way it should be for implementation. *Data physicalization* in this sense means rampant changes to the data independent of any logical data structure. I have seen situations where the technical staff rigidly controls the database. Change requests from the business and application developers are made to this technical staff, they rule on these requests, and accept or reject requests as they see fit. They add and delete foreign keys at will, and they add, remove, and replicate data attributes at their sole discretion. The result is a disastrous set of conflicting data relations and redundant data.

> A proper data structure follows formal design techniques.

This process is the only course of action when there are no formal data structure design techniques. Formal design techniques are needed to ensure a proper data structure and prevent the impacts of improper data structures. These formal techniques include data normalization, data denormalization, primary and foreign keys, semantic statements, data cardinalities, and an integrated data structure.

Data Normalization

Data normalization, as mentioned above, is the process that brings data into normal form that minimizes redundancies and keeps anomalies from entering the data resource. It provides a subject-oriented data resource that is based on business objects and events. There are very precise principles that are powerful and important for normalizing a data structure, but they are too extensive to present in detail here. Only the basic concept is provided.

> Data normalization consists of three formal techniques.

The first technique is to find repeating groups and move those groups to another data entity. For example, an employee can register for many different training classes during their tenure with an organization. Training Class is a repeating group that becomes a separate data entity from Employee. Note that valid semantic statements help identify repeating groups.

The second technique is to find partial key dependencies and move those dependencies to another data entity. Each data attribute must be uniquely identified by the entire primary key for the data entity. When there are multiple data attributes in a primary key and all of those data attributes are not needed to uniquely identify a data attribute, then that data attribute must be moved to another data entity. For example, the primary key of a Training Class is the training course name, such as assertiveness training, and the training class date. Training Class contains a data attribute for the date the training course was first established, which is dependent only on the training course name. It is redundant for all Training Classes and should be moved from Training Class to Training Course. This is why the proper identification of primary keys is important.

The third technique is to find inter-attribute dependencies and move those dependencies to another data entity. For example, Employee contains data attributes for the pay range level, such as 8, and pay range value, such as $3000 per pay period. The pay range value depends on the pay range level and should be moved to a Pay Range data entity so that it is not stored redundantly in Employee. In simple terms, any data attributes that comprise a code table, such as race, ethnicity, management level, education level, and so on, should be defined as a separate data entity. Notice that formal data names help identify the data attributes that belong in another data entity.

There is considerable discussion about additional techniques for data normalization. Some of these techniques are important and others are quite esoteric. The bottom line is that if you follow these three basic techniques, the data structure will be substantially correct and the majority of data structure problems will be resolved. This is the point of diminishing returns where the process should move on to development of the deployment and physical schema. If development of a logical data structure continues beyond this point, there is an increased risk of the paralysis by analysis that is typical in many organizations today. The logical data structure does not have to be absolutely perfect, just good enough to move on with development of the data resource.

Data Denormalization

Data denormalization, as mentioned above, is the process of adjusting the data structure for optimum performance in a particular operating environment without compromising the logical design. Like data normalization, there are very precise principles that are important for denormalizing a data structure, but they are too extensive to present in detail here. Only the basic concept is provided.

> Data denormalization consists of three techniques
> for optimum performance.

The three basic techniques are that every data entity becomes a data file unless an exception applies, every data attribute becomes a data item unless an exception applies, and every data occurrence becomes a data record unless an exception applies. The acceptable exceptions and their alternatives are specific for each physical environment in an organization. Listing them is beyond the scope of this book.[6]

Note that the intent of data denormalization is to adjust for optimum performance, not peak performance. There is often considerable discussion about achieving peak performance to the detriment of the normalized data structure. The bottom line is that if you follow the basic techniques, the physical data structure will perform optimally and will adequately support the business information demand. The balance is between optimum, not peak, performance and not compromising business understanding portrayed in the logical data structure.

Primary Keys and Foreign Keys

The designation of primary keys has followed an interesting route. Before the emergence of database management systems, primary keys were either never designated or were a *physical key* often generated by the data processing staff and were referred to as surrogate keys. As data structures became more business oriented, the designation of primary keys became more business oriented and data attributes meaningful to the business were used for *business keys*. As databases grew in size, the business oriented primary keys caused performance problems and a system-assigned identifier was used.

> Both business and physical primary keys are needed
> for a proper data structure.

---

[6] Refer to *Practical Data Design* for an explanation of the data denormalization techniques.

I have heard many discussions, and a number of heated arguments, about the pros and cons of business keys versus physical keys. These discussions center around which one should be used. The simple answer is that they both are very important and much needed, and both should be used.[7] The business key is needed for business understanding and proper data normalization. The physical key is needed for optimum performance. The business key belongs with a normalized logical data structure and the physical key belongs with the denormalized physical data structure. Both must be designated and maintained, and presented to the appropriate audience.

A *foreign key* is simply the primary key of a parent data entity that is contained in a subordinate data entity to identify its parent data occurrence. If both a business primary key and a physical primary key are designated, then both a business foreign key and a physical foreign key are designated in a subordinate data entity. Again, one is useful for business understanding and the other is useful for performance.

Semantic Statements

Semantic statements can add value for understanding the business and developing a data structure that supports the business if they are used properly. There are three basic principles for the proper use of semantic statements.

> Semantic statements must add value to data structures.

First, semantic statements must be meaningful with respect to the business rather than just repeating the general data cardinality. They must add value to the data structure or they become unnecessary detail. Second, semantic statements can appear on the data relation in an entity-relation diagram, with the foreign key in the data attribute structure, or as separate statements. There is no one place where the semantic statements should appear. They belong to the data structure and can be shown wherever they are most useful for the intended audience. Third, semantic statements should appear on the logical data structures that are related to the business, but should not appear on the physical data structures related to database implementation.

---

[7] I am not aware of any requirement that states there must be one and only one primary key for a data entity.

Data Cardinalities

Data relations and semantic statements indicate general data cardinalities. They appropriately belong with the data structure because they help people understand the business and the data that support the business. After considerable thought and discussion regarding specific data cardinalities, it was determined that they are a feature of data integrity and not a feature of the data structure. They are more appropriate to the formation of precise data integrity rules because they deal with the identification and enforcement of specific requirements, not an understanding of the business.

> Specific data cardinalities are a data integrity issue,
> not a data structure issue.

Please take note that specific data cardinalities are not being discarded as some people claim. They are extremely useful for defining and enforcing specific requirements for data value quality and are being placed with the development of precise data integrity rules for that purpose. The next chapter on Precise Data Integrity explains specific data cardinalities in more detail.

Integrated Data Structure

The data structure must be integrated across an organization so that there is only one common data structure for the entire data resource. That integrated data structure must contain all the detail necessary for all audiences within the three-tier five-schema concept. That detail can then be segmented by business topic and filtered for the intended audience. Each of these subsets are taken from the common data structure and are not developed or maintained as separate, independent data structures. The evolution of data resource design tools that have the capability to transform, segment, and filter will be a great help.

> There must be one integrated data structure
> for the entire data resource.

The common data structure must include the entire data resource and cover the full scope of business activities. The data structure may be developed on a priority basis depending on the resources available. Those resources, however, should be spent on covering the entire data resource rather than developing redundant, conflicting data structures for the same segment of the data resource. The common data structure is part of one integrated, organization-wide, common data architecture.

The data definitions must be stored separately from the data structure. Every data entity and data attribute is defined only once and that definition applies to each existence of that data entity or data attribute. This works like a glossary in a book. A term is defined once in the glossary and that definition applies each time that term appears throughout the book. A term is not defined each time it appears in the book. This approach minimizes the redundancy and inconsistency that frequently occurs when data definitions are stored with each existence of a data entity or data attribute.

The data structure must also be integrated with formal data names, comprehensive data definitions, and precise data integrity rules to provide a complete understanding of the data resource. The data names, data definitions, and data integrity rules are also integrated within the common data architecture. Specific logical and physical data models are prepared for a specific scope of the business, for specific audiences, for a specific purpose by drawing the appropriate detail from the common data architecture. All enhancements are made to the common data architecture and are then available for inclusion in any specific data models.

> The common data architecture contains all the detail
> for specific data models.

A variety of different notations are available for developing data models. It is not important which notations are used, and different notations may be used for different audiences. What is important is that the notations used are appropriate for the audience and that the data models are presented to the audience in a technically correct–culturally acceptable manner. The data models must correctly represent the business and the data resource that supports the business, and they must be readily accepted by the intended audience. If either one of these objectives is not met, the data model has not served its purpose.

Proper Data Structure Benefits

There are several benefits from developing a proper data structure that include an improved business representation, reduced data disparity, improved productivity, and success motivation. These benefits continue to build on the benefits explained in the previous chapters. Each of these benefits is explained below.

Improved Business Representation

The development of a proper data structure provides an improved understanding of the business and the data resource required to support that business. It builds on formal data names and comprehensive data definitions to provide a high-quality data resource. Formal data names and comprehensive data definitions support the proper structuring of data. In turn, the proper structuring of data support the development of formal data names and comprehensive data definitions. It is a symbiotic relationship between the data architecture components.

> Proper data structures improve both data understanding
> and business understanding.

Developing one integrated data structure, segmenting it for a specific business topic, and filtering the detail for the intended audience also improves the business representation. Using a presentation format that is technically correct and culturally acceptable further improves the business representation. Combining these techniques draws people into the process of designing a data resource that supports the current and future business information demand.

Reduced Data Disparity

The data disparity is reduced with development of an integrated data structure. The redundancy is eliminated, and the conflicts and uncertainty resulting from that redundancy are eliminated. Everyone in the organization who uses the data resource contributes to the development of an integrated data structure rather than doing their own thing and increasing the data disparity.

> A proper data structure limits the disparate data cycle.

Developing an integrated data structure further limits the disparate data cycle. Building a proper data structure on formal data names and comprehensive data definitions substantially slows the disparate data cycle and substantially improves in the comparate data cycle. *It is the turning point between a predominantly disparate data resource and a predominantly comparate data resource!*

Improved Productivity

Improving the business representation and reducing the data disparity result in improved productivity for both business clients and information technology staff. More people become involved in contributing to a high-quality data resource rather than just doing their own thing. They have a better understanding of the data resource and how it supports the business information needs and are readily drawn into the process.

> Proper data structures improve productivity.

The time that was spent understanding the data and resolving conflicts that resulted from the data disparity is spent on more important value-added tasks. Seldom are people laid off or reassigned to other duties as a result of improved productivity, as some people claim. They usually move on to more value-added tasks that move the business ahead.

Best Practices

The good practices for developing proper data structures emphasize developing an integrated data structure that represents the business and includes all the detail for understanding the business and implementing the data resource to support the business. They also emphasize targeting the audience with the appropriate level of detail and understanding the techniques for developing proper data structures. But, like the development of formal data names and comprehensive data definitions, developing proper data structures for all data at the organization's disposal cannot be done all at once. The best practices to achieve early successes with a minimum effort are explained below.

Focus on Core Business Functions

Prioritize the development of a proper data structure by starting with data supporting the critical business functions that were used for developing formal data names and comprehensive data definitions. From there, move to less critical business functions, and then into historical data and the analysis of business trends and patterns. The development of proper data structures should follow the same sequence for developing formal data names and comprehensive data definitions.

The starting point may be the operational data supporting business transactions, historical data used in data warehouses and data marts, business dimensions and measures for evaluating the business, and so on. The specific starting point is different for every organization and may change from time to time within the same organizations. Each organization must determine where to start developing proper data structures that will provide the most benefit to the organization.

Use the Three Tiers

Begin with the strategic tier and work down through the tactical tier to the detail tier. Beginning with the business and including business people in the development of proper data structures ensures that the resulting data resource will adequately represent the business. Within the detail tier, move from the logical schema through the deployment schema to the physical schema. Avoid any brute-force physical development at all costs.

If business clients are interested in the information provided to the business, the business schema may be included in the early efforts. The business schema representing a critical business function could be combined into an information model for that business function. This approach should be followed only if an information model provides immediate benefits.

Target the Audience

Develop one integrated data structure for the entire data resource that contains all the detail necessary to understand the business and implement the data resource. Identify audiences for the data structures and present the appropriate level of detail to those audiences. Present that detail in a format that is acceptable to that audience. By all means, avoid an approach of one data structure fitting all audiences.

The integrated data structure should be developed within a single common data architecture for the organization. The best approach is to use the business critical data structures to begin development of the common data architecture. One misconception about the common data architecture is that it must be developed completely for all data at the organization's disposal before it can be used. This is not true. The common data architecture can be, and should be, developed incrementally based on critical business needs.

Provide Formal Training

Provide formal training for business clients and information technology staff. The training should include the concepts, principles, and techniques for understanding the business and developing a data structure to support that business. The savings in productivity alone will more than cover the cost of the training.

One major concept to be presented in formal training is that the data structure does not have to be exact in every detail to move forward. Too much effort is being spent to get a perfect data structure rather that an acceptable data structure, resulting in delays associated with paralysis by analysis. A point of diminishing returns needs to be established where an improvement in the data structure is not feasible based on the level of effort involved and the delay that is created. This does not mean that a brute force physical data structure should be developed and implemented quickly to avoid delays. It does mean that there is a reasonable point where further development of a logical and a physical data structure does not provide benefits that are worth the effort.

Summary

The bad habits leading to improper data structures, the impacts of those bad habits, the good practices for proper data structures, the benefits of those good practices, and the most beneficial best practices are summarized below. The list is also contained in Appendix A.

> Bad habits leading to an improper data structure:
>> Detail overload—excessive detail on the entity-relation diagram.
>>> Useless semantics.
>>> Data cardinalities.
>>> Data attributes.
>>> Primary key notations.
>> Wrong audience focus.
>>> Wrong level of detail for the audience.
>>> Poor presentation format.
>>> All audiences not covered.

Inadequate business representation.
   Incomplete business detail.
   Incomplete business coverage.
   Redundant business coverage.
Poor data structuring techniques.
   Data normalization and denormalization.
   Primary key designations.
   Data definition inclusion.
   Incorrect data structure.

Impacts of an improper data structure:
   Poor business understanding.
   Poor performance of the hardware and system software.
   Continued data disparity.
   Lower productivity of both business clients and information technology staff.

Good practices for a proper data structure:
   Data structure components.
      Entity-relation diagram.
      Data attribute structure.
   Proper detail to each audience.
      Five-schema concept.
      Three tier concept.
      Combined three-tier and five-schema
   Formal design techniques.
      Data normalization.
      Data denormalization.
      Primary keys and foreign keys.
      Semantic statements.
      Data cardinalities.
      Integrated data structure.

Benefits of a proper data structure:
   Improved business representation and understanding.
   Reduced data disparity.
   Improved productivity for business clients and information technology staff.

Best practices for success motivation:
   Focus on core business functions first.
   Use the three tiers—move down through the strategic, tactical, and detail tiers.

Target the audience with the appropriate level of detail.

Provide formal training for key business clients and information technology staff.

The bad habits, good practices, and best practices for data structures can be used to evaluate the status of an organization's data resource. Fill in the horizontal bar (below) to show the degree to which the bad habits exist and the degree to which the good practices and the best practices have been implemented. You can provide definitions for the Poor, Fair, Moderate, Good, and Excellent headings to suit your organization, or you can use a numeric scale if it is more appropriate. You can also select the items that are important for your organization, but don't be too hasty at excluding items, because they may be valuable later. This list is also contained in Appendix B.

	P	F	M	G	E
Bad Habits					
Detail overload					
Useless semantics	☐	☐	☐	☐	☐
Data cardinalities	☐	☐	☐	☐	☐
Data attributes	☐	☐	☐	☐	☐
Primary key notations	☐	☐	☐	☐	☐
Wrong audience focus					
Wrong level of detail for audience	☐	☐	☐	☐	☐
Poor presentation format	☐	☐	☐	☐	☐
All audiences not covered	☐	☐	☐	☐	☐
Inadequate business representation					
Incomplete business detail	☐	☐	☐	☐	☐
Incomplete business coverage	☐	☐	☐	☐	☐
Redundant business coverage	☐	☐	☐	☐	☐
Poor data structure techniques					
Data normalization and denormalization	☐	☐	☐	☐	☐
Primary key designations	☐	☐	☐	☐	☐
Data definition inclusion	☐	☐	☐	☐	☐
Incorrect data structure	☐	☐	☐	☐	☐
Good Practices					
Understand the concepts					
Entity-relation diagrams	☐	☐	☐	☐	☐
Data attribute structure	☐	☐	☐	☐	☐

	P	F	M	G	E
Identify the audience					
Five-schema concept	☐	☐	☐	☐	☐
Three-tier concept	☐	☐	☐	☐	☐
Combined three-tier five-schema concept	☐	☐	☐	☐	☐
Use proper techniques					
Data normalization	☐	☐	☐	☐	☐
Data denormalization	☐	☐	☐	☐	☐
Primary keys and foreign keys	☐	☐	☐	☐	☐
Semantic statements	☐	☐	☐	☐	☐
Data cardinalities	☐	☐	☐	☐	☐
Integrated data structure	☐	☐	☐	☐	☐
Best Practices					
Core business functions	☐	☐	☐	☐	☐
Use the three tiers	☐	☐	☐	☐	☐
Target the audience	☐	☐	☐	☐	☐
Formal training	☐	☐	☐	☐	☐

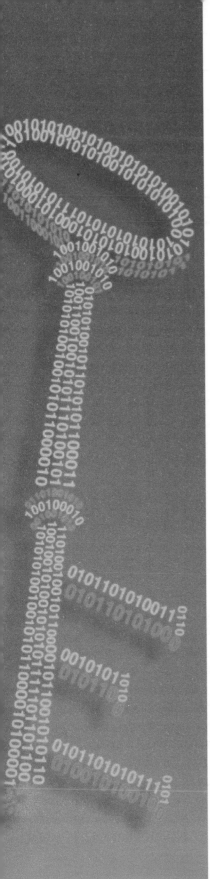

CHAPTER 5

Precise Data Integrity Rules

> Precise data integrity rules ensure
> high data quality.

After proper data structure, the fourth way to achieve **data resource quality is through the development of precise data integrity rules. Data integrity rules specify the criteria that need to be met in order to have high-quality data values that support business needs. They are one component of overall data architecture quality. The other components are data accuracy and data completeness, which will be explained later.**

Traditionally, data integrity rules are defined and enforced in the form of data edits. Many of these data edits are non-specific, incomplete, unenforced, redundant across applications using the same database, and out of date. They have been weak and are getting weaker as the technology evolves to networks, enterprise resource planning applications, and data warehouses. The data value quality is declining and the business operations are being impacted. The definition of precise data integrity rules overcomes this declining situation and improves data value quality.

The concept of formal data integrity rules has been evolving since the early days of data processing and data edits. I separated the specification of data rules from the specification of process rules in the mid-1980s. Others have contributed to the concept of business rules during the 1990s. The specification of precise data integrity rules to ensure data value quality builds on these efforts. This chapter provides an overview of the bad habits that lead to low data integrity and how those bad habits can be turned into good practices that improve data integrity.

Imprecise Data Integrity Rules

Integrity is the state of being unimpaired, the condition of being whole or complete, or the steadfast adherence to strict rules. *Data integrity* is a measure of how well the data are maintained in the data resource after they are captured or created. It indicates the degree to which the data are unimpaired and complete according to a precise set of rules. *Data integrity rules* specify the criteria that need to be met to ensure that the data resource contains the highest data quality necessary to support the business.

Imprecise means not precise, not clearly expressed, indefinite, inaccurate, incorrect, or not conforming to proper form. *Imprecise data integrity rules* are data integrity rules that do not provide adequate criteria to ensure high-quality data and result in data errors. Low data integrity results from the poor specification, poor enforcement of data integrity rules, or both. There are eight prominent bad habits leading to imprecise data integrity rules. Each of these bad habits is explained below.

Ignoring a High Data Error Rate

The foremost bad habit is ignoring a high frequency of data errors. A *data error* is a data value that provides incorrect or false knowledge about the business, or about business objects and events that are important to the business. An *explicit data error* is a data error that is readily visible and known. They are routinely identified and made apparent through data edits. An *implicit data error* is a data error that is hidden and is only known through real-time discovery. They are not routinely identified through data edits and are not readily apparent.

> The true data error rate in most organizations
> is far higher than expected.

The explicit data error rate is often quite high in a disparate data resource and is relatively easy to calculate. The implicit data error rate, however, may be even higher and is relatively difficult to calculate. My experience with the known data error rate in many disparate data resources is that 50% of the data records will fail with one or more data errors following the application of reasonable data integrity rules. This does not mean that all the data values in a data record are in error; it means that one or more of them are in error. A tightening of the data integrity rules, in many cases, can raise the error rate close to 100%, meaning that nearly every data record has one or more data errors. Worse yet, this is only the known error rate from data edits and real-time discovery. The true error rate, including both explicit and implicit errors, could be even higher.[1]

In many organizations the data error rate is high and there is no active effort to review the data errors, identify the problem, and resolve the problems that cause the high data error rate. People routinely correct the data errors, day after day, with no attempt to solve the problem. Valuable resources are being used to correct data errors with no effort toward a self-correction process that prevents the data errors.

One caution about a low data error rate. It may not mean that appropriate data integrity rules are in place to catch and correct the data errors. It may mean that the people involved in capturing or creating data are doing an exemplary job. Should these people leave the organization or move on to another job, the data error rate could skyrocket. I have seen just this situation happen in several organizations that were overly comfortable with their low data error rate.

Incomplete Data Integrity Rules

Most organizations do not have complete, routinely applied data integrity rules in place to identify data errors. Most data edits are limited in some respect and do not fully check for all possible data errors. They were usually developed hastily near the end of information system implementation and are often disparate across different information systems that use the same data resource. Like data definitions, data integrity rules are weak, inconclusive, incomplete, uninterpretable, nonexistent, or out of date with business changes. Many data integrity rules are not consistent with data names, data definitions, and the data structure.

---

[1] I have not done any studies regarding the percentage of errors across all data values in a data record or across all data values in the data resource.

> There are numerous reasons for incomplete data edits.

There are many reasons for incomplete data integrity rules. The most common is an orientation toward completing an information system implementation that is typically overdue and over budget. Just get some data edits in place and worry about data quality later. The perception is that nobody is really interested in data integrity rules anyway. The fact that there are no formal data integrity rules is usually known somewhere within the organization, although that fact is seldom openly admitted. Nobody really wants to readily admit that the data their business is dependent on has no formal data edits.

Another prominent reason that data integrity rules are incomplete is that business clients are seldom involved in developing data integrity rules. A high percent of the knowledge about data value quality is vested in the business clients, not in the information technology staff. The exclusion of business clients from the development of data integrity rules severely impacts data value quality.

Try something the next time you are on the phone placing an order or giving information for a survey. Purposely give a phone number that does not match your address or zip code, or give an address that does not match the zip code, or a zip code that does not match the city, or some other relatively obvious error. See if the recipient of that information catches the error while you are still on the phone. This will let you know whether they have formal, real-time edits in place.

Delayed Data Error Identification

Many organizations have some level of data edits, but the identification and correction of data errors is done long after the data are captured or created. The identification and correction of data errors is delayed to the point that it impacts the business in two ways. First, unless there are rigid controls on data edits that ensure the data will be edited before they are made available, the data may well be in use before the error is identified and a correction made. The longer the delay in identifying and correcting data errors, the greater the risk to the business from using incorrect data. Second, if the data are not made available until they are corrected, it could delay processing and other business actions, which could have an equal impact on the business.

After-the-fact data error identification
does not support the business.

I was in an organization where they were gaining customer numbers so rapidly that they would have cornered all customers in that market sector within a few years. Although this appeared to be spectacular business growth, the growth rate was totally unreasonable. In addition, problems were beginning to surface with quantity discounts for customers and commissions for the sales staff. The problem was traced back to the creation of customer numbers. Neither the sales staff nor the customer readily knew their customer number, so it was left blank on the order form presuming that the office staff would locate and enter the correct number. After all, that is what the office staff is supposed to do. The office staff, on the other hand, had instructions that a blank customer number meant a new customer and the next available customer number was assigned. The ripple effect on discounts and commissions was rapidly getting out of control.

Default Data Values

The use of default data values is a wide-spread habit in many organizations. A *default data value* is a data value that is automatically entered when no other data value is readily available. There are several reasons for the use of default data values, such as providing some data to avoid blank data fields, reducing the error rate, and so on. Default values have their place, but they are often overused and abused.

For example, a default for an indicator could be an N except for a rare situation. If the situation arises, the indicator is set to Y. In this situation a default of N would be acceptable. I have seen some really poor default data values, however. One example is entering a default race of Caucasian if no other race was available. One of the worst examples I have ever found was a default birth date of January 1, 1900 if no other birth date was available. Both of these situations result in data errors that could be disastrous to the business. In most situations a blank is better than incorrect data.[2]

---

[2] I do not want to get into a discussion of the difference between blanks and nulls. For practical purposes, I use the term *blank* to simply mean the absence of a data value.

> Default data values often cause more harm than good.

A prominent cause of hidden data errors is the uncontrolled use of default values because they do not accurately represent the real world. In many situations, people are not generally aware that default data values are being entered. Default data values are usually not documented, or are not documented so they are readily available. The fact that a default data value can be entered and the situations under which a value is entered are seldom documented. The actual insertion of a default data value is seldom tracked or reported. The result is that people are unaware that default values can be inserted or that they have been inserted in specific instances.

It was mentioned in the chapter on Proper Data Structures that a data attribute should only represent one fact. This rule is often violated with default data values. For example, a data field should contain a valid date, but a default data value of Not Known or Not Provided is often inserted into the date field. This results in a date field that represents multiple facts. The reason for no date should be stored in a separate data attribute.

Nonspecific Data Domains

A *data domain* is a set of allowable values for a data attribute. The data domain is usually defined as a general data type. The data domain that is relevant to the business is seldom defined. The conditions under which certain data values are allowed or the relationship between the data values in different data attributes are rarely defined. These situations lead to incorrect data.

> Data domains are usually nonspecific in most databases.

A *database data domain* specifies the values allowed with respect to the database management system. It is usually the general data type, such as text, integer, or date, and is applied in all situations. A *mathematical data domain* specifies the data values that are mathematically possible in a data attribute. It is usually the maximum range of data values allowed, and is usually applied in all situations. A *business data domain* specifies the data values that are allowed with respect to the business and the conditions under which those data values are allowed. It represents what is reasonable for the business and provides more accurate data.

For example, the length of a cargo trailer in feet is two digits. The database data domain is either text or integer, the mathematical data domain is 0 to 99 feet, but the business data domain is 20 to 60 feet. There are no 0-foot cargo trailers, or 5-foot cargo trailers, or 90-foot cargo trailers.

Nonspecific Data Optionality

Data optionality traditionally shows whether a data value is required or is optional. In many situations these labels are not specific. For example, the received date for a product order is usually listed as optional because it is not available at the time the product was ordered. The received date, however, is actually prevented when the product is ordered, but it is required when the product is received by the customer. It is not optional, but is either prevented or required under certain conditions.

> Data optionality is incomplete or inaccurate in most databases.

There is a difference between the traditional database data optionality and business data optionality. *Database data optionality* is a general statement about the requirements of a data value with respect to a database management system. The choices are usually required or optional because the database management system cannot handle specific conditions, at least at this level of their development. *Business data optionality* is a specific statement about the presence of a data value, including the conditions under which that data value will be present. The choices are required, prevented, or optional. There are very few situations where a data value is truly optional; most data values are required or prevented under specific situations.

Undefined Data Derivation

Data that are calculated, generated, created, or otherwise derived in some manner are seldom documented. The contributing data attributes, the algorithm for derivation, and the timing of the derivation, if documented, are usually not readily available to people using the data resource. The data derivations that are documented are frequently out of synch with the process that is actually deriving the data. The processing is often changed to meet changing business needs without changing the documentation. Frequently, there are conflicting data derivations in different applications that are using the same database, or applications that are deriving the same data value and storing them in different databases. All of these situations lead to inaccurate data.

> The derivation of data is seldom formally documented
> or readily known.

The rederivation of data is rarely documented. Derived data values are volatile and become out of synch with the real world. In some situations volatile data values are routinely rederived to accurately represent the real world. In other situations volatile data values are infrequently rederived or are not rederived at all. Volatile data values may be rederived at different times in different applications or different data bases. These situations also lead to inaccurate data.

Uncontrolled Data Deletion

Operational data are usually discarded after their usefulness is over. Data values are replaced, and data occurrences are deleted with no consideration for their future value to the organization. The emergence of data warehousing shows the critical need for high-quality historical data to analyze trends and patterns in the business. When people look for these historical data, they are not always available or cannot be trusted because there is no formal control over the retention of operational data that were obsolete.

> Obsolete operational data are seldom retained for historical analysis.

There are seldom any rules or procedures for the deletion of obsolete operational data. Much of the data necessary for historical analysis is gone forever. Many organizations are starting today to formally retain and manage their obsolete operational data so they can perform historical analysis in the future.

Imprecise Data Integrity Rule Impacts

The existence of imprecise data rules and the resulting low data integrity is a highly undesirable state of the data resource. The impacts of imprecise data rules can be devastating to business operations and planning. The data resource can have formal data names, comprehensive data definitions, and a proper data structure, but imprecise data rules will ruin much of the beneficial effects. The worst impacts to the business are a bad perception, inappropriate business actions, and lost productivity. Each of these impacts is explained below.

Bad Perception

Citizens and customers often form a perception of the service and products based on the data they encounter. If those data have low integrity, the perception is that the services and products provided by that organization also have low integrity. The ready access to data on line and through third parties increases the risk of low data integrity and resulting bad perceptions. One little glitch in the data can cast a bad perception about the organization.

> Citizens and customers often perceive that data integrity is low.

It is not important whether the service and products are actually low quality. It is the perception that citizens and customers have about the service and products that really counts. The quality may be there, but if it is perceived as not being there, it is essentially the same as not being there, and citizens and customers will respond accordingly.

Inappropriate Business Actions

Imprecise data integrity rules and the resulting low data integrity result in inappropriate business actions and missed business opportunities. Informal data names, vague data definitions, and improper data structure resulted in inappropriate business actions and lost opportunities because the data were not readily identified or understood. Imprecise data integrity rules result in inappropriate business actions and lost opportunities because the data values do not accurately represent the real world.

> Imprecise data integrity rules lead to
> inappropriate business actions.

The employees in both public and private sector organizations can take inappropriate actions based on data values that do not accurately represent the situation. They are unable to correctly evaluate the situation and respond in an appropriate manner. These inappropriate actions result in lost customers in the private sector. In the public sector, citizens usually do not have an opportunity to go elsewhere, so they file legal appeals, perform demonstrations, take legal action, or elect another public official.

Lost Productivity

The time spent identifying and correcting data errors is lost productivity. If an organization is not proactive at preventing data errors, it continues to lose productivity by routinely correcting the same data errors. The time spent finding and resolving data errors far exceeds the time spent putting precise data integrity rules in place and proactively preventing data errors.

> Imprecise data integrity rules result in lost productivity.

The time spent resolving bad perceptions, reclaiming lost customers, and rebuilding confidence in citizens is lost productivity. The time spent resolving inappropriate business actions and handling responses to inappropriate business actions is also lost productivity. The use of computer resources to identify data errors, notify people of those data errors, and resolve the data errors is a loss of those resources. The indications are that more resources are lost due to imprecise data integrity rules and data errors than are lost to informal data names, vague data definitions, and improper data structure combined.

Precise Data Integrity Rules

Precise means clearly expressed, definite, accurate, correct, and conforming to proper form. A *precise data integrity rule* is a data integrity rule that precisely specifies the criteria for high-quality data values and reduces or eliminates data errors. The consistent application and enforcement of those rules ensure high-quality data values.

Data integrity, data accuracy, and data completeness are the three components of data architecture, known as *data fidelity*. Data integrity is a measure of how well the data values are maintained after they are captured or created, as explained above. ***Data accuracy*** is a measure of how well the data values represent the real world at a point in time. ***Data completeness*** is a measure of how well the scope of the data resource meets the scope of the business information demand.

The development of precise data integrity rules resolves most of the problems with data integrity and some of the problems with data accuracy. The data accuracy problems that are due to obtaining the data values from the real world cannot be identified or resolved with data integrity rules. For example, if a person gives you their birth date, you can verify that the date is a valid date, but you cannot verify if that date is the person's true birth date.

Data Rule Concept

I began developing and using precise data rules in the mid-1980s. It was known back then that traditional data edits were not providing the desired data value quality. A different orientation toward data architecture quality, not toward the process of finding and correcting data errors after-the-fact, was needed. The orientation was changed from correcting errors to preventing errors. Therefore, the concept was changed from data editing as a process to data rules as a specification of the criteria for high-quality data values.

> Data rules are a formal subset of business rules.

The concept of business rules has been evolving during the 1990s. The concept is excellent, and many good approaches and notations have been presented for defining business rules. The orientation, however, is more toward processes, procedures, and policies than toward data quality. To resolve this situation, business rules were subdivided into six categories representing the six columns on the Zachman Framework for Enterprise Architectures, providing data rules, process rules, network rules, people rules, time rules, and motivation rules.

Shortly after these six categories of business rules were defined and circulated, I was meeting with network designers and technicians. During the conversation the question arose about whether business rules could apply to the network. All the examples these people had seen were oriented toward data or business processes. There were no examples related to networks. I explained the six categories of business rules and how network rules applied to the network column of the Framework. This concept opened a whole new door to network quality for this group of people. It substantiated that defining six categories of rules for the six columns of the Framework was valid and allowed a more precise definition of the rules within each column.

> Data integrity rules are a formal subset of data rules.

A **data rule** is a subset of business rules that deal with the data column of the Zachman Framework. They specify the criteria for maintaining the quality of the data architecture. It became apparent during the specification of precise data rules that there were several broad categories of data rules. There are data rules that pertained to data integrity, data sourcing, data extraction, data transformation, and data deployment. This realization led to formally defining five broad categories of data rules. The discussion of the other categories of data rules other than data integrity rules is beyond the scope of this book.[3]

People frequently ask me if I expect them to formally name and specify all data integrity rules. After all, there could be thousands of those rules to specify. My response is yes, if you want a high-quality data resource. I can remember about 15 or 20 years ago the same question was being asked about naming and defining every data attribute; after all, there could be thousands of them. The answer then was yes, and those organizations that did name and define their data are far better off today. Those organizations that precisely specify data integrity rules today will be better off in the years to come.

Data Integrity Rule Names

Data integrity rules are named according to the data naming taxonomy and supporting vocabulary that were explained in the chapter on Proper Data Names.

---

[3] The author is preparing a definitive book on data rules for maintaining a high-quality data resource.

For example, a data integrity rule that specifies the criteria for changing an employee's name would be Employee. Name, Change! and a data integrity rule for deleting stream flow data occurrences might be Stream Flow. Delete!.

There are several common words that can be used in the data rule name component, such as Change, Delete, Inactive, Calculate, and so on. When the data integrity rule is stored separately from the data it pertains to, the formal data rule name is required for identification. When the data integrity rule is stored with the data it pertains to, the formal data name is not needed, and the common word is used to identify the data rule. The examples below (in the Data Integrity Rule Types section) illustrate this convention.

The data integrity rules need to be normalized so that a formal data name can be provided, similar to the way that data entities and data attributes need to be normalized after they are named. A data integrity rule is normalized to the data component that it represents or on which it takes action. For example, the data integrity rule about an employee's name change normalizes to Employee. Name. The data integrity rule for calculating a customer's account balance normalizes to Account. Balance even though the contributing data attributes are the Account Transaction. Amount.

People occasionally ask me if there is ever a conflict where a data rule normalizes to more than one data component. So far, I have not encountered any such conflict. Every data rule that I have defined normalizes to only one data component.

Data Integrity Rule Notation

The notations for specifying data integrity rules are built on a few basic principles. First, the notation must be acceptable and understandable to business clients. They are the ones that provide the basic criteria for data integrity and they should be drawn into the process to gain their knowledge and experience. Second, the notations must be based on standard mathematics and logic notations where practical. They must be based on sound theory, yet acceptable to all audiences. Third, any symbols in the notations used must be readily available on a standard keyboard. Although there are many symbols in mathematics and logics that could be used, only those that are available on the keyboard should be used.

The symbols used for data integrity rule notations are shown below. These are not the same symbols used in data names, with the exception of the carets, so there is no conflict between the symbols used for data names and the symbols used for data integrity rules.

Mathematical symbols:

+	addition
–	subtraction
*	multiplication
/	division
**	power

Logical symbols:

<	less than
>	greater than
<=	less than or equal to
>=	greater than or equal to
=	equal to
<>	not equal to
&	and
|	or
~	relationship

Set symbols:

{ }	a set
n{ }m	a set with minimum and maximum values
( )	a grouping of elements

Data Integrity Rule Types

There are six broad categories of data integrity rules. They are briefly explained below, but a complete discussion of data integrity rules is beyond the scope of this book. The specification of data integrity rules is evolving, and the notations shown below are the best at the time of this writing. Work is continuing with business clients, data architects, data analysts, and database technicians to refine these specifications.

Data Value

Nonspecific data domains are a bad habit that results in low data integrity. Nonspecific data domains are resolved with the specification of a data value rule or a conditional data value rule. A ***data value rule*** specifies the domain of allowable values for a data attribute that applies for all situations. There are no conditions or exceptions placed on the allowable values.

The domain of allowable values is often specified as the mathematical data domain rather than the business data domain, as explained above. For example, if a trailer length is specified as two-digit numeric, the data domain is likely specified as zero to 99 meaning that a trailer could be zero feet to 99 feet long. Mathematically this is correct, but the business domain for a trailer is 20 to 60 feet. It is the business data domain that is of interest in developing data value rules.

The basic notation for a data value rule is:

minimum allowed value <= actual value <= maximum allowed value

The basic data value rule for the length of a trailer using this notation is shown below. The data attribute name is shown between the minimum and maximum values. Note that this notation is more precise than the traditional 20 to 60 feet.

20 <= Trailer. Length <= 60

Since data names can be rather long, the formal data name is replaced with the common word *value* to shorten the notation. The data value rule is then placed below the data attribute name, as shown below.

Trailer. Length
   20 <= value <= 60

The data value rule below is often used with names. It catches the common errors with name attributes where the first character is blank. Note that there are two criteria in this rule and they are connected with an ampersand. This is acceptable for data integrity rules.

Company. Name
   5 characters <= text <= 30 characters & first character <> blank

An indicator data value rule is shown below. Note the statement about a default value. The insertion of default data values must be specified in data value rules so that people readily understand the origin of data values.

Product. Audit Indicator
   { 'Y' | 'N'} Default 'N'

Other data value rules are shown below. Notice the different notations that can be used to specify the data value rules. Notice that the terms *text*, *real*, and *integer* can be used in a data value rule to indicate the data type.

1 character

valid Date

January 1, 1996 <= date <= December 31, 1998

36.75 <= real <= 72.25

Conditional Data Value

A *conditional data value rule* specifies the domain of allowable values for a data attribute when there are conditions or exceptions that apply. It specifies both the conditions for optionality and the conditions for a relationship between data values in different data attributes.

The optional criteria in a database management system is overused and is not specific to many business situations. It is relatively easy to say that a data value is optional and worry about the data integrity later. But, there are very few data values that are truly optional. There are usually different business conditions under which they are either required or prevented. Therefore, it is the business data optionality, not the database data optionality, that is important for defining conditional data value rules.

For example, a Product Order has a Sale Date, a Actual Ship Date, and an Actual Delivery Date. When the Product Order is made the Sale Date is Required but the Actual Ship Date and Delivery Date are not known. They are not optional, they are actually prevented because they are not known. The conditional data value rule is shown below.

When Product Status = 'Confirmed'

    Product Order. Sale Date is Required

    Product Order. Actual Ship Date is Prevented

    Product Order. Actual Delivery Date is Prevented

When Product Status = 'Shipped'

    Product Order. Sale Date is Required

    Product Order. Actual Ship Date is Required

    Product Order. Actual Delivery Date is Prevented

When Product Status = 'Delivered'

    Product Order. Sale Date is Required

    Product Order. Actual Ship Date is Required

    Product Order. Actual Delivery Date is Required

Notice the use of When rather than If in the rule. Required means that a data value is mandatory and essential and must be entered. Prevented means that a value is prohibited or disallowed and must not be entered. Optional means that the value is truly elective and at the discretion of the person entering the data. True data optionality usually occurs with comment or explanation data attributes.

The relationship between data attributes within the same data entity or between data entities is also specified in a conditional data value rule. Using the Product Order dates above, the following rules might be specified.

> Product Order. Actual Ship Date >= Product Order. Sale Date
> Product Order. Actual Delivery Date >= Product Order. Actual Ship Date

Data Structure

A **data structure rule** specifies the data cardinality for a data relation when there are no conditions or exceptions that apply. Remember it was mentioned in the last chapter on Proper Data Structure that data cardinality was a data integrity feature, not a structural feature. The data structure rule is where the data cardinality is specified so that the data structure is easier to understand.

For example, a Stream has many Stream Segments and each Stream Segment must belong to only one Stream, as shown by the data relation on an entity-relation diagram. In actuality, a Stream must be composed of two or more Stream Segments. The data cardinality is shown in the data structure rule below, which specifies that each Stream must have two to many Stream Segments and each Stream Segment must belong to one and only one Stream. In spite of the apparent mathematical notation of this statement, many business clients readily accept the notation.

> 1{Stream} 1 ~ 2{Stream Segment} M

Semantic data modeling would have the two semantic statements shown below. Notice that the data structure rule and the semantic statements are in synch, and that the semantic statements are more explicit and meaningful when they do not have words like Contains and Belongs between the data entity names.

> A Stream must have two or more Stream Segments
> A Stream Segment must belong to one and only one Stream

Conditional Data Structure

A **conditional data structure rule** specifies the data cardinality for a data relation when conditions or exceptions apply. For example, an entity-relation diagram may show a one-to-many data relation between Student and Degree. If there is a semantic statement or specific data cardinality, it may specify that the degree is optional, meaning that the student may have zero, one, or many degrees. Although this data relation appears proper, it is not accurate. An undergraduate student, by definition, cannot have a degree; a graduate student, by definition, must have one or more degrees. These conditions can be shown on an entity-relation diagram, but they are more explicit when specified as a conditional data structure rule.

In the example below, the first rule states that a Student is either an Undergraduate Student or a Graduate Student. Note the use of the data naming taxonomy for the two subsets of Student and the or symbol between the two subsets. The second rule states that an Undergraduate Student must have zero Degrees, as noted by the minimum and maximum values. The third rule states that a Graduate Student must have one or more Degrees, as noted by the minimum of 1 and a maximum of M. These data rules are precise and there is no optionality.

    Student = {[Undergraduate] Student | [Graduate] Student}
    1{[Undergraduate] Student} 1 ~ 0{Degree} 0
    1{[Graduate] Student} 1 ~ 1{Degree}M

Conditional data structure rules can show the optionality for coded data values, which is often difficult to show on an entity-relation diagram. For example, an Education Level. Code in Employee is required for middle managers, executives, and appointed officials, but is prevented for salaried employees and classified employees. The first data rule below specifies the optional relationship between Employee and Education Level. The second data rule specifies the conditions under which the Education Level. Code value is required and prevented.

    0{Employee} M ~ 0{Education Level} 1

    Employee
        Education Level. Code
            Required when Management Level. Code = {'M' | 'E' | 'A'}
            Prevented when Management Level. Code = {'S' | 'C'}

If the Race. Code in Employee is truly optional, meaning at the discretion of the employee, the data integrity rule would be specified as shown below. The first rule shows that the relation between Employee and Race is optional. The second rule shows that the data value is optional. Notice the change in syntax from the previous example. These notations make the data integrity rules easy to understand.

0{Employee} M ~ 0{Race} 1

Employee
    Race. Code is Optional

Data Derivation

Undefined data derivation is a prominent cause of low data integrity. A *data derivation rule* specifies the contributors, the algorithm, and the conditions for deriving a data value. It also specifies the conditions for rederiving those data values if necessary. The examples below show the derivation of a count, total weight, and average weight.

Product Shipment. Product Count = Count of unique Products in Product
                               Shipment
Derive when Product Shipment Status. Code = 'C'

Product Shipment. Total Weight = Sum of all Product Load. Weights in
                              Product Shipment
Derive when Product Shipment Status. Code = 'C'

Product Shipment. Average Product Weight =
    Product Shipment. Total Weight / Product Shipment. Product Count
    Derive when contributors are available

A derived data value may need to be rederived when the conditions change or the contributors change, so that it accurately represents the real world. This situation occurs more frequently in a dynamic business environment. The data value may be rederived on a periodic basis, such as every day, or when an event happens, such as a deposit or withdrawal for a checking account. The algorithm and the contributors are usually the same, but the timing of the rederivation needs to be specified.

Data Retention

Uncontrolled data deletion was also mentioned as a cause of low data integrity. A *data retention rule* specifies how long data values are retained in a particular database and what is done with data values when their usefulness in that database is over. The usefulness is with respect to where the data values are located and the retention is with respect to the organization at large. For example, school attendance data may be useful in the school's operational database only during the current school year, but may need to be retained as historical data in the school district for five years, and with the State Superintendent for 10 years. After ten years the data can be purged.

A *data occurrence retention rule* specifies how long the data occurrence is retained and what is done with that data occurrence when its usefulness is over. The rule applies to all data values in that data occurrence. The data occurrence retention rule for customer purchase data is shown below. Notice the data rule names within the Customer data entity.

```
Customer
    Customer. Inactive!
    When no Customer Purchase activity for 180 days
        Delete Customer occurrence
    Customer. Delete!
        Move Customer occurrence to Customer History
        Delete Customer Purchase occurrences

Customer History
    When Current Date >= Customer History. Date + 36 Months
        Purge Customer History occurrence

Customer Purchase
    Customer Purchase. Delete!
        Move Customer Purchase occurrence to Customer Purchase History
```

A *data attribute retention rule* specifies how long the data values are retained and what is to be done with those data values when their usefulness is over. The rule applies to specific data values rather than to the entire data occurrence. A data attribute retention rule is shown below for a customer's name change.

```
Customer. Name, Change!
    Save current Customer. Name in Customer History
    Replace current Customer. Name with the new Customer. Name
```

Fundamental Data Integrity Rules

Fundamental data integrity rules can be developed and inherited the same as fundamental data definitions. A *fundamental data integrity rule* is a data integrity rule that can apply to many specific data values. The data integrity rule is defined once and is applied to many different situations. A *specific data integrity rule* is a data integrity rule that is defined specifically for one situation.

Fundamental data integrity rules provide quality and consistency.

For example, a data integrity rule can be defined for longitude domain, such as Longitude. Degrees, Domain! −180.0 <= value <= 180.0. The data integrity rule for a wellhead longitude domain would be Well Head. Longitude Degrees, Domain! = Longitude Degrees. Domain!. The result is maximum quality and consistency with minimum data integrity rules.

Data Integrity Rule Enforcement

Data integrity rules are meaningless for ensuring high-quality data values unless they are implemented and enforced. A *data integrity violation* is the situation where a data integrity rule is violated. There are five good practices for implementing data integrity rules and managing data integrity violations.

There are five good practices for enforcing data integrity rules.

One Set of Rules

There is only one set of data integrity rules for the data resource, and those rules are defined within the common data architecture. Data integrity rules must not be specified independently in each application using the data resource. They may be implemented through one or more applications, and they may be implemented in many different places, but they are specified only once for the data resource. This principle prevents redundant and conflicting data integrity rules.

Apply to All Data

Data integrity rules must be routinely and consistently applied to all data entering the data resource. There are no exceptions, exemptions, or waivers for the consistent enforcement of data integrity rules. As soon as the enforcement of data integrity rules is relaxed to any degree, the probability of data errors increases dramatically. No matter what the argument or excuse, the data integrity rules must be applied to all data.

Apply Close to Capture

The data integrity rules must be enforced as close to the initial capture of the data as possible. This approach allows early identification and correction of potential data errors. It prevents data errors from entering the data resource and avoids the whole process of identifying and removing the data errors after the fact. Remember that prevention is less expensive than correction.

Violation Actions Defined

The action to be taken when a data integrity rule fails or is violated must be specified. The specification of precise data integrity rules and the consistent enforcement of those rules is useless if the actions to be taken when the rule fails is not specified. It also wastes resources to identify the error and then let it pass to be corrected later. Once the data error is in hand, it must be corrected to prevent any impact on the business operations.

There are two actions to be taken when a data integrity rule is violated; a violation action and a violation notification. A ***data integrity violation action*** is the action taken with the data that fail the rule. The typical data actions are to override the error with meaningful data, to suspend the data pending further correction, to apply a default data value, to accept the data, or to delete the data. A ***data integrity violation notification*** is the action taken to notify someone that a data integrity rule has been violated so that further preventive action can be taken. The typical notifications are to notify someone immediately, log the failure and the data action taken for later review, or to ignore the failure and the data action taken.

When I explain the necessity of specifying these actions to people, I often get a rather uninterested response. It is bad enough to have to do the data integrity rules specifications, but to define the actions when a data integrity rule is violated is just too much. So I suggest that a default action of delete the data and ignore any notification be used for all violations because it will keep the data resource free of data errors with minimum effort. The reality of this approach usually gets people's attention rather quickly and they begin to define the violation and notification actions.

Default Values Specified

Default data values can be applied, but those data values must be as meaningful as possible to the business. Bad default data values like those mentioned above must not be allowed. That is why default data values and the conditions under which they are applied must be specified in a data rules. The insertion of a default data value must also be documented so the situation can be reviewed and appropriate adjustments made to the application of default data values.

Proactive Data Quality Management

The management of data quality must be proactive to make optimum use of resources and minimize the impacts to business operations. Allowing data errors to enter the data resource, identifying the errors, and making corrections is a reactive approach that should not be tolerated in today's dynamic business environment. It was the reason for changing from a reactive data edit orientation to a more proactive data integrity rule orientation. There are three good practices for proactive data quality management.

> There are three good practices for proactive
> data quality management.

Rapid Identification

The data errors must be rapidly identified and corrected. The sooner that data errors are identified and corrected, and the closer to the source of the data where that action is taken, the more accurate they will be and the less impact they will have on the business. The data rule enforcement principle for implementing the data integrity rules as close to the source as possible supports the principle of early detection and correction.

Apply to Entire Data Resource

Precise data integrity rules must be applied to the entire data resource. The rules cannot apply to part of the data resource, or part of the data sources, or be enforced part of the time. The data integrity rules must be specified for all the data and be enforced all the time to ensure high integrity data. The capability to extract and move data that is provided by networks makes it mandatory to apply data integrity rules to the entire data resource.

Document Default Values

The data that fail the data integrity rules and the insertion of default data values must be documented. The documentation must be reviewed on a regular basis to determine if any actions can be taken to reduce the data error rate and the need for default data values. The emphasis is on preventing data errors from entering the data resource and eventually preventing data errors from trying to enter the data resource.

These three good practices provide a self-correction approach that routinely reviews data errors and takes steps to prevent the reoccurrence of those data errors. They provide a major emphasis toward lowering the data error rate by actively tracking down data errors that have entered, or tried to enter, the data resource and resolving the problem that caused those errors. It is only through a proactive, self-correction process that the data error rate and their impact on business operations can be reduced.

Precise Data Integrity Rule Benefits

Precise data integrity rules provide four basic benefits: higher data value quality, limited data disparity, improved productivity, and success motivation. You should notice by now that the same set of benefits keep reappearing as the bad habits are turned into good practices. At the risk of being redundant, the benefits are repeated so that people will be fully aware of the benefits for implementing the good practices.

Higher Data Quality

The specification and enforcement of precise data integrity rules produces higher quality data that provide better support to the business. Data error rates are lower, the proactive self-correction process ensures a continued emphasis on reducing data errors, and fewer inappropriate business actions are taken. Organizations that have established a program to develop precise data integrity rules see a steadily declining data error rate and an improved use of the data resource.

Limited Data Disparity

Formal data names, comprehensive data definitions, and proper data structures limit data disparity by improving the understanding of data, which increases the use of those data. Together they make a significant step toward limiting data disparity and promoting a comparate data resource. Precise data integrity rules limit data disparity even further by improving the quality of the data values, which further increases the use of the data. They work in parallel with the data names, definitions, and structure to further reduce data disparity and promote the comparate data cycle.

Improved Productivity

The result of improved data value quality and limited data disparity is an improvement in productivity. Fewer inappropriate business decisions are made, and missed business opportunities are minimized. Less time is spent on a proactive approach than was spent on a reactive approach, even when the time to specify the precise data integrity rules and enforce them is included. This fact alone should convince organizations that they should immediately implement a program to specify precise data integrity rules.

Best Practices

The good practices for developing precise data integrity rules emphasize the development of data integrity rules for the entire data resource, applying them as close to the data source as possible, and specifying actions to be taken when the data rules are violated. Specifying precise data integrity rules is an overwhelming task. It is often more overwhelming than formally naming, comprehensively defining, and properly structuring data. The task is so overwhelming because there are very few data integrity rules that are specified, and many of those are buried in application code that is difficult to interpret. Many organizations have no idea where or how to start.

Focus on Core Business Functions

Development of data integrity rules should begin with the data supporting the core business functions. The approach is similar to that for data names, definitions, and structures. Start with the operational data supporting the core business functions or the historical data used in data warehouses. Then move through the less critical business functions in an orderly manner. Develop the data integrity rules along with the data names, data definitions, and data structure. Include business clients in the process of identifying the data supporting the critical business functions and developing the data integrity rules.

Focus on Largest Impact

Identify the major sources of errors in the data supporting the critical business functions and the types of errors that have the largest impact on the business. Specify the data rules that resolve these major errors. Then move on to the next set of data errors that are causing the largest impact on the business. This approach provides the biggest successes that are readily visible to the business.

Proactive Approach

Establish a proactive approach that continues to identify the data errors that have the largest impact on the business, and target those problems. Do not stop resolving data errors when the first set of high-impact data errors are resolved. Data quality improvement is an ongoing process that constantly identifies data errors that impact the business and resolves those errors.

Once this approach is started, it is easy to continue. Correcting data errors increases the motivation to continue finding additional data errors to correct. As the first priorities are resolved, the specification of precise data integrity rules can move on to ancillary and historical data, it can move to less major sources of data errors, and it can move from data value rules into structural rules, derivation rules, and retention rules. The specific directions can be prioritized based on the impact on the business, the resources available, and the resources saved.

Summary

The bad habits leading to imprecise data integrity rules, the impacts of those bad habits, the good practices for precise data integrity rules, the benefits of those good practices, and the most beneficial best practices are summarized below. The list is also contained in Appendix A.

> Bad habits leading to imprecise data integrity rules:
>> Ignoring a high data error rate.
>> Incomplete data integrity rules.
>> Delayed data error identification and correction.
>> Default data values frequently used.
>> Nonspecific data domains.

Nonspecific data optionality.

Undefined data derivations.

Uncontrolled data deletion.

Impacts of imprecise data integrity rules:

Bad perception about the service and products offered by the organization.

Inappropriate business actions for both citizens and customers.

Lost productivity for business clients, information technology staff, and hardware.

Good practices for precise data integrity rules:

Data rule concept.

Data integrity rule names.

Data integrity rule notation.

Data integrity rule types.

Formal names for data integrity rules.

Specific notations for data integrity rules.

Six types of data integrity rules.

Data value rule.

Conditional data value rule.

Data structure rule.

Conditional data structure rule.

Data derivation rule.

Data retention rule.

Fundamental data integrity rules.

Data integrity rule enforcement.

One set of rules.

Apply to all data in the data resource.

Apply close to data capture.

Violation actions defined.

Default data values specified.

Proactive data quality management.

Rapid identification of data errors.

Apply to entire data resource.

Document default values that are inserted.

Benefits of precise data integrity rules:

Higher data quality.

Limited data disparity.

Improved productivity.

Best practices for success motivation:
   Focus on core business functions first.
   Focus on errors with the largest impact on the business.
   Proactive approach to identify data errors with the largest business impact.

The bad habits, good practices, and best practices for data integrity rules can be used to evaluate the status of an organization's data resource. Fill in the horizontal bar (below) to show the degree to which the bad habits exist and the degree to which the good practices and the best practices have been implemented. You can provide definitions for the Poor, Fair, Moderate, Good, and Excellent headings to suit your organization, or you can use a numeric scale if it is more appropriate. You can also select the items that are important for your organization, but don't be too hasty at excluding items, because they may be valuable later. This list is also contained in Appendix B.

	P	F	M	G	E
Bad Habits					
Ignoring a high data error rate	☐	☐	☐	☐	☐
Incomplete data integrity rules	☐	☐	☐	☐	☐
Delayed data error identification	☐	☐	☐	☐	☐
Default data values	☐	☐	☐	☐	☐
Nonspecific data domains	☐	☐	☐	☐	☐
Nonspecific data optionality	☐	☐	☐	☐	☐
Undefined data derivations	☐	☐	☐	☐	☐
Uncontrolled data deletion	☐	☐	☐	☐	☐
Good Practices					
Data rule concept	☐	☐	☐	☐	☐
Data integrity rule names	☐	☐	☐	☐	☐
Data integrity rule notation	☐	☐	☐	☐	☐
Data integrity rule types					
Data value rule	☐	☐	☐	☐	☐
Conditional data value rule	☐	☐	☐	☐	☐
Data structure rule	☐	☐	☐	☐	☐
Conditional data structure rule	☐	☐	☐	☐	☐
Data derivation rule	☐	☐	☐	☐	☐
Data retention rule	☐	☐	☐	☐	☐

	P	F	M	G	E
Fundamental data integrity rules	☐	☐	☐	☐	☐
Data integrity rule enforcement					
One set of rules	☐	☐	☐	☐	☐
Apply to all data	☐	☐	☐	☐	☐
Apply close to data capture	☐	☐	☐	☐	☐
Violation actions defined	☐	☐	☐	☐	☐
Default values specified	☐	☐	☐	☐	☐
Proactive data quality management					
Rapid identification of data errors	☐	☐	☐	☐	☐
Apply to entire data resource	☐	☐	☐	☐	☐
Document default values that are inserted	☐	☐	☐	☐	☐
Best Practices					
Focus on core business functions	☐	☐	☐	☐	☐
Focus on largest impact	☐	☐	☐	☐	☐
Proactive approach	☐	☐	☐	☐	☐

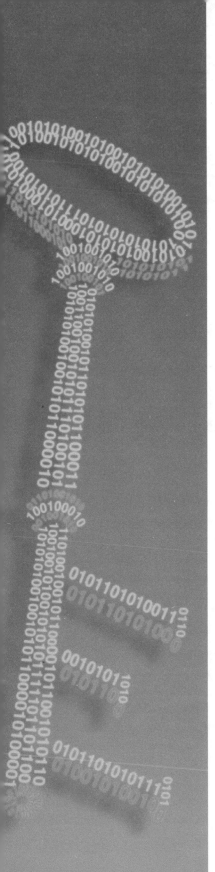

CHAPTER 6

Robust Data Documentation

> Robust data documentation raises awareness
> of the data resource.

After precise data integrity rules, the fifth way to achieve data resource quality is through the development of robust data documentation. People may do an excellent job of naming data, defining data, structuring data, and even developing data integrity rules, but if the results of those efforts are not documented and made readily available, people are not fully aware of the data resource and will continue to do their own thing. It is the awareness that people have about the data resource that is important to fully utilize the data resource.

Much of the current knowledge and understanding about the data resource is vested in people. Very little information is formally documented in any manner, let alone readily available to anyone interested in using the data resource. Many of these people who have an understanding of the data resource are leaving the organization for better jobs or retirement. This is a permanent loss of institutional memory about the data resource that cannot be recovered. It is not something that is likely to happen; it is happening in many organizations today.

This chapter describes the bad habits leading to limited documentation of the data resource and the impacts of limited data documentation. A new concept for data documentation is presented, and the good practices supporting that concept are explained. This is not a detailed discussion about data documentation or repositories for holding that documentation, but it provides an overview of the bad habits and how those bad habits can be replaced with good practices.

Limited Data Documentation

Limited data documentation includes any documentation about the data resource that is sparse, incomplete, out of date, incorrect, inaccessible, unknown, poorly presented, poorly understood, and so on. Documentation has typically been an after-the-fact task that needed to be done to complete a project. It has not been considered an important task for getting an information system designed, implemented, and operational. The result is that minimal, disparate data documentation has been collected over the years.

The prominent bad habits leading to limited data documentation are explained below. You should understand these bad habits to determine if limited data documentation exists in your data resource.

Data Documentation Not Complete

The data documentation in most organizations is incomplete at best. The information that does exist is vested in people and documented in a variety of notes, documents, data files, and documentation applications. It is scattered throughout the organization and is extremely difficult to locate, let alone integrate, for a complete understanding of the data resource. People cannot readily understand and use the data if they cannot obtain complete documentation.

> Most documentation about the data resource is very incomplete.

The worst situation I have ever encountered was an organization that had no documentation for their data resource; I mean nothing. There were very short physical data names in the database that provided little understanding about the data. We started by looking at the domain of values for each data item and the frequency of those values to get a general idea about what each data item represented, such as name, date, number, description, and so on. We looked at reports and took information from the column headings to help us understand the data items, and examined some of the source documents that went through data entry. In some situations we even looked at application code to gain information. We then began asking business clients for additional information about what the data items represented. It was a slow, arduous, painful process, but we made progress with understanding the contents of the data resource.

Much of the understanding about the data resource is leaving the organization on a regular basis as employees move on to other jobs and retirement, and contractors move on to other engagements. This is a permanent loss of information about the data resource that can never be replaced. It is resulting in data documentation that is less complete over time; a most undesirable situation.

> Knowledge about the data resource is being permanently lost
> as people leave the organization.

Documentation about the data resource is disparate, and the situation is getting worse rather than better. The good news is that people are beginning to independently capture and maintain formal documentation about the data resource. The bad news is that people are independently capturing and maintaining that documentation. As new documentation tools become available and more data megatypes emerge, such as spatial data, textual data, imaging data, and so on, the volume of documentation is increasing, but it is being stored in a variety of different locations in a variety of different formats. The situation is changing from minimal documentation that is being lost to rapidly increasing quantities of disparate documentation.

Data Documentation Not Current

The data documentation in most organizations is not current. At best, the documentation is developed once and then is considered to be valid for the life of the data resource. The situation is very similar to the situation described for data definitions. Once developed, the documentation is not kept current with the changing business. The data documentation may be acceptable in many respects, but it is just out of date with the current business. It does not accurately represent the data resource or its support of the business today.

> Most data documentation is not kept current with the business.

I became aware of a situation in a hospital where the number of in-patients in maternity made a dramatic increase. The obvious answer was that there were either more births in the geographic area that the hospital served, or people were coming to the hospital from a wider geographical area. This was not true, because the birth rate was largely unchanged in spite of the increase in patients. The answer was in a decision to treat each newborn as an additional in-patient, where previously they were not considered to be an additional in-patient.

A similar situation occurred with a drug rehabilitation center. There was a sudden increase in the number of admissions for drug rehabilitation that caused concern in the community. Was the addition due to an increase in the use of drugs? The answer again was a change in the business from one admission for treatment, whether in-patient or out-patient, to one admission for in-patient treatment and a separate admission for out-patient treatment.

These are simple examples illustrating that a change in the business is seldom documented in the data resource that supports that business. Simply, the documentation is out of date with the business.

Data Documentation Not Understandable

The data documentation that does exist is not thoroughly understandable to all audiences. The data documentation may be complete and current, but it may not be understandable. Much of the documentation that does exist is oriented toward the physical database and may be understandable to database technicians. This documentation, however, is not appropriate for business clients and data analysts who need to understand the data resource from a business perspective. The documentation pertains to a limited audience.

> Most data documentation is not understandable to all audiences.

The problem may be with the method of presentation, similar to the situation explained earlier about data structures. Good information presented in a poor manner can be as bad as no information at all. For example, data definitions and data integrity rules can be excellent, but if their presentation is inappropriate for the audience they are essentially useless. One data analyst told me that his data documentation was a mish-mash of random, unrelated facts and it was hard to decipher any meaning from the mess.

You may have faced the situation with instructions for assembling, using, or repairing some household product. You read the instructions, and they make no sense at all. The instructions frequently do not match the diagram, and the diagram may not match the product itself. You struggle through the instructions and wish the writer had gotten his act together to make things understandable.

Data Documentation Redundant

It may be surprising, but with the limited data documentation that exists in most organizations, there is frequently redundant data documentation. This redundant data documentation is often inconsistent and causes additional confusion when people attempt to understand the data resource. The redundant data documentation may be scattered across different documentation products, or it may be contained within one documentation product.

> Redundant data documentation causes additional confusion.

A typical example is the redundant storage of data definitions in a design or documentation application. Some applications force the redundant creation and storage of data definitions, such as for every instance of the data attributes in a foreign key. These redundant data definitions may be consistent when they were first created, but they soon become out of synch because they are not consistently updated. The problem is further magnified if the data definitions are not consistent when they were first created. People are unable to determine the correct data definitions.

The problem is not limited to data definitions. I mentioned in previous chapters that data definitions, data structures, and data integrity rules are often redundant. For example, some segments of the data resource have been modeled five or six times. If each of these models is documented and made available to the organization, there is considerable confusion about which is the correct version that most accurately represents the business and the data resource. This is one reason why data documentation has not been made available to all audiences.

Data Documentation Not Readily Available

Data documentation may be complete, current, and understandable, but if it is not readily available to all audiences, it is relatively useless. Unavailable documentation can be truly inaccessible, or it can be very difficult to access. I encountered a situation where relatively good data documentation existed, but that documentation was not available to anyone other than data analysts and database technicians; that was company policy. I was unable to determine what that policy was attempting to achieve.

> A large quantity of data documentation that exists
> is not readily available.

Data documentation is often stored in large data repositories or data dictionaries. These products are difficult to access, even though they may be readily available to all audiences. A person needs to access the product, log on, go through a lengthy menu, and select the data needed, all before getting any results. This process is just too cumbersome for most people who want to quickly understand the data, and the product is seldom used by anyone other than technicians. All too often, otherwise good data documentation is locked away in a product or database that is difficult to access.

These data repositories and data dictionaries are often isolated from production systems. A person working in a production application who needs information about a data attribute or a set of data codes cannot readily find that information unless he or she logs out of that production application and enters the data documentation product. Most people just will not make this effort and will forge ahead with their current understanding.

As mentioned above, much of the data documentation is scattered across a variety of products, particularly when the data resource contains a variety of different data megatypes, like tabular data, spatial data, and imaging data. Each product contains their own data documentation and there is seldom any integration across these products. People seldom access one product to find information about the data resource; they surely will not access several different products for that information.

Data Documentation Existence Unknown

The existence of documentation about the data resource may be unknown to many people in the organization. The data documentation may be complete, current, understandable, and readily available, but the existence of that document may not be generally known. If people do not know the data documentation exists, or all the locations in which that data documentation does exist, they cannot use that documentation to understand the data resource.

> The existence of the data documentation may not be known.

It is a simple situation of *If we only knew what we know about the data resource*. Knowing that documentation about the data resource exists is the key to accessing and using that documentation in order to understand the data resource. It is also the key to understanding the level of data documentation that actually exists and to making an effort to increase and improve that documentation to the benefit of the business.

Limited Data Documentation Impacts

If the data documentation is limited by one or more of the bad habits described above, it is the same as no data documentation. Limited documentation about the data resource results in three major impacts on the organization. Each of these impacts is described below.

Limited Awareness

Limited data documentation severely hampers people's awareness of the data resource. When people are not aware of the data resource, they do not understand the data and they do not fully utilize the data resource. They do not share the data and they do not contribute to building and maintaining a data resource that meets the current and future business information demand. No matter what the quality of the data resource, it is useless if the data documentation is not readily available to people using the data resource.

> Limited awareness decreases understanding, quality, and use of the data resource.

Informal data names prevented the ready identification of data in the data resource. Vague data definitions inhibited the understanding of data in the data resource. Improper data structures misrepresented the business. Imprecise data integrity rules resulted in low-quality data values. Limited data documentation hinders people's awareness about the data resource. No wonder the data resource in many organizations is low quality.

Continued Data Disparity

Limited data documentation further perpetuates the disparate data cycle and the natural drift of the data resource toward disparity. It results in a lack of trust in the data resource and an incomplete use of the data resource, which in turn encourages people to create their own data. If people are not aware that data exist, understand the data, and trust those data, they will build their own data.

> Limited awareness results in continued data disparity.

The concept of documenting the data resource has been around since the early days of computing, and particularly since the emergence of database management systems. It has been in the design specifications and project plans for at least 30 years. However, there has been relatively little concern about enforcing the preparation and maintenance of good data documentation. The independent and often redundant collection of data documentation is also causing an increase in data disparity. The lack of good documentation about the data resource is a leading cause of the disparate data cycle.

Lost Productivity

The result of limited awareness about the data resource and continued data disparity is a loss of productivity. Both business client and information technology staff productivity is lost when they are not fully aware of the data resource. Business clients spend unnecessary time finding data, understanding data, developing their own data, and resolving inappropriate business actions. Information technology staff spend unnecessary time maintaining disparate data, helping people understand the data, and helping business clients create disparate data.

> Limited awareness results in a loss of productivity.

The loss of productivity from limited data documentation is different than the loss from informal data names, vague data definitions, improper data structure, and imprecise data integrity rules. It is a loss due to the lack of awareness about the data resource. Even when data names, definition, structure, and integrity rules are developed, a lack of awareness about their existence can cause a loss of productivity.

Robust Data Documentation

Robust data documentation is documentation about the data resource that is complete, current, understandable, non-redundant, readily available, and known to exist. Achieving robust data documentation requires a new approach to designing and managing data documentation. The traditional approaches are not working and will not work as the data resource continues to increase in size and complexity.

Data Resource Data Concept

Documentation about the data resource is often referred to as **metadata,** which is commonly defined as *data about the data*. This term has been misused and abused to the point that the real definition is often unclear. Recently, people cannot even spell *metadata* correctly or define it consistently. It is ironic that a concept as important to understanding and using the data resource as documentation, cannot be spelled or defined consistently within the discipline.

An increased emphasis on metadata is not solving the problem of limited data documentation. This emphasis only promotes the concept that *metadata* are something different from the *real data*. They must be designed and managed independent of the real data. They must be treated with different principles and techniques than the real data. This approach is self-defeating.

> Data resource data are any data about
> the organization's data resource.

I started using the term *data resource data* in a conversation with middle managers to get them to understand the importance of thoroughly documenting the data resource. I explained that data resource data were no different than financial data, customer data, or human resource data. They are a major segment of the organization's data resource that are designed, developed, managed, stored, retrieved, and used the same as any other segment of the data resource. There was immediate interest, and one manager commented, "Is that what this metadata thing is all about? I can sure support that concept."

Data resource data are any data that document the data resource. They are designed and managed within a common data architecture the same as any other segment of the data resource. There is nothing magical, mythical, or different about data resource data. All of the good practices described throughout this book for naming data, defining data, structuring data, and so on, apply to data resource data the same as any other data contained in the data resource. Data resource data are developed within the common data architecture the same as any other data.

Some people believe that data resource data are relatively esoteric and cannot be documented like other data. They believe that the documentation of data resource data is best left to data repositories and other products that capture and store data resource data. They believe that there is no reason for anyone to understand data resource data, particularly business clients. This belief is really an abdication of the responsibility to fully understand and manage data resource data.

> High-quality data resource data are mandatory for managing
> a high-quality data resource.

Data resource data support the business of managing the organization's data resource just like human resource data support the business of managing the organization's human resource. Business clients and information technology staff need high-quality data resource data to perform their business activities just the same as finance, human resource, or marketing people need high-quality data to perform their business activities. High-quality data resource data are mandatory for proper management of an organization's data resource.

Data Resource Data Aspects

There are two major aspects to data resource data: a technical or physical aspect and a semantic or logical aspect. Robust data resource data require that both aspects be captured and maintained. The term *aspect* is used rather than *category* because the boundaries between the technical and the semantic data are blurred; there is no finite distinction between the two aspects. Some people refer to the semantic aspect as the business aspect because that is what business people consult to understand the data resource. Business people, however, do consult the technical aspect, so the terms *technical* and *semantic* were used to represent the two aspects of data resource data.

> Data resource data have a business aspect and a technical aspect.

Technical data resource data are the data that technicians need to build, manage, and maintain databases. They include things like physical data names and structures, data types and formats, file specifications and sizes, blocking factors, access methods, use statistics, and so on. Technical data resource data are also referred to as *corporeal data* or *physical data* that represent the physical database.

Technical data resource data are relatively easy to capture and maintain. They can often be captured and maintained automatically by many applications and database management systems. Many methods concentrate on technical data resource data because they are relatively easy to capture and maintain, and they are necessary to keep the database functioning. It is this orientation toward technical data resource data, however, that limits use of the data resource.

Semantic data resource data are the data that help people understand the data resource and use that data resource to support business activities. They are the data that people need to fully utilize the data resource. They include things like primary data names, data definitions, logical data structure, and so on. Semantic data resource data are also referred to as *business data* or *logical data* that represent the logical data resource.

Semantic data resource data are relatively difficult to capture and maintain. They are difficult to capture and maintain automatically because they represent the content and meaning of the data. There have been numerous attempts to automate the capture and storage of semantic data, but they have been minimally successful. These techniques work relatively well for the technical data, but the content and meaning are nearly impossible to capture and maintain automatically.

Most organizations are relatively strong on technical data and relatively weak on semantic data because the semantic data require an extra effort to capture and maintain. It is actually the lack of good semantic data that perpetuates the disparate data cycle. An organization can have the best technical data possible, but if the semantic data are missing, the disparate data cycle will be in full swing.

Complete Data Documentation

Data resource data must be complete. They must include both semantic and technical data resource data. They must include core business data and ancillary data, operational and historical data, manual and automated data, current and historical data, tabular and non-tabular data, and so on. They must include data definitions, data structure, data integrity rules, logical design and physical design, and so on. Data resource data must include all information pertaining to the data resource.

> Data resource data must completely document
> the entire data resource.

Since data resource data are part of the data resource, they must also be documented. I have seen a number of organizations that have done an excellent job of documenting their data resource, but have failed to document their data resource data. One major aspect of raising the awareness of the data resource is to thoroughly document the data resource data. When people readily understand the data resource data, they can thoroughly understand the data resource.

Current Data Documentation

Data resource data must be kept current with the business. They must reflect the current state of the data resource for both technical people and business people. Both the business and the technology are dynamic, and the data resource adjusts to meet the changing business information needs. The data resource data must adequately represent the current state of both the support to the business and the technical management.

> Data resource data must be current with the business.

The data resource data must also represent historical changes to the data resource. Maintaining historical data resource data is no different than maintaining historical employee data or historical customer data. They track how the data resource has changed over time the same as the environment and legislation have changed over time. Eventually, historical data resource data can be analyzed for trends and patterns the same as other data, and management of the data resource will rise to a new high.

Understandable Data Documentation

Data resource data must be understandable to all audiences. They must present the correct detail for the intended audience. Technical people must see any technical or semantic data that help them build and maintain the database. Business people must see any semantic or technical data that help them understand the data resource and use it to support their business activities.

> The data documentation must be understandable to all audiences.

The data resource data must also be presented in an acceptable manner for the intended audience the same as any other business data. The data resource data must be segmented to represent the portion of the business that is of interest, such as affirmative action or customer orders. They must be filtered to present the correct detail for the intended audience, such as business definitions or file specifications. They must be presented in a manner that is culturally acceptable for that audience. The understanding of otherwise very good data resource data can be compromised by poor presentation techniques.

Non-Redundant Data Documentation

Data resource data must be non-redundant. There must be a single version of truth about both the semantic aspect and the technical aspect of the data resource. Data resource data will eventually need to document the data redundancy that exists in the disparate data and indicate the correct source for official data. Documenting the existing data redundancy is not creating redundant data resource data. There is still only one version of the documentation about the existing redundant data.

Data resource data must be non-redundant.

Data resource data may need to be replicated in different locations for ready access, but that replication is different from redundant versions of data resource data. **Data replication** is the consistent copying of data from one official source to multiple secondary sources. The replicated data are in synch with each other and the primary data source and represent the same version of truth about the data resource. **Redundant data** are inconsistently developed from multiple sources or by different methods. They are not in synch and represent conflicting versions of truth about the data resource.

The best way to ensure that the data resource data are not redundant is to develop the data resource data within the common data architecture. The data resource data may be stored in different products or different databases, but they must be integrated within the common data architecture to remain non-redundant. In other words they are designed within the common data architecture, but their storage is deployed to a variety of different locations for ready access.

Data resource data, as mentioned above, are designed, managed, stored, and used just like any other data in the data resource. The concept, principles, and techniques for managing data resource data are the same as for managing the real data. Yet I have not seen a formal model for data resource data that covers both semantic and technical data resource data for all data contained in an organization's data resource. There are models and standards for small segments of data resource data and for the exchange of data between software products, but there is no overall, comprehensive model for data resource data.

I developed an initial, high-level entity-relation diagram for data resource data in a previous book.[1] I continue to develop and enhance a data resource data model to cover all of the different aspects of data resource data and the unique situations I encounter. I have helped many people incorporate parts of this data

---

[1] Brackett, Michael H., *The Data Warehouse Challenge: Taming Data Chaos*, John Wiley & Sons, 1996.

resource data model into their organization. A comprehensive model of data resource data could benefit many organizations and could be used to design or customize a data repository product to support data documentation.

Readily Available Data Documentation

Data resource data must be readily available to all audiences. The location where the data resource data are stored is not important. What is important is that they are readily available with respect to presentation to an audience. The data resource data may be stored in different products or databases, as mentioned above, but they must be readily available to all audiences. If they are stored in different locations or in locations that are difficult to access, there should be a front-end application that makes them readily available to the recipient.

> Data resource data must be readily available to all audiences.

"Readily available" means available when and where they are needed. For example, a person entering data on a screen should have the data definitions readily available. They should be able to double-click or press a function key and have a window open with the definition. When data fail a data integrity rule, the data that fail, the integrity rule, and corrective action should be presented at the time of the failure. This concept applies to all semantic and technical data.

Generally, data resource data are not privileged in any way and should be readily available to anyone who wants information about the data resource. There are some situations, however, where just knowing that data exist could pose a threat to an organization. In these situations, the data resource data can be considered privileged and either secured with a password or stored in a separate secure location. These situations, however, should not become an excuse not to develop and maintain good data resource data. Good data resource data must be developed and maintained for the entire data resource.

Data Documentation Known to Exist

Data resource data must be known to exist for the organization at large. Everyone in the organization who contributes to or uses the data resource in any way must know that robust data documentation exists and how to access that documentation. The best data resource data possible may be available, but if people do not know that those data are available and how to access them, they are relatively worthless. There should be an ongoing awareness program to familiarize people with the existence of data resource data and how to access those data.

> Data resource data must be known to exist.

I worked with one international organization that has an excellent corporate network. One segment of this network is dedicated to documentation about the business and the data resource supporting the business. As we determined what was needed to document the data resource, those features were added to this segment of the network, the data resource data were captured and stored and were made readily available to anyone in the organization. The awareness was built right into the main menu on their network. This is an ideal approach.

Ancillary Data Documentation

There are several additional good practices that help people understand and use the data resource. These good practices support the prominent good practices mentioned above and provide an added benefit to the business clients.

Data Subject Thesaurus

A *thesaurus* is a list of synonyms and related terms that help people find a specific term that meets their needs. A *data subject thesaurus* is a list of synonyms and related business terms that help people find the data subjects that support their business information needs. It is a list of business terms and alias data entity names that point to the formal data subject name. Any business term that could be used in the organization is listed with a reference to the data subject or data subjects that may be related to that term.

> A data subject thesaurus equates business terms
> to formal data subject names.

For example, there is a data subject for Timber Stand that represents a contiguous stand of similar trees. The data subject thesaurus might have the terms

Woodlot, Forest, Trees, Timber, Vegetation, and so on, that refer to Timber Stand. Similarly, there is a data entity for Product that represents the products that are produced and marketed by an organization. The data subject thesaurus might have the words, Item, Commodity, Goods, Merchandise, and so on, that refer to Product.

One approach to identifying a topic of interest is the use of a keyword in context (KWIC) list. Words or terms that are in the context of the material are extracted and listed as an index to that material. The data subject thesaurus uses keywords in the context of the name, but it also uses key terms out of context (KTOC) as shown in the example above. Any possible business term that could lead people to the proper data subject is put in the thesaurus, not just the key words that exist in the name.

It was mentioned in the chapter on Formal Data Names that business clients contributed extra time to get meaningful business terms for the best possible data names. These same business clients found out that a data subject thesaurus was being prepared, and literally took over that thesaurus to get all the business synonyms entered. They saw the value of readily identifying the data and proceeded to contribute their expertise.

The data subject thesaurus needs to be kept up-to-date with changing business terms. Any term that is encountered in the business can be added to the data subject thesaurus with a reference to one or more data entities. There is no limit to the number of business terms or synonymous data subject names that can be listed in a data subject thesaurus. The only criteria is that if people might use that term to access the data resource, then it should be added to the thesaurus.

Data Characteristic Thesaurus

A **data characteristic thesaurus** is a list of synonyms and related terms that help people find the data characteristics that support their business information needs. It is generally less useful than the data subject thesaurus, but can provide considerable benefit as the volume of comparate data grows. Creation of a data subject thesaurus provides the major benefit for finding data in the data resource and creation of a data characteristic thesaurus provides a secondary benefit. Usually when people find the correct data subject, they can easily find the correct data characteristic.

> A data characteristic thesaurus supports a data subject thesaurus.

A data characteristic thesaurus could be used to cross-reference all alias data names to the primary data characteristic name. Data that already exist in the disparate data resource can be referenced to the formal data characteristic name. This allows the formal data names to be applied to the data that exist in the disparate data resource, and even to data that are available outside the organization. A complete discussion of the cross-referencing process for disparate data is beyond the scope of this book.[2]

Business Term Glossary

A **business term glossary** provides a list of terms and abbreviations used in the business and a definition of each of those terms and abbreviations. There are often as many synonyms, homonyms, and abbreviations in the business world as there are in the data resource. One way to help business clients understand these business terms and abbreviations and identify the official business terms is to develop a comprehensive business term glossary. It goes hand-in-hand with the development of a data subject thesaurus. A good librarian with input from knowledgeable business clients or a newcomer to the organization can produce an excellent business term glossary.

A glossary of business terms provides meaningful definitions.

A business term glossary does not include the data definitions or the references between business terms and the data resource. It does not contain all of the common words used in preparing formal data names or the abbreviations of words used in formal data names. It does contain a definition of business terms and abbreviations and cross-references between business terms. It helps resolve the uncertainty and conflict involved in synonymous business terms and abbreviations. It helps people identify prominent business terms and prepare formal data names that are meaningful to the business.

---

[2] Techniques for cross-referencing data can be found in Brackett, Michael H., *The Data Warehouse Challenge: Taming Data Chaos*, John Wiley & Sons, 1996.

Robust Data Documentation Benefits

Robust data documentation that is complete, current, understandable, readily available, and known to exist provides several benefits to the organization, including increased awareness of the data resource, halting the data disparity, improving productivity, and success motivation. Each of these benefits is explained below.

Increased Awareness

Robust data documentation increases awareness about the state of the data resource and the contents of the data resource. Increasing awareness of the data resource helps people understand the data resource and fully utilize it to meet the business information demand. It provides a single version of the truth that builds confidence in the data resource and encourages people to contribute to improving the quality of the data resource.

> Robust data documentation increases data resource awareness.

Robust data documentation based on the new concept of data resource data breaks the myths and mystique about traditional metadata. It provides a whole new perspective about capturing and maintaining documentation about the data resource. It treats data resource data the same as any other segment of the data resource and promotes the development of high-quality data resource data.

Halted Data Disparity

Robust data documentation is the final blow that substantially halts the disparate data cycle. Formal data names provided better data identification, comprehensive data definitions helped people understand the data, proper data structures provided better business representation, and precise data integrity rules improved data value quality. Each helped to progressively slow the disparate data cycle. Robust data documentation makes all that information readily available to people to limit confusion and build confidence in the data resource.

> Robust data documentation is the final blow to data disparity.

Robust data documentation ensures that the compare data cycle is in full swing and the natural drift of the data resource has been turned away from disparity. It helps draw people into the process of understanding the data resource and contributing their efforts toward improving that data resource. It substantially discourages them from continuing to create disparate data.

Improved Productivity

The result of increasing awareness about the data resource, halting any further creation of disparate data, and developing of a comparate data resource is increased productivity. When business clients and information technology staff are aware of the data resource and fully utilize that data resource to meet business information needs, productivity improves. More appropriate business actions are taken, missed opportunities are reduced, and less productivity is lost on non-value-added tasks. There is also a better use of the computer resources.

> Robust data documentation provides the final boost in productivity.

Each of the good practices described in the previous chapters improves productivity. The data resource data build on the previous good practices and takes productivity to new heights. The good practices described in the remaining chapters continue to boost productivity, but the major gains have been made.

Best Practices

The good practices for developing robust data documentation emphasize capturing technical and semantic data resource data and making those data readily available to anyone in the organization interested in understanding and using the data resource. Data documentation, like data names, data definitions, data structure, and data integrity rules, cannot be developed all at once. There is just too much discovery and understanding that needs to take place to put all the data resource data in place in a short time. The best approach is to establish a priority for developing data resource data.

Document Current Activities

First, document anything that is being done with formal data names, comprehensive data definitions, proper data structures, and precise data integrity rules. Whatever their priority, that is the first priority for developing data resource data: capture and maintain data documentation as it is being developed. Do not wait until the tasks are done and then capture the documentation after-the-fact. Capture the data resource data, using whatever tools are available, as they are being developed.

Documentation Readily Available

Second, make the data resource data readily available to all audiences, and let the organization at large know that the data resource data are readily available. The state of the data resource should be opened up so that people can see what is and what is not there, and can respond accordingly. A *no-blame no-whitewash approach* encourages people to put their effort into developing a comparate data resource. It is not important whether the current data documentation is perfect or not; it is important that people are encouraged to contribute to documentation about a comparate data resource.

Provide Documentation Support

Third, provide initial support for understanding the data resource through a data subject thesaurus and a business term glossary. Provide people with the means to readily access the data resource based on terms they are familiar with and understand. Provide whatever is necessary to help them find the data they need to support their business activities. The data characteristic thesaurus will fall into place in due time.

Data Resource Data Architecture

The most important practice is to begin building a data resource data model within the common data architecture. Determine what data resource data are needed, design those data like any other data, and build, buy, or customize an application to maintain those data. A discussion of the tools that capture or store data resource data is beyond the scope of this book, but it is important to have some supporting application and database for data resource data that follows the good practices laid out above.[3] The ultimate success motivation is seeing a consistent, integrated, robust, well-understood data resource data architecture unfolding.

A data resource data model is not an information model as some people claim. As mentioned earlier in the Proper Data Structure chapter, an information model consists of the business schema for a particular business function. A data resource data model is a model of the data resource data that contains formal data names, comprehensive data definitions, proper data structure, precise data integrity rules, and is documented the same as any other data. These components are also documented as data resource data the same as any other data model. In other words, the data resource data document themselves.

The data resource data model is not a meta-data model, a meta-model, or a meta-meta-model. It is these concepts that make the traditional concept of *meta-data* appear academic and esoteric. (I once overheard a discussion about *meta-data* where a person was talking about the benefits of a *meta meta data data model model*. That is getting pretty esoteric.) The term *metadata* may never be completely replaced, but if business clients and information technology staff begin thinking *data resource data* when they hear the term *metadata,* there will be a better understanding of the concept and better documentation about the data resource.

Summary

The bad habits leading to limited data documentation, the impacts of those bad habits, the good practices for robust data documentation, the benefits of those good practices, and the most beneficial best practices are summarized below. The list is also contained in Appendix A.

> Bad habits leading to limited data documentation:
>> Data documentation not complete.
>> Data documentation not current with the business.
>> Data documentation not understandable to all audiences.
>> Data documentation is redundant.

---

[3] The section Start Within Current Budget in the chapter on Appropriate Data Recognition explains how one organization made a quick-start with its own repository and then made a smooth migration to a commercial repository.

   Data documentation not readily available.

   Data documentation existence largely unknown to the organization.

Impacts of limited data documentation:

   Limited awareness about the data documentation.

   Disparate data cycle continues.

   Lost productivity continues.

Good practices for robust data documentation:

   Data resource data concept replaces 'metadata'.

   Data resource data aspects for business and technical data.

   Complete data documentation.

   Current data documentation.

   Understandable data documentation.

   Non-redundant data documentation.

   Readily available data documentation.

   Data documentation known to exist.

   Ancillary data documentation.

      Data subject thesaurus.

      Data characteristic thesaurus.

      Business term glossary.

Benefits of robust data documentation:

   Increased awareness of data resource data.

   Halted the disparate data cycle.

   Improved productivity.

Best practices for success motivation:

   Document current activities.

   Documentation readily available.

   Provide documentation support.

   Data resource data architecture.

The bad habits, good practices, and best practices for data documentation can be used to evaluate the status of an organizations data resource. Fill in the horizontal bar (below) to show the degree to which the bad habits exist and the degree to which the good practices and the best practices have been implemented. You can provide definitions for the Poor, Fair, Moderate, Good, and Excellent headings to suit your organization, or you can use a numeric scale if it is more appropriate. You can also select the items that are important for your organization, but don't be too hasty at excluding items, because they may be valuable later. This list is also contained in Appendix B.

	P	F	M	G	E
Bad Habits					
Data documentation not complete	☐	☐	☐	☐	☐
Data documentation not current	☐	☐	☐	☐	☐
Data documentation not understandable	☐	☐	☐	☐	☐
Data documentation redundant	☐	☐	☐	☐	☐
Data documentation not readily available	☐	☐	☐	☐	☐
Data documentation existence unknown	☐	☐	☐	☐	☐
Good Practices					
Data resource data concept	☐	☐	☐	☐	☐
Data resource data aspects	☐	☐	☐	☐	☐
Complete data documentation	☐	☐	☐	☐	☐
Current data documentation	☐	☐	☐	☐	☐
Understandable data documentation	☐	☐	☐	☐	☐
Non-redundant data documentation	☐	☐	☐	☐	☐
Readily available data documentation	☐	☐	☐	☐	☐
Data documentation known to exist	☐	☐	☐	☐	☐
Ancillary data documentation					
Data subject thesaurus	☐	☐	☐	☐	☐
Data characteristic thesaurus	☐	☐	☐	☐	☐
Business term glossary	☐	☐	☐	☐	☐
Best Practices					
Document current activities	☐	☐	☐	☐	☐
Documentation readily available	☐	☐	☐	☐	☐
Provide documentation support	☐	☐	☐	☐	☐
Data resource data architecture	☐	☐	☐	☐	☐

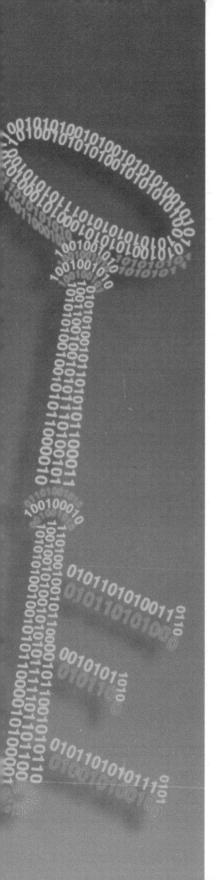

CHAPTER 7

Reasonable Data Orientation

> A reasonable data orientation
> promotes business understanding.

The previous five chapters explained five ways to achieve data resource quality from an architectural perspective. There are an additional five ways to achieve data resource quality from a non-architectural perspective. These five ways pertain to the availability and management of the data resource.

After robust data documentation, the sixth way to achieve data resource quality is through a reasonable orientation for development of the data resource. A reasonable orientation is focusing on a long-term objective to meet the current and future business information demand rather than a short-term objective to meet current needs. Continuing to focus on short-term objectives compromises the long-term stability of the data resource; a situation that is happening in most organizations today.

A reasonable orientation relates largely to the structure of a data resource but includes cultural aspects related to that structure. This chapter explains the bad habits that contribute to an unreasonable orientation, how they impact the business, and the good practices that can be used to ensure a long-term focus on the business.

Unreasonable Data Orientation

The six bad habits leading to an unreasonable data orientation center around short-term objectives and a narrow focus for the data resource. Each of these bad habits is explained below.

Physical Orientation

The first bad habit is a profound orientation toward physical design, data storage, and hardware performance. There is little or no consideration for the business support provided by the data. The emphasis is on the physical schema at the exclusion of the other data schema explained in the chapter on Proper Data Structure. The other data schema are not developed and there is no transformation to the physical schema. This is what is referred to as a *brute-force physical approach*.

> A physical orientation largely ignores business support.

A profound physical orientation is usually a very short-term orientation. The major concern is current performance on the hardware that is available in the organization today. There is seldom any consideration for future performance, future hardware acquisition, or changes in hardware technology. In many situations there is an objective, hidden or known, to minimize any additional expenses for hardware acquisition. The business will just have to live with the hardware that is available.

A profound physical orientation may be due to a lack of training, or training that is oriented toward the generation of code for developing the physical database. Many methods today are oriented solely toward cutting the code for generating the physical database. Any other activity that is not directly related to generating the physical database is totally unnecessary. The perceived purpose of many data models is simply to get enough data to automatically develop the physical database.

I was sitting in a data design session that was oriented toward the client's business. The technical manger was becoming frustrated that no deliverables were being produced. After all, a design to meet the business needs was not a deliverable; the code and the physical database were the deliverables. We were trying to explain the benefits of understanding the business and then designing the data to support the business. Finally, in a fit of frustration, the manager jumped up and said "Just cut the crap and cut the code" and left the room. I have heard many different versions of this phrase, but the message is always the same.

The impacts of a physical orientation can be disastrous. Performance can be worse than a well-designed database that supports the business. There are often considerable redundant data created just to optimize performance. There are unnecessary, meaningless, and even incorrect data relations developed by the random insertion of foreign keys just to improve access. There is usually a total lack of precise data integrity rules with only data types and mathematical domains specified.

I was involved with one organization that had a profound physical orientation for the information system they had just developed. After a brief review, I mentioned that it would likely result in poor performance. They responded that there already was poor performance, and they had turned off referential integrity with no material gain in performance. I asked if that impacted the data quality, and they responded that they had previously removed all data edits in an attempt to gain performance. They had even moved all of the operational reporting to another replicated database in an attempt to improve performance. They had achieved a slight improvement in performance but had substantially delayed the timeliness of operational reporting.

Multiple Fact Orientation

Another bad habit that is related to a physical orientation, but deserves separate mention, is the creation of multiple fact data attributes. A ***multiple fact data attribute*** is a data attribute that contains more than one fact. Many times a physical orientation results in putting multiple facts in one data attribute. For example, a birth date attribute may have a date or the terms Not Available or Not Necessary. This is a combination of two facts; one for the date a person is born and another for the availability of that date.

> Multiple fact and multiple value
> data attributes cause many problems.

Multiple fact data attributes result in two basic problems. First, they are very difficult to edit because a data integrity rule needs to specify a valid date or one of two character strings. Second, there are problems with any calculations that are performed on the date, such as the calculation of age. It is difficult to calculate age on a character string that says the date is not available. Only the valid dates would need to be selected for calculation, and the character strings would need to be ignored.

A bad habit very similar to multiple fact data attributes is multiple value data attributes. A ***multiple value data attribute*** is a data attribute that contains multiple values of the same fact or of different facts. For example, a data attribute may contain a string of names for the people who worked on a team, such as J. Smith, K Jones, T Jackson. These data values are just as difficult to edit as multiple fact data attributes.

The worst example that I have encountered is the concatenation of multiple facts related to problem reporting. There can be a variety of problems that occur during manufacturing and each of these problems have many different parameters specific to that problem. The problem parameters are not consistent across all manufacturing problems. The physical approach was to collect the parameters related to a specific manufacturing problem, concatenate them into one text string, and store that string in a textual description field. This textual description field was then displayed on the screen and people interpreted the parameters as best they could according to a key of parameter names and length for a specific manufacturing problem.

We began to tear these description fields apart for each manufacturing problem to define specific data attributes and found another interesting situation. The same parameter might occur in more than one problem, but the format and the name of that parameter was often different from one manufacturing problem to the next. There was no consistent name or format for the parameters across manufacturing problems, and there was no data edit of any kind. The identification and documentation of these parameters took one person several weeks to complete.

One clarification about multiple fact data attributes that is worth mentioning: An address data attribute often contains multiple facts, such as building number, street name, cardinal direction, and apartment number. These multiple facts are closely related and can be placed in the same data attribute, if it is appropriate for the business, and the name and the definitions accurately reflect these multiple data attributes. Many emergency response systems and crime analysis systems separate an address into single fact data attributes because that is the level of business support required.

Process Orientation

The third bad habit is a strong orientation toward specific processing that is performed on the data. The processing may be a business activity, reporting, or some other use of the data. This orientation is claimed to be an orientation toward the business, but it is an orientation toward a specific use of the data, not toward general support of the business.

> A process orientation meets only one of many business needs.

One situation I encountered was the processing in a distribution center where products could be cross-docked or warehoused. When a shipment of products arrived from a vendor, the products could be cross-docked and immediately shipped out or they could be warehoused and shipped later. If they were cross-docked, the data were placed in one data file and if they were warehoused the data were placed in a different data file. If for some reason the shipment did not conform to the purchase order, the data were placed in a third data file. Data records were moved from one data file to another as appropriate. This orientation prevailed throughout the entire operational database. There were far more data files than were necessary to track the distribution of products. The result was substantial performance problems.

A process orientation toward one specific use of the data is usually to the detriment of other uses of the data. In the example above, the data may have been useful for tracking products during distribution, but it was very difficult for developing reports about the distribution of those products, or for finding all the products related to a specific shipment. When the data starts looking like the activities that are being performed, the reports being developed, or some other specific use of the data, there is a process orientation.

Another situation I encountered was an organization that was having performance problems in their operational database. On first review there appeared to be way too many data files for the scope of the database. On close examination they had created a data file for each state of each data entity and were moving data records from one data file to another as the state of the data entities changed. For example, when a product was ordered the order went into an order data file, when the order was confirmed the data record was moved to the order confirmed file, when the order was shipped the data record was moved to the order shipped data file, and so on. This approach does not result in very efficient processing.

I was walking down the hallway between cubicles in an organization one day and heard two people talking about the location of a particular data item. One person said that they had expected the data item to be in a particular data file because that is where it would be easier for them to obtain. The other person responded that it was totally ridiculous to be in that data file because he needed it in the data file where it was currently located. The first person responded that maybe they could write a request to have the data item replicated in both data files so they each could have easy access.

Operational Orientation

A fourth bad habit is an intense orientation toward operational processing. There is no consideration for any processing other than what is necessary to support the day-to-day operations of the organization. There is no consideration for capturing and maintaining historical data for the future analysis of trends and patterns. When the operational usefulness is over, the data are discarded. This situation was mentioned in the chapter on Precise Data Integrity Rules.

> An operational orientation shows no consideration for the future.

An intense orientation toward current operational data totally ignores the emergence of data warehousing and data mining technologies, and any in-depth analysis of the business. Many organizations have decided to move into data warehousing to analyze the trends and patterns in their business, and make future projections about their business, only to find that there are no meaningful historical data available. The operational data were discarded because their usefulness was over.

In situations where historical operational data do exist, those data are often moved directly into a data warehouse for the analysis of trends and patterns. The operational data are disparate and are considered a *house of cards* by some organizations. The evaluational data in the data warehouse is also disparate, as described earlier.[1] The result is that a data warehouse is simply *a house of cards built on the roof of a house of cards.*

I was in one organization that had no historical data about their business. The operational data were totally discarded after their operational usefulness was

---

[1] Operational and evaluational data are defined and explained in more detail in the chapter on Expanded Data Vision.

over. Even the audit trails that contained some historical data were saved only for a short period of time until their usefulness as operational backup was over and they were discarded. There was a total lack of concern for the future value of any operational data. When I questioned people about this situation, I received an intense response that the sole purpose of the database was to support current operational processing.

Independent Orientation

A fifth bad habit is an orientation toward the independent development of databases. The data structures for each database are independent and there is no concern or interest for developing these structures within any consistent data architecture for the organization. This situation is commonly known as *stovepipe systems* or *islands of data*. There is minimal, if any, coordination between information systems and their databases.

> An independent orientation severely limits data sharing.

There are two aspects to an independent orientation. First, there is independence within the major types of data, such as tabular, spatial, imaging, and so on. Each information system has its own databases that contain their own data. Second, there is independence across the major types of data. Even if there is some coordination within the major data types, there is seldom any coordination across the major data types.

There are many reasons for an independent data orientation. There is often a lack of formal training about developing an enterprise-wide data architecture or the concepts of data sharing. Training is often oriented toward the physical implementation of specific data types. Seldom do you find training on integrating the design of tabular, spatial, and imaging data within a single data architecture.

There is often a lack of organization-wide concern. The concern is only about a specific system that needs to be developed. There may be time or resource constraints that limit any coordination or integration with other systems, which is short-sighted at best. There may be the physical or process orientations mentioned above that prevent any coordination or integration even if there were an interest.

An independent orientation results from everyone doing their own thing within a narrow scope and a short term. Rapid application development often adds to the problem. Let's get this system built quickly. Who needs an overall data architecture? We know how to get it up and running. We do not need to share our data with anybody else, and nobody better be messing with our data. Just get it done and implemented. We will worry about tomorrow when tomorrow comes. I have heard these and similar comments more times than I care to count.

Inappropriate Business Orientation

The sixth bad habit is an orientation that is not appropriate for business client involvement. This orientation can range from the total exclusion of business clients to a physical database that is totally driven by business clients. Neither approach is appropriate for designing a data resource that supports the business needs.

> The exclusion of business clients
> excludes their knowledge of the business.

I was in one organization that had a very physical orientation to their databases. I asked about business client involvement and received a very negative response. Why should business clients be involved in the design of the database? What do they know about building efficient databases? Who needs joint application development? The inclusion of business clients would only slow down the process and delay implementation.

This organization followed the traditional approach of a design specification developed by the business clients. That design specification was given to the technical staff, and they developed the database as they interpreted the design document. There was no interaction with the business clients. If any additional information was needed, a document was sent back to the business clients requesting that information. I asked the business clients about this situation and they responded that it has always been that way and that they prided themselves in trying to get the specification correct in the first document.

The other extreme is databases that are designed by business clients with minimal or no involvement of the technical staff. Business clients dominate the design and demand that the database be built a certain way, and the technical staff simply carries out that demand without question. What the business client wants is what the business client gets. In some situations, business clients simply build their own databases without any technical staff. The result in both situations is a blend of the orientations mentioned above, and most notably no coordination or integration between information systems or databases.

Business clients may thoroughly understand their business but they seldom understand the entire business, particularly in a large organization. They usually lack the basic principles and training for developing an organization-wide data resource that supports the entire business. In many situations they exercise their authority to take over because of the exclusion mentioned above and the impacts of that exclusion. It is a situation of *they had their way, now I'm going to have my way* that does not resolve the basic problems.

Unreasonable Data Orientation Impacts

The impact of these unreasonable orientations is a loss of business focus, the promotion of data disparity, performance problems, and lost productivity. These impacts can often be severe and, in some situations, can do more harm to the business than the impacts of the architectural bad habits mentioned in the previous chapters.

Lost Business Focus

The prominent impact of unreasonable orientations is a loss of focus on the business that the data resource is intended to support. Physical and process orientations, independent orientations, and inappropriate business orientations take their toll on the business support. These orientations are very narrow, very short-term, and are often very personal. They create a lose-lose situation with respect to the business at large.

> Inappropriate orientations lead to a lose-lose situation.

One of the things that I have noticed in some public and private sector organizations is a strong onslaught from the technical staff when their orientation is questioned. Their response is often intense, threatening, arrogant, and emotional. I have noticed an equally strong reaction from many business people when their orientation is questioned. Both of these responses result in a loss of business focus. They polarize people, lead to increased defensiveness, and ultimately lead to actions that are not in the best interest of the business.

Continued Data Disparity

Another impact of an unreasonable orientation is a continuation of data disparity. In addition to the architectural impacts, orientations toward the physical database and data use, and toward uncoordinated and independent development, are promoting continued data disparity. Implementing the good practices from the previous chapters can resolve many of the problems, but if people will not cooperate and develop a common data resource, the data disparity will continue.

> Unreasonable orientations promote
> data disparity even with good practices.

In spite of all the architectural principles and techniques that are available, the fact remains that when people do not cooperate and integrate their efforts toward the business at large, data disparity will continue. When people proceed on their own agendas and their own schedules, the business ultimately suffers. Regardless of past practices, regardless of who is to blame for the current situations, regardless of any hidden personal agendas, when people operate independently the business suffers.

Performance Problems

An unreasonable orientation leads to overall performance problems. Even though the orientation may be toward improved performance in a specific situation for the near term, the overall performance decreases. It was mentioned in the first chapter on The State of the Data Resource that the demand for information is constantly changing and often comes on very short notice. Any specific performance orientation for the near term will become obsolete with the dynamic demand for information.

> Unreasonable orientation leads to overall poor performance.

In some situations a physical or process orientation was taken with the intent of achieving good performance. After implementation, the result of that orientation is a realization that the desired performance was not achieved. Then, as the demand for information changes, the performance gets worse. The flip side is that performance problems can indicate a physical or process orientation.

There is one caution about performance problems. One reason for poor performance is a true hardware limitation; the current hardware will simply not handle the workload. This situation cannot be resolved with any type of orientation. It can only be resolved with additional hardware. A second caution is that a hardware limitation is often blamed for poor performance that is really due to an unreasonable orientation. An organization needs to look in depth at performance problems to determine if they are due to true hardware limitation, to unreasonable orientations, or to both.

Lost Productivity

The ultimate impact of a loss of business focus, continued data disparity, and performance problems is a loss of productivity. Like the previous sets of bad habits, unreasonable orientations impact productivity sooner or later. The productivity of both business clients and information technology staff is less than optimal. No one in the organization is immune from productivity loss due to an unreasonable orientation.

> Unreasonable orientations ultimately impact productivity.

The only way that this productivity loss can be corrected is for attitudes to change along with the development techniques. Both the business and information technology staff must understand that their orientations are impacting the data resource, which impacts their productivity, which impacts the business, which could impact their job security. When they corporate and use reasonable data orientations, the situation will begin to improve.

Reasonable Data Orientation

A reasonable data orientation is one that is oriented primarily toward the business and long-term support of the business information demand. The primary objective is support of the current and future business information demand. A reasonable data orientation includes good practices for a business subject orientation, a business client orientation, a new five-tier concept, detailed data normalization, an architectural orientation, and single fact data attributes.

Business Subject Orientation

The data resource must be oriented toward business subjects, as mentioned in the State of the Data Resource chapter and the Proper Data Structure chapter. A subject-oriented data resource is built with data subjects that represent business objects and business events about which the organization is involved or interested. *Any true support to the business comes from a data resource that is primarily oriented to the business objects and events that are important to that business!*

> A business subject orientation
> ensures continued support for the business.

Any other orientation, however important it may appear to be, is secondary to a business subject orientation. All of the concepts, principles, and techniques presented in the previous chapters support a primary orientation to the business with secondary orientations to other issues like involvement, integration, and performance.

Business Client Orientation

A business subject orientation requires an appropriate orientation to business clients. The extremes of totally excluding business clients from any direct input into design of the data resource to their total control of database development is not acceptable. Business client knowledge of what the business does, where it is today, and where it is going in the future is critical to developing a successful data resource. Information technology staff involvement in how to develop and implement a data resource that supports the business is equally critical.

> Appropriate business client
> inclusion supports a business orientation.

Both business clients and information technology staff must be included in the right mix to ensure a successful data resource. Concepts like a team approach, cooperative development, joint development, dynamic teams, and so on, promote the proper mix of knowledge and skills at the proper time for a successful data resource. A team of knowledgeable business clients and skilled technologists is the only way to develop a subject-oriented data resource that will meet the current and future business information demand.

Five-Tier Concept

The three-tier five-schema concept was explained in the chapter on Proper Data Structure. That concept can be expanded beyond the operational data to resolve the problems associated with an operational orientation and the loss of historical data. A new five-tier concept includes two tiers added below the three-tier concept, as shown in Figure 7.1.

The third tier of the three-tier concept becomes an *operational tier* oriented toward the data necessary to maintain the day-to-day business operations. Mathematically, it is considered to be in the data space. The fourth tier is an *analytical*

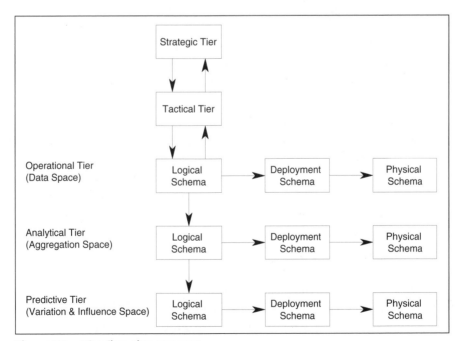

Figure 7.1   The five-tier concept.

tier oriented toward verifying or disproving known or suspected trends and patterns. It supports true data warehousing and is considered to be in the aggregation space. The fifth tier is a ***predictive tier*** oriented toward discovering unknown or unsuspected trends and patterns. It supports true data mining and is considered to be a combination of the variation and influence spaces.

> The five-tier concept ensures a business
> orientation and a consistent architecture.

The primary benefit of this five-tier concept is that each tier has a logical schema, a deployment schema, and a physical schema. Each logical schema is built from the logical schema in the tier above it to ensure that the entire data resource is built within the same data architecture. There is no independent development of the logical schema in the tiers. The progression is from the strategic tier, to the tactical tier, to the operational tier, to the analytical tier, to the predictive tier.

The secondary benefit of this five-tier concept is that each tier has an initial logical design, followed by deployment, followed by denormalization and physical implementation. There is no brute-force-physical development from the operational physical schema, to the analytical physical schema, to the predictive physical schema. Many of the discussions in the literature and at conferences deal with techniques for moving down the physical schema without a corresponding logical design. This should not be allowed in favor of a normal progression down the logical schema and then horizontally to the physical schema.

The logical schema are developed with respect to their mathematical space. The logical schema in the operational tier are developed with traditional relational modeling. The logical schema in the analytical tier are developed with dimensional modeling. The logical schema in the predictive tier are developed with rotational modeling. A discussion of the different types of data modeling is beyond the scope of this book, but it is important to say that these different types of data modeling are evolving and that the five-tier concept provides a framework for that evolution.

The column of logical schema from the strategic tier down through the predictive tier replaces the traditional conceptual schema. In other words, the traditional conceptual schema has been expanded into five more precise schema with specific orientation. It was mentioned earlier that the term *conceptual schema* had lost its meaning to many people because it was used for many different orientations. The implementation of the five-tier schema and specific names for each tier resolves this confusion.

Each of the lower three tiers also have a business schema and a data view schema, even though they are not shown on the diagram. The information model mentioned earlier actually includes the three business schema in the operational, analytical, and predictive tiers. It is a model of the information that is needed by the business. It is the bridge between the data resource tier and the information tier in the business intelligence value chain. Again, techniques are evolving in this area, and the five-tier concept provides a framework for that evolution.

Data Normalization

Data normalization is largely ignored in the unreasonable orientation bad habits. Consistently applying the techniques for bringing the data into normal form is mandatory for the development of a subject-oriented data resource that is built within a common data architecture. Formal data normalization resolves many of the unreasonable orientation bad habits.

Data normalization must be
extended to include the two new tiers.

Data normalization, however, is different for the logical schema in the operational, analytical, and predictive tiers. There has been considerable discussion about denormalizing the data from the operational tier to the analytical and predictive tiers, but this is an inappropriate use of data denormalization. This discussion results from progressing down through the physical schema in the operational, analytical, and predictive tiers. As mentioned above, the progression should be down the logical schema and across through the deployment schema to the physical schema.

Data normalization is simply bringing the data into a normal form for the intended purpose. Traditionally this meant a third normal relational form for operational data. Data normalization, however, also means bringing data into a normal form for analytical processing and for predictive processing. The term *data normalization*, like *conceptual schema*, has lost its meaning and needs to be further refined to be meaningful.

Traditional, third normal form, relational data normalization is now referred to as *operational data normalization*, meaning bringing data into normal form for operational processing. *Analytical data normalization* is bringing data into normal form for analytical processing. *Predictive data normalization* is bringing data into normal form for predictive processing. These three types of data normalization are different, but they are relevant to the type of processing being performed.

The progression down through the operational, analytical, and predictive tiers is a renormalization of the data for a specific purpose using operational, analytical, and predictive data normalization. The logical schema are renormalized for a different purpose and are then deployed and denormalized for a specific operating environment. Techniques are evolving in this area and are beyond the scope of this book; however, the five-tier five-schema concept provides a framework for that evolution.

Single Architecture Orientation

The data resource must be developed within a single enterprise-wide data architecture. All data from all tiers and all schema must be designed, implemented, and managed within a single data architecture. Any data modeling effort should draw from and enhance a single common data architecture. If the data are not defined in the common data architecture, they should be added and then drawn out for a specific data model. This approach prevents the development of independent, redundant, and inconsistent data structures by building on and enhancing the common data architecture.

> The data resource should be
> developed within a single data architecture.

The logical schema in the common data architecture must be structurally independent of any processes or hardware. The concept of data independence has been around for many years, but is seldom followed. The logical data structure must be orthogonal to the business activities and the hardware structure so that data can be readily shared across all business activities and deployed across a variety of hardware environments. Maintaining logical structural independence ensures that the data resource meets a wide variety of business needs in many different locations. It supports the concept of a central architecture with local deployment.

A common data architecture also avoids an operational orientation where the data are only considered useful for operational processing. The five-tier concept and the development of precise data integrity rules ensures that historical data are available for the analysis of trends and patterns. They ensure that the usefulness of data is considered for the organization at large, not for a specific purpose. The result is a value-added data resource that meets the current and future business information demand of the organization.

A common data architecture helps the development of a structurally stable data architecture. One thing we have learned over the last few years is that a logical data structure can be structurally stable while supporting changing business needs. This discovery destroyed the myth that the logical data structure needs to constantly change with the changing business. *A structurally stable–business flexible data architecture can be developed so that it remains quite stable while supporting changing business needs!*

The basic principle is that the logical data structure is stable across changing business needs and it is stable across changing technology. The current business can change with only minor changes in the logical data structure. If the organization acquires new lines of business or drops lines of business, there would certainly be major changes in the logical data structure. The technology can also change with minimal changes in the logical data structure. The physical data structure would certainly change to match the changing technology.

Single Fact Orientation

Data attributes must be ***single fact data attributes*** that represent single facts and single values of those facts with respect to the business needs. Multiple facts and multiple values cannot be shoved together in data attributes due to some physical or process orientation. This habit came from the 80-column card and fixed field length days where there was an orientation to saving space. This is no longer valid with today's sophisticated database management systems.

> Data attributes must contain single facts and single values.

The business needs determine how facts are placed in data attributes. For example, Address. Line 1 might be defined as A combined data attribute consisting of Address. House Number, Address. Street Name, Address. Street Cardinal Direction, and Address. Unit Designation. It is acceptable for mailing and contains a closely related set of facts. Emergency response and crime analysis, however, might require that these facts be stored separately. If an organization has both requirements, the single-fact data attributes and the combined-fact data attributes would both appear in the data architecture.

A good practice to follow with combined fact data attributes is to describe the combination of the single fact data attributes in the comprehensive data definition, as shown above. The single fact data attributes are also defined, even if they are not intended for use. In other words, a single fact data attribute is defined for each fact, and then those single-fact data attributes are concatenated into a combined-fact data attribute to meet business needs.

Traditional data normalization only deals with the placement of data attributes in the proper data entity. It does not address the proper placement of facts within a data attribute. Data normalization must be extended to include the placement of a single fact within a data attribute, and then the combination of those single fact data attributes into combined fact data attributes as necessary for business support. This approach ensures the formal naming and comprehensive definition of all business facts and the formal combination of these facts.

Two data attributes should be defined for closely related facts. Using the date example above, there should be one data attribute for the date and another data attribute for the reason the date is not available. These two data attributes are mutually exclusive, as defined in the data integrity rules. When a date is entered, the reason for no date is prevented and when a date is not entered, the reason for no date is required.[2]

Reasonable Data Orientation Benefits

The benefits of a business orientation are most rewarding for the organization at large in the long term. Many of the bad habits were rewarding for small segments of the organization for a short period of time, but they were not rewarding for the entire organization in the long term. The good practices result

---

[2] Again, I am not going to get involved in the difference between blanks and nulls. These are conditions under which values are required or prevented.

in improved business support, promotion of compare data resource, improved productivity, and success motivation. All of these benefits support the benefits of the architectural good practices mentioned in the previous chapters.

Improved Business Support

The good practices for a reasonable orientation of the data resource provide improved support for the business. Taking a business subject orientation and developing teams with the right mix of business knowledge and technical skills results in the development of a data resource that meets business needs. Creating that right mix of knowledge and skills stops polarizing people and creates a win-win situation. After all, both parties are after the same thing.

> A business focus improves business support.

Developing a single, organization-wide, common data architecture for the entire data resource also provides improved business support. All models are developed as a subset of that common data architecture, which strongly supports the concept of model reuse. The information is filtered to provide the proper detail to the target audience. The correct perspective of the business is constantly portrayed to all audiences.

Developing a data resource that is structurally stable and business flexible helps draw business people into the process. It allows people to discuss business issues and the future direction of the business so that the data resource can meet those needs. It promotes the benefits of a data resource that is shared across business activities and hardware environments. Presenting the data architecture in a technically correct–culturally acceptable manner further encourages business people to become involved. The ultimate benefit is improved business support.

Promotion of Compare Data Resource

A reasonable data orientation also promotes development of a compare data resource. Most of the data disparity has been stopped, or can be stopped, with the architectural good practices. Taking a reasonable data orientation encourages both business and information technology staff to become involved and develop a compare data resource. This personal involvement blends both techniques and culture into development of a data resource that supports the current and future business information demand.

> A reasonable data orientation
> promotes the comparate data resource.

Providing the comprehensive five-tier five-schema concept also helps both the cultural and technical development of a comparate data resource. People can see how the operational, analytical, and predictive tiers of the data resource can support the current and future aspects of the business. The techniques provided with the five tiers give people the ability to develop and maintain a comparate data resource that extends far beyond operational support. Hopefully, this concept will prevent data disparity from happening as these technologies evolve.

Improved Productivity

The result of improved business support and the promotion of a comparate data resource is an improvement in productivity. The productivity of both business and information technology is improved beyond the gains achieved from the architectural best practices. These may not be monumental gains in productivity, but they are significant in the sense that the culture of the organization is being changed toward the cooperative development of a single common data architecture.

> A reasonable data orientation
> provides a cultural productivity improvement.

The overall database and hardware performance can also be improved with the good practices of a reasonable data orientation. There may or may not be improvement for specific business activities, but there is an overall improvement in performance for the organization at large. Using the proper normalization and denormalization techniques within the five-tier five-schema concept will optimize the performance for any specific business activity.

Best Practices

The good practices for achieving a reasonable data orientation emphasize a change in attitude toward a business perspective and formal techniques. A reasonable data orientation contributes to the success motivation provided by the architectural best practices. An intense physical or process orientation is avoided with the promotion of a strong business orientation. This switch in orientations is one of the strongest motivators for the continued development of a comparate data resource. The technical good practices described in the previous chapters provided a technical success motivation, but a reasonable data orientation provides a strong cultural success motivation.

> A real business orientation provides strong success motivation.

Like the architectural good practices, the reasonable data orientation best practices cannot all be implemented at once. The most important good practice, by far, is to take a business subject orientation for development of the data resource. The involvement of business knowledge and technical skills in the development team provides a strong business focus. This strong focus on the business ensures that the data resource will support the business. The other good practices will fall into place relatively easy with a strong business focus.

Summary

The bad habits leading to an unreasonable data orientation, the impacts of those bad habits, the good practices for a reasonable data orientation, the benefits of those good practices, and the most beneficial best practices are summarized below. This list is also contained in Appendix A.

Bad habits leading to an unreasonable data orientation:
  Physical database orientation.
  Multiple fact, multiple value data item orientation.
  Process orientation toward use of the data.
  Operational orientation with no consideration for historical data.
  Independent database development orientation.
  Inappropriate business orientation.

Impacts of an unreasonable data orientation:
   Loss of business focus.
   Continuation of data disparity.
   Unnecessary performance problems.
   Loss of productivity.

Good practices for a reasonable data orientation:
   Business subject orientation based on business objects and events.
   Business client orientation.
   Five-tier concept for the data resource.
   Data normalization to include the five tiers.
   Single fact data attribute orientation.
   Single data architecture orientation.

Benefits of a reasonable data orientation:
   Improved business support.
   Promotion of a comparate data resource.
   Improved productivity for business and information technology staff.

Best practices for success motivation:
   Take a business subject orientation.
   Involve business knowledge in design.
   Include technical skills in design.

The bad habits, good practices, and best practices for data orientation can be used to evaluate the status of an organization's data resource. Fill in the horizontal bar (below) to show the degree to which the bad habits exist and the degree to which the good practices and the best practices have been implemented. You can provide definitions for the Poor, Fair, Moderate, Good, and Excellent headings to suit your organization, or you can use a numeric scale if it is more appropriate. You can also select the items that are important for your organization, but don't be too hasty at excluding items, because they may be valuable later. This list is also contained in Appendix B.

	P	F	M	G	E
Bad Habits					
Physical orientation	☐	☐	☐	☐	☐
Multiple fact orientation	☐	☐	☐	☐	☐
Process orientation	☐	☐	☐	☐	☐

	P	F	M	G	E
Operational orientation	☐	☐	☐	☐	☐
Independent orientation	☐	☐	☐	☐	☐
Inappropriate business orientation	☐	☐	☐	☐	☐

Good Practices

	P	F	M	G	E
Business subject orientation	☐	☐	☐	☐	☐
Business client orientation	☐	☐	☐	☐	☐
Five-tier concept	☐	☐	☐	☐	☐
Data normalization expansion	☐	☐	☐	☐	☐
Single fact data attribute	☐	☐	☐	☐	☐
Single data architecture	☐	☐	☐	☐	☐

Best Practices

	P	F	M	G	E
Take a business subject orientation	☐	☐	☐	☐	☐
Involve business knowledge	☐	☐	☐	☐	☐
Include technical skills	☐	☐	☐	☐	☐

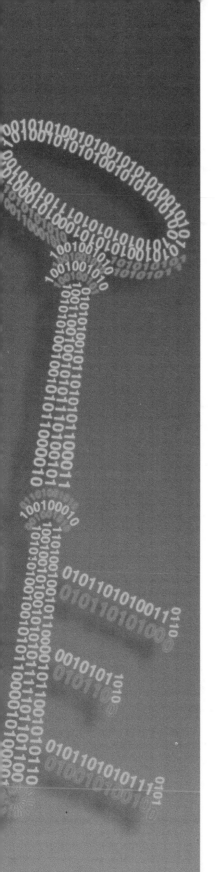

CHAPTER 8

Acceptable Data Availability

> Data must be readily available so
> they can be shared across the business.

After reasonable data orientation, the seventh way to achieve data resource quality is through an acceptable level of data availability. The data may not be readily available or may be too readily available. If the data are not readily available, they cannot be used to support business activities. If they are too readily available, there can be unauthorized access and changes to the data that could impact the business. The data resource could have very good quality resulting from many good practices; but if the data are not at the right level of availability, the business will be impacted.

Data availability applies to the business data as well as the data resource data. Since data resource data are part of an organization's data resource, and are designed and managed the same as business data, they are subject to the same availability criteria as the business data. If the data resource data do not have the right level of availability, the use of the business data is affected and the business is impacted accordingly.

This chapter presents the second set of non-architectural bad habits that organizations have and how those bad habits can be turned into good practices. The bad habits are related to the availability aspects of the data resource and have a strong bearing on how well the data are shared across the business. The degree of data sharing has a strong influence on whether people will support the development of a comparate data resource or continue doing their own thing and perpetuate the disparate data cycle.

Unacceptable Data Availability

Data availability is the process of ensuring that the data are available to meet the business information demand while properly protecting and securing those data. The data must be readily available to support business activities, but they must be protected enough to ensure proper access and recoverability in the event of a human or natural disaster. The bad habits leading to unacceptable data availability are described below.

Data Not Readily Accessible

The data may not be readily accessible by people needing those data to perform their business activities. Data that are not readily accessible may range from data that are totally unavailable, to data that are available but difficult to access, to data that are easy to access but whose access process is very cumbersome. In each of these situations, people will just not access the data because of some type of hardware or system software constraint.

> Data that cannot be easily accessed cannot be readily shared.

Another aspect of data not being readily accessible is employees not being authorized to access the data they need to perform their business activities. An employee may have full business authority to access and to add, change, or delete data in line with their duties, but just not have the proper system authority to access those data. In other words, the system or database security are not aligned with an employee's business authority to use the data resource.

An issue that is related to data availability is a lack of trust or confidence in the data. Even if the data are available or moderately available, if the people do not trust or have confidence in the data, they will find a reason not to use those data. The limited availability of data in one form or another may be one of those hidden reasons for claiming the data are unavailable so they can develop their own data. When people claim that data are not readily available, you should look deeper to determine if the data are really unavailable or if there is an apparent unavailability due to another reason.

Inadequate Data Protection

In some situations, the data are too accessible and are not readily protected. Employees who do not have business authority can look at data that they do not need to perform their business activities. Employees may be allowed to add, change, or delete data when they are not authorized to do so. In many organizations there are inadequate procedures for ensuring that employees can access the data for the right purposes.

> Data can be overly accessible or not have adequate protection.

There is also a high probability of inadequate protection from the unauthorized access, destruction, or deletion of data by non-employees. The development of security procedures, such as firewalls and passwords, that offer protection from the intentional acts of hackers and other disgruntled people is often not in place. These people can find ways into the databases and either use the data to their advantage, or alter or destroy the data to the detriment of the organization's business.

Many of the problems with data availability are internal employee related, rather than external non-employee related. Most of the data destruction that actually occurs is done unintentionally by employees in the normal course of performing their duties. The data resource is seldom protected from these unintentional mistakes.

Inadequate Data Recovery

The data backup processes are inadequate in many organizations. The frequency of backups may not be sufficient to match the fast pace of changes in today's dynamic business environment. Considerable business may transpire between formal database backups. The use of database logs and audit trails may cover the business transactions between formal database backups. In many cases, however, these logs and audit trails do not adequately cover the business or are not themselves properly backed up.

The portion of the data resource that is backed up may also be inadequate. The data supporting critical business functions may be adequately backed up, but the data for other less critical functions may not be adequately backed up. Many organizations are evaluating their backup and recovery procedures solely on the data supporting critical business functions rather than on the entire data resource.

> If data backup is not adequate,
> the speed of recovery is of little importance.

The data recovery processes are also inadequate in many organizations. Should something happen to the data resource, whether human-, hardware- or software-related, or environment related, the data cannot be recovered fast enough and completely enough to continue supporting the business. While the data resource is being recovered, the business may not be able to keep going at the same level it would if the data resource were available. Even if the business does continue with manual processing, the data resource may not be able to be brought up to date with the hand processing once recovery has been completed.

This issue is very critical in many public sector organizations. It is one thing not to be able to order your CDs or have your lawn mower parts delivered on time. It is a totally different thing not to have the National Crime Information System (NCIC), the Emergency Medical Service (EMS) system, or a poison control system available because its database is down. The length of time the data resource is unavailable and the degree to which it can be recovered is critical in many public sector organizations.

Unprotected Privacy and Confidentiality

An individual's or organization's right to privacy is not adequately protected by many organizations. Data are often released that should not be released, and data that should be released are often withheld. In some situations data are withheld because they are deemed to be privileged by the organization, when in fact they are not privileged by law. In other situations data are released inappropriately even though they are privileged by law. It is not always clear which data are privileged and which data are not privileged. This has traditionally been a problem in public sector organizations, but is becoming a problem in private sector organizations.

> There are few controls on the release of privileged data.

There are numerous state and Federal laws and regulations pertaining to the proper disclosure of data. These disclosure laws and regulations specify data that must be released when they are requested and data that can only be released under specific circumstances. These laws and regulations are constantly changing, and many organizations are not aware of the current status of the laws and regulations or that they even exist. They are just forging ahead with their own perceptions or their own internal policies without due regard for the existing laws or regulations.

A related issue in the public sector is the right to charge for the data that are provided to citizens or private sector organizations. One side of the issue is that these data were collected and maintained with public funds and should be readily available and a nominal charge. The other side of the issue is that some individuals or organizations use these data for personal gain or profit and that they should not be allowed to do so at the public's expense. The issue is not easily resolved, but the resolution does have an impact on the proper disclosure of data.

Inappropriate Data Use

The data may be used inappropriately for purposes other than legitimate business activities. Data can be sold or traded that could compromise business strategies or a person's or organization's right to privacy. There are many possible inappropriate uses for an organization's data and many different reasons for those uses. Numerous stories appear in the trade journals about the inappropriate use of data by employees that have access to those data. These stories are not about non-employees who breach security and access the data, but about employees who have access to the data and use those data for other than normal business activities.

> The data are often used inappropriately for other than normal business activities.

Many organizations do not regularly review the use of their data to ensure they are being used appropriately and ethically. Usually they are caught off-guard when they discover, directly or indirectly, such uses of their data. In most cases it is too late to take any action to correct or resolve the specific problem. The organization can only learn from the incident and be better prepared in the future.

Unacceptable Data Availability Impacts

There are four major impacts that could result from the unacceptable data availability bad habits, including limited data sharing, encouraging data disparity, impact on the business, and impact on people. Each of these impacts is explained below.

Limited Data Sharing

Data that are not readily available cannot be readily shared across business activities. Certain data may be privileged or restricted for one reason or another, even within an organization, but a large portion of the data resource can be shared across business activities. If the data cannot be readily shared across business activities, they do not meet the objective for a comparate data resource.

> Unavailable data limit the sharing of data across business activities.

Limited data sharing applies to both the data resource data and the business data. When the data resource data are not readily available, people are not aware of business data that exist in the data resource and cannot readily share those business data. Data sharing, therefore, begins with sharing the data resource data and then continues with the sharing of business data.

Encourage Data Disparity

Limited data sharing encourages continued data disparity. Even though the architectural best practices are in place, if the data cannot be readily shared across the business, the creation of additional disparate data is encouraged. When either the data resource data or the business data are limited in any manner, other than legitimate privileged data, data disparity is encouraged. This is a cultural encouragement to continued data disparity compared to the architectural reasons described in previous chapters.

> Limited data sharing encourages continued data disparity.

People that really want to do their own thing with data will find any excuse to be able to do their own thing. Any of the bad habits described in this book can be used as an excuse for people to develop their own data. Any reason related to the unavailability of data, such as difficult access, confidentiality, the possibility of unauthorized access, and so on, can be used as an excuse for people independently developing their own data.

Impact on Business

The worst impact of unacceptable data availability is not being able to perform the business activities. Anytime that the data are not readily available to meet the business information demand, the business is impacted. The impact may be minor or serious, and it could range from prices not being available to customers to life-threatening situations. It could result in inappropriate business actions, lost opportunities, and lost productivity to resolve those actions. Whether the reason is inadequate data protection, inadequate data recovery, or difficult access, unavailable data do not support business needs.

> The impact of unavailable data can be devastating to the business.

John Zachman tells the story of going to a restaurant one evening. The host and waiters were just standing around, and there were no customers in the restaurant. He asked if they were open for business and the host responded that they were. He asked why there were no other customers and the host responded that the computer was down. They were unable to process any orders or to prepare any receipts, both of which were done electronically. John asked if they could take the orders by hand and complete receipts by hand. The host responded that they did not know how to process orders or receipts by hand.

Impact on People

The impact on citizens and customers could be more severe than the impact on business activities. The impact of releasing privileged data about a person can be emotionally devastating to that person and could result in civil or criminal actions against the organization. It could also result in people providing false information in order to protect their right to privacy. Many people purposely provide the wrong information to organizations just because they do not trust the organization and do not want the correct information inadvertently released.

The situation with credit ratings is rapidly getting out of control. Credit bureaus are all too willing to get data about bad credit risks into their database and all too lax about removing those data. The transfer of credit data from one credit bureau to another makes it even more difficult for people to resolve bad credit ratings. Organizations that initiated the bad credit are often lax at initiating the removal of that bad credit when the situation has been resolved. These actions impact people unnecessarily.

> The impact of unavailable data can be life threatening.

The unavailability of data can impact a person's welfare and may even be life threatening. The restaurant situation described above may be acceptable in a restaurant. It may be acceptable for ordering products or services on the phone, but it is totally unacceptable for any emergency response. Can you imagine calling 911 and being told that there would be a delay in dispatching a medic unit or fire truck because the database was down? Can you imagine a delay in emergency response because alternate routes were not taken when the database containing road repair data is down? Can you imagine a hazardous materials team being delayed in containing a chemical spill, one that is toxic to people and hazardous to the environment, because their chemical database is unavailable?

Acceptable Data Availability

The bad habits leading to an unacceptable level of data availability can be turned into good practices for ensuring an acceptable level of data availability. The good practices include adequate data accessibility, adequate data protection, adequate data recovery, protected privacy and confidentiality, and appropriate data use. Each of these good practices is described below.

Adequate Data Accessibility

The data resource can be so secure that nobody can access the data. Obviously, there will be no problems with the data if no one can access those data, but the business will not be able to operate. The other extreme is that everyone has full access to the entire data resource, wherever those data may reside. This may cause problems with nationwide or multinational organizations and could cause problems with the quality of those data. Either of these extremes will eventually impact the business and people. Between these two extremes there is an acceptable level of data availability that ensures high-quality data to support business needs, allows reasonable protection of the data resource, and provides a reasonable protection for a person's or organization's right to privacy.

> The data resource must be readily
> available to support business activities.

The key is identifying and maintaining the right level of data accessibility. The data must be available to help employees perform their activities and keep the business operating. The data must be available to help citizens and customers use the services and acquire the products they need. Establishing the appropriate level of data accessibility is up to each organization based on where the data are located and what data are needed to support the business. Developing an organization-wide common data architecture significantly enhances the appropriate designation of data availability.

Adequate Data Protection

The data resource must be protected from unauthorized access, alteration, or destruction. Every reasonable effort should be made to prevent both the unintentional destruction of data by employees and the intentional access to alter or destroy data or to use the data for non-business purposes. Techniques such as authorizations, passwords, security checks, firewalls, and so on should be used to protect the data resource. Security breaches should be identified and analyzed to provide a better level of protection.

> The data resource must be adequately
> protected from alteration or destruction.

Adequate data protection means not going overboard with an unnecessary level of protection that impacts the business, and not being negligent about providing a reasonable level of protection that impacts the business. The data resource data should document who has the authority to access data, enter data, change data, and delete data. They should also document the conditions under which the data should be entered, changed, or deleted. Again, establishing an organization-wide common data architecture significantly improves the development of adequate data resource protection.

Adequate Data Recovery

The data resource must be recoverable in the event that data are altered or destroyed by man-made or natural disasters. The purpose of adequate data backup and recovery is to reinstate the data resource as quickly and completely as possible to keep the business operating. The data resource must be regularly backed up with a frequency that matches the dynamics of the business. Database logs and audit trails must be maintained to match the dynamics of the business and the data resource backup frequency, and must also be backed up in case they are altered or destroyed. Recovery procedures should be in place to reinstate any portion of the data resource that is altered or destroyed.

> The data resource must be rapidly and completely recoverable.

Procedures should be in place to continue the business through manual processes while the data resource is unavailable. When the data resource has been recovered, there must be procedures in place to bring it current with the manual processing that was done during the outage so that it reflects the current state of the business. Priorities should be established for the recovery of the data resource and for bringing the data resource up to date with the manual transactions. These priorities should be based on business needs and may change as the business needs change.

Protected Privacy and Confidentiality

The data must be protected from any disclosure that violates a person's or organization's right to privacy and confidentiality. One objective of a compare data resource is the sharing of data across business activities. Most data can be readily shared across the organization, with other organizations, and with customers or citizens. There are, however, some important exceptions related to an individual's or organization's right to privacy. Data that violate a person's or an organization's right to privacy must not be readily shared.

> A person's and organization's right to privacy must be honored.

Each organization must be aware of the current laws and regulations pertaining to data privacy and confidentiality and provide protection according to those laws and regulations. Since these laws and regulations are constantly changing, each organization needs to remain aware of the changes and adjust their protection accordingly. It is also helpful to remain aware of current court cases and any precedents that are established relating to the disclosure of confidential data.

The data resource data should document the laws and regulations pertaining to the definition of confidential data and the proper disclosure of those confidential data. They should document the confidential data attributes that can be disclosed and the conditions for that disclosure. They should also document the data stewards that are responsible for approving the disclosure of confidential data.[1]

Appropriate Data Use

There must be a constant review of the appropriate and ethical use of the data. Many organizations ignore this aspect of data availability because they consider it to be part of the process documentation that identifies which data attributes are created, used, or updated by automated processes. Ethical use of the data is, however, a data availability issue because it ensures that the data resource is being used in an appropriate manner for legitimate business activities. It ensures that the data resource is not being used for personal gain or for purposes that are not

---

[1] Data stewards are described in the next chapter on Adequate Data Responsibility.

related to the organization's business. Those business activities may or may not be part of an information system.

> The data resource must be used
> in an appropriate and ethical manner.

Appropriate data use also includes specifying the intended uses of data that are released to other organizations or individuals. Organizations should obtain non-disclosure or non-compete agreements from organizations and individuals that receive data. They should obtain use agreements that specify the conditions under which the data will be used by the recipient and the manner in which the data will be destroyed when their usefulness is over. These agreements should specify whether the data can be further disclosed, sold, traded, or given away.

Acceptable Data Availability Benefits

There are three major benefits of an acceptable level of data availability, including better use of staff, a shared data resource, and fewer impacts on business and people. Each of these benefits is described below.

Better Staff Use

There is more than enough work to go around for everyone interested in building and maintaining a comparate data resource. Business people do not need to dabble in the technical aspects of the data resource and technical people do not need to dabble in the business aspects. *Both business clients and technical staff need to combine their knowledge and skills to develop a quality data resource that will support the business needs!*

> The business and technical staff
> must combine their skills and knowledge.

The business people should identify the authority to access, enter, change, and delete data with respect to business needs. They should identify the appropriate levels of data protection, and the desired frequency of backup and speed of recovery, from a business perspective. They should identify the laws and regulations pertaining to data confidentiality and disclosure and the people who have authority to disclose confidential data. The business people need to concentrate on avoiding impacts to the business rather than on the technical aspects of the physical database.

The technical people should implement the access authority, the levels of data protection, the backup procedures, and the recovery procedures. They should understand all the possible ways that people can intentionally and unintentionally alter or destroy data. They should stay current with the technology and the techniques for preventing the alteration or destruction of data. This is a challenging area for the technical staff as networks evolve and a greater portion of the business is conducted over networks.

Shared Data Resource

One major benefit of an acceptable level of data availability is the emphasis on a shared data resource. The development, documentation, and implementation of access control procedures, data protection procedures, data backup and recovery procedures, and a constant review of appropriate data use builds confidence in the data resource. People feel comfortable with the data resource and confident that the data are protected and used appropriately. They will tend to contribute to developing one high-quality data resource rather than doing their own thing.

> Acceptable data available is a
> cultural encouragement to share data.

Sharing data promotes the development of a comparate data resource. It is a cultural encouragement for people to pull together for the common good of the organization. It adds to the other cultural encouragements and supports the architectural good practices. The data resource becomes smaller because it is less disparate, it becomes better because there is less disparity to manage, and it is more fully utilized.

Fewer Impacts

An acceptable level of data availability results in less impacts on the business and on people, and the impacts that do occur are less severe. Employees are more comfortable with the data, and citizens and customers are more comfortable with the organization because they know the data are high-quality and are used appropriately. Citizens and customers are more willing to provide the correct information which ultimately benefits the business and results in fewer impacts.

> Acceptable data available results in fewer impacts.

The business flows smoother when there are fewer impacts and the impacts are less severe. There is a proactive theme of preventing problems rather than a reactive theme of resolving problems. People begin to realize that problem prevention takes less resources than problem resolution and is far less frustrating. The biggest benefit of fewer impacts is that productivity continues to improve and the time spent resolving problems can be spent on more value-added business activities.

Best Practices

The good practices for an acceptable level of data availability emphasize a balance between sharing data and protecting an organization's or individual's right to privacy. It also emphasizes appropriate backup and recovery to ensure that the data are readily available. It is difficult to implement all the good practices for acceptable data availability, just like it is with the other sets of good practices. Unlike the other sets of good practices, there is no one practice that is better to start gaining acceptable data availability, but there are priorities.

> Sharing data and minimizing impacts
> provides a cultural success motivation.

Target Greatest Impacts

The first priority is to find the real hot spots that are causing the greatest impacts on the business. If data confidentiality and disclosure is a major issue, it should receive major emphasis. If ready access is causing a major impact, it should receive major emphasis. The major emphasis may be related to the priorities established for the architectural good practices, or they may be in other non-architectural good practices. The first priority may not always be related to the critical business data.

Backup and Recovery

The second priority is to make sure the data are backed up regularly and that data recovery can be done quickly and completely according to business needs. The critical areas of the data resource that support critical business functions should be targeted for regular backup and rapid recovery. The backups should be done as frequently as necessary to ensure that no business data are lost. The recovery should be done quickly and include any manual processing that was done during the outage. When the data supporting critical business functions are adequately covered, then the less critical data can be addressed.

Adequate Protection

The third priority is to make sure the data are protected from intentional or unintentional alteration or destruction, or from the disclosure of confidential data. The best approach for protection is to begin with the business critical data and ensure that they are adequately protected, and then work toward the less critical data. The best approach for disclosure is to identify the data that could be privileged and ensure that they are adequately protected from inappropriate disclosure.

Establishing the priorities in this manner provides the greatest benefit for the effort expended. The most severe impacts are resolved first, which contributes to a cultural success motivation for people to keep improving and utilizing a shared data resource. As one woman told me after we made major improvement in one segment of an organization's data resource, "It's like a breath of fresh air on a spring day."

Summary

The bad habits leading to unacceptable data availability, the impacts of those bad habits, the good practices for acceptable data availability, the benefits of those good practices, and the most beneficial best practices are summarized below. The list is also contained in Appendix A.

> Bad practices leading to unacceptable data availability:
>> Data are not readily accessible.
>> Inadequate protection of the data.
>> Inadequate recovery of the data.

Unprotected right to privacy and confidentiality.
Inappropriate use of the data.

Impacts of unacceptable data availability:
Data sharing is limited.
Data disparity is encouraged.
Impact on the business.
Impact on people.

Good practices for acceptable data availability:
Adequate accessibility to data to support business activities.
Adequate protection of the data resource.
Adequate data recovery for continued business support.
Protect privacy and confidentiality of individuals and organizations.
Appropriate use of the data.

Benefits of acceptable data availability:
Better use of the business and technical staff.
Shared data resource across business activities.
Fewer impacts on the business and on people.

Best practices for success motivation:
Target greatest impacts on the business.
Backup and recovery of data critical to the business.
Adequate protection from alteration, destruction, or improper disclosure.

The bad habits, good practices, and best practices for an acceptable level of data availability can be used to evaluate the status of an organization's data resource. Fill in the horizontal bar (below) to show the degree to which the bad habits exist and the degree to which the good practices and the best practices have been implemented. You can provide definitions for the Poor, Fair, Moderate, Good, and Excellent headings to suit your organization, or you can use a numeric scale if it is more appropriate. You can also select the items that are important for your organization, but don't be too hasty at excluding items, because they may be valuable later. This list is also contained in Appendix B.

	P	F	M	G	E
Bad Habits					
Data not readily accessible	☐	☐	☐	☐	☐
Inadequate data protection	☐	☐	☐	☐	☐

	P	F	M	G	E
Inadequate data recovery	☐	☐	☐	☐	☐
Unprotected privacy and confidentiality	☐	☐	☐	☐	☐
Inappropriate data use	☐	☐	☐	☐	☐

Good Practices

	P	F	M	G	E
Adequate data accessibility	☐	☐	☐	☐	☐
Adequate data protection	☐	☐	☐	☐	☐
Adequate data recovery	☐	☐	☐	☐	☐
Protect privacy and confidentiality	☐	☐	☐	☐	☐
Appropriate data use	☐	☐	☐	☐	☐

Best Practices

	P	F	M	G	E
Target greatest impacts	☐	☐	☐	☐	☐
Backup and recovery	☐	☐	☐	☐	☐
Adequate protection	☐	☐	☐	☐	☐

CHAPTER 9

Adequate Data Responsibility

> Adequate data responsibility is
> mandatory for proper control of data resource.

After acceptable data availability, the eighth way to achieve data resource quality is through the development of adequate responsibilities for the data resource. There is in most organizations a distinct lack of formal responsibilities for management of the data resource and a distinct lack of enforcement for any responsibilities that do exist. A resource as critical to the organization's welfare as the data resource is substantially deficient in adequate responsibilities to manage that resource.

Organizations have a chief financial officer who is responsible for the financial resource and is held accountable for following formal accounting principles. There is a human resource director who is responsible for the human resource and is held accountable for following current regulations and laws. Similar positions exist for other critical resources in the organization, such as real property. But there is seldom an equivalent position for the data resource.

I am often asked: Who is ultimately responsible for the data? Who in the organization owns the data? Who has control of the data resource? The answer should be that there is a collective responsibility by all the stakeholders in the organization that is carried out through authorized representatives. The fact, sadly enough, is that there are seldom any formal or collective responsibilities for management of the data resource. By formal responsibilities, I mean responsibilities equivalent to those for the finances, human resource, and real property.

This chapter presents the third set of non-architectural bad habits that organizations have related to the inadequate responsibility for managing the data resource. These bad habits impact the organization in many different ways. Turning these bad habits into good practices that provide adequate responsibilities for managing the data resource are presented. The benefits of implementing these good practices far offset any effort involved in implementing those good practices.

Inadequate Data Responsibility

Inadequate means insufficient, or not adequate to fulfill a need or meet a requirement. *Inadequate data responsibility* is the situation where the responsibility as defined does not fulfill the need for properly managing a shared data resource. The responsibility is casual, lax, inconsistent, uncoordinated, and not suitable for the current environment of a shared resource. Any responsibilities that do exist are usually developed independently, are incomplete, and are largely unknown to the organization at large. Simply put, there are no formal responsibilities for the management of a critical resource.

There are three primary bad habits that result in inadequate data responsibilities, including no centralized control, no management procedures, and no data stewardship. Each of these bad habits is explained below.

No Centralized Control

There is seldom any formal centralized control of the data resource. Each organizational unit or each person in the organization is doing their own thing with data; they are *thinking locally and acting locally*. Their approach to managing data is independent, unilateral, arbitrary, and self-centered. This may be a harsh statement, but it is all too often true. The approach is not oriented toward sharing data for the good of the organization.

> Few organizations have centralized
> control over their data resource.

I have been in many public and private sector organizations where there is minimal centralized control of the data resource. Each department, division, or unit does their own thing with their data for their business activities. There is little coordination with any data other than the critical business data, and there is not any real coordination for the critical business data. Not surprisingly, these are the organizations that are screaming the loudest about not being able to get the information they need to properly run the business.

A related situation is centralized control that is improperly placed in the organization. Data processing traditionally supported core business functions, such as finance or human resource, and was managed by the chief financial officer or human resource director. This situation still exists in many organizations today, and the orientation of the data resource is primarily toward support of those business functions. This primary orientation to a specific business function results in a narrow focus that causes people to develop their own data because they cannot get the support they need.

No Management Procedures

There is a general lack of procedures for managing the data resource. In many situations there may be some degree of centralized control over the data resource, or at least an attempt at centralized control, but there are minimal procedures in place for people to follow. If there are no formal procedures in place, there is nothing other than word-of-mouth for people to follow. No matter how good the intention for centralized control of the data resource, that control just will not happen.

> Few organizations have formal,
> usable procedures for their data resource.

If finances and human resources were managed the same way that data are managed, there would be terminations, civil suits, and possibly criminal charges. Nobody would consider allowing anyone in the organization to manage the finances as they saw fit for their business activity. Nobody would consider allowing anyone in the organization to hire, terminate, and promote people as they deemed necessary. There would be financial and employee chaos.

Another aspect of no management procedures is the issuance of mandates for managing the data resource. On occasion I encounter the situation where someone with authority issues a mandate for control of the data resource. Procedures are laid down from on high, and they will be followed. The implication is that if they are not followed there will be punishment.

The one thing that is glaringly obvious with mandates is that there are far more workers than there are mandators, and the workers have the tools to do what they want. They will take whatever action is necessary to support their business activities. Every time that I encounter a mandate situation, or any procedures that sound like a mandate, I see a failure in the making. I am not aware of any organization that has mandated procedures for data resource management that has been fully successful in establishing a comparate data resource. There may have been some progress toward a comparate data resource, but little success at fully establishing a comparate data resource.

No Data Stewardship

Generally there are no people in the organization with formally designated responsibilities for managing the data resource. Even if there is an initiative for centralized control of the data resource and formal procedures for managing the data resource, there will be no real management of the data resource if there are no formally assigned responsibilities. The responsibility often defaults to the information technology staff and is performed by database technicians with minimal experience in coordination. No wonder the state of the data resource is chaos.

> Few organizations have formal
> responsibilities for managing the data resource.

As stated above, the financial resource has a chief financial officer, the human resource has a human resource director, the real property has a facilities director, and so on. Each of the critical resources in an organization has formally designated responsibilities for ensuring that the resource is properly managed. Finance has people in charge of payables, receivables, budgets, and so on. Human resource has people in charge of training, affirmative action, and so on. Real property has people in charge of long-range planning, maintenance, disposal, and so on. The data resource is the only critical resource that is used throughout the organization that does not have formally assigned responsibilities for controlling that resource.

Inadequate Data Responsibility Impacts

In the absence of any formal responsibilities, people take the initiative and develop their own data resource. The good news is that they are taking the initiative and developing the data they need to perform their business activities. The bad news is that they are taking independent initiatives to develop uncoordinated data. The existence of inadequate data responsibilities impacts the organization by limiting data sharing and encouraging data disparity. Each of these impacts is explained below.

Limited Data Sharing

Any time that there is no centralized control over the data resource, a lack of formal procedures for managing the data resource, or no assigned responsibilities for managing the data resource, there will be limited data sharing. Inadequate responsibilities encourage people to develop their own data. When people are not encouraged to take part in developing a shared data resource, they will not be a team player and will tend to do their own thing.

> An inadequate level of data responsibility limits data sharing.

A narrow business focus or constant focus on the same business function alienates people. Mandates for managing the data resource result in a lack of comradery for developing a single integrated data resource. Punishment for not following mandates further alienates people to the point they feel they are not part of a shared data resource. In many respects, people are pushed into building their own data for their own activities.

Data Disparity Encouraged

The lack of centralized control, formal procedures, and assigned responsibilities is an open ticket for people to continue creating disparate data. After all, who is going to stop them? Who is going to tell them to do otherwise and risk impacting their specific business activity? Who is going to tell them that they cannot do whatever is necessary to support their business activities? Do technical people in information technology think they are going to tell business people how to manage their data? Does anyone really have the authority to tell business people how to manage their data? These are the attitudes of many people I have encountered in organizations where there is no real control over the data resource.

> Inadequate data responsibility encourages data disparity.

People often say that it is too expensive to establish centralized control, implement formal procedures, and assign responsibilities. Do you realize what that will cost us? Do you realize the effort involved in putting such an initiative in place? My response is to ask about the costs of disparate data and their impact on the business. The problem lies in the fact that disparate data impacts are hidden costs, and implementing adequate responsibility is a visible cost. I wonder what would happen if an organization did zero-based budgeting, or a similar approach, and included the costs of disparate data and their impacts as line items in the budget?

Adequate Data Responsibility

The bad habits and their impacts must be resolved and turned into good practices for establishing adequate data responsibilities. The good practices include data stewardship, reasonable management procedures, and centralized control. Each of these good practices is explained below.

Authorized Data Stewardship

Adequate data responsibility begins with the establishment of authorized data stewards. *Steward* came from the old English term *sty ward*; a person who was the ward of the sty. Such people watched over the stock and were responsible for the welfare of the stock, particularly during the night when the risks to the welfare of the stock were high. *Steward* is a good term for the data resource because it implies a keeper of the data who is watching over the welfare of the data for the organization.

A *data steward* is a person who watches over the data and is responsible for the welfare of the data resource and its support of the business, particularly when the risks are high. There are many terms that could be used, such as data guardians, data custodians, data coordinators, data analysts, data trustees, data curators, data administrators, data facilitators, data negotiators, data interventionists, and so on. I have seen these terms and many more that are basically saying the same thing, but *data steward* appears to be the most acceptable term.

Many people promote the concept of data ownership and that the data owners are responsible for the data resource. *Data ownership* is not used because it implies all the rights that come with ownership in general. The data owner would have the right to change the data, sell the data, buy additional data, and so on. That is not the intent in designating responsibility for the data resource. Therefore, *data steward* is used rather than *data owner*.

The job of a data steward is larger than one person can possibly manage in a dynamic business environment. The data resource is too large and too complex for one person to comprehend and control. The business knowledge and the information technology skills must be combined into a data stewardship initiative that encompasses the entire data resource. This initiative includes two basic levels of data stewardship: a strategic level and a detail level. Each of these levels are explained below.

Strategic Level

A **strategic data steward** is a person who has legal and financial responsibility for a major segment of the data resource. That person has decision-making authority for setting directions and committing resources for that segment of the data resource. The strategic data steward is usually an executive or upper-level manager and usually has responsibility along organizational lines, much as the director of human resource is the strategic data steward for human resource data.

Strategic data stewards do not need to be knowledgeable about the detail of the data resource. They do not need to thoroughly understand the data definitions, data structure, physical implementation, and so on. They do need to be generally familiar with a major business function and the data required to support that business function. They need to be familiar with the laws and regulations pertaining to the data. They need to be familiar with the data resource problems and the resources available to resolve those problems.

> Strategic data stewards set direction and commit resources.

I remember one situation in a large university where the registrar took the strategic data steward responsibility very seriously. He collected all the federal, state, and local laws and regulations pertaining to student data and compiled them into a rather impressive notebook. After reviewing what he had collected, he would not release the results. What he discovered was that there were many things that they were doing with student data that they should not have been doing. Also, there were many situations where they were withholding student data when they had no right to withhold those data. When the initial shock wore off, he set about correcting the problem by specifying what could and could not be done with student data.

The strategic data stewards collectively manage the organization's data resource. The best managed data resources I have encountered are those that are managed by a team of strategic data stewards who collectively decide how the data resource is to be developed for the good of the organization at large. They collectively look at the problems with the data resource, the needs of the business, and the resources available and make commitments to building a shared data resource.

Detail Level

The **detail data steward** is a person who is knowledgeable about the data by reason of having intimate familiarity with the data. That person is usually a knowledgeable worker who has been directly involved with the data for a considerable period of time. The detail data steward is responsible for developing the data architecture and the data resource data. That person has no decision making authority for setting directions for the data resource or committing resources to data resource development.

> Detail data stewards build the
> data architecture and data resource data.

Detail data stewards may cross organizational boundaries. It is not important where they currently work; it is important that they understand the data resource and have knowledge about the data resource. Their assignment as a detail data steward is based on their knowledge about the data, not their position in the organization. Detail data stewards can be business clients for the business aspects of the data architecture and information technology staff for the technical aspects of the data architecture. They collectively contribute to development of the data architecture and the data resource data.

The detail data stewards must interact with each other to develop an integrated shareable data resource. They must work within one common data architecture for the organization. They are actually building different parts of the same organization-wide data architecture, and all the pieces need to fit together. Where possible, they should define and use common sets of data to encourage data sharing.

I was in one organization that had an initiative to document their data resource and that was searching for knowledgeable people to contribute to that documentation. They were looking for people to start building the data resource data. There was little success because the effort was concentrated on the current technical staff and current business clients who would have the time to contribute to the initiative. These people were good at their current job, but they had little knowledge of the past and little in-depth knowledge of the data resource.

I also noticed that a number of older business clients and information technology staff nearing retirement had been pushed aside into jobs that were not in the mainstream until they were eligible for retirement. They were considered too technically obsolete to remain in the mainstream of the business, but too dedicated to terminate before retirement. There was little benefit to training them because there would be minimal benefit to the organization after they retired.

I began talking to these people and found a wealth of knowledge about the data resource and the support it provided to the business. I began drawing these people in as the detail data stewards to begin building the data resource data. I encountered considerable opposition to this approach because these people were technically obsolete and were about ready to retire. Why would I involve them in anything as important as documenting the data resource?

I persisted, and after several weeks of effort we had developed a tremendous quantity of data resource data. The volume of data resource data was growing rapidly and was building interest as it grew. People were becoming interested in both the semantic and technical aspects of the data resource data because they began to understand the data. In the end, several of these technically obsolete people stayed beyond retirement to continue their contribution to the data resource data.

Maintaining Two Distinct Levels

It is important that these strategic and detail levels of data stewardship not be confused or combined. They are totally different, though related, functions. I have seen situations where executives were appointed as data stewards because the organization wanted executive awareness of the data resource. As these executives began working on data architecture tasks, like data definitions and data structure, they began to delegate the task to appropriate individuals. When a decision arose as to the direction for the team or resource commitments to the initiative, the delegates needed to contact the executives for approval. This usually resulted in a prolonged process to set direction or commit resources, which delayed the initiative.

> The two distinct levels of data stewardship must be maintained.

The flip side of this problem is getting knowledgeable people involved in an initiative to develop data resource data. They start working on the data architecture tasks, like data definitions and data structure, and make considerable progress. When the need for a decision arises about the direction or resource commitment, these knowledgeable workers are forced to contact executives for decisions and the scenario described above evolves. This time, however, it is a little more difficult because the executives are not known. The knowledge workers need to find the appropriate authority to set direction and commit resources, which delays the initiative.

Therefore, it is important that the strategic and detail data stewardship functions remain distinct. The strategic data stewards form a team to set the overall direction for the data resource and commit resources to development of the data resource. The detail data stewards build a sharable data resource within a common data architecture according to the directions and resources set by the strategic data stewards.

Large Organizations

In very large organizations, particularly nationwide and multi-national organizations, the data steward task can be overwhelming. An international organization faces a situation called *data globalization*. There are many things to consider when an organization becomes multi-national, such as languages, measurement units, time zones, monetary units, local laws and customs, holidays, and so on. All the cultural, political, and geographical considerations must be included in management of the data resource. The strategic and detail data stewards must consider all these aspects of the organization to ensure that the data resource supports the entire organization.

> Larger organizations need a
> more robust structure for data stewards.

One of the problems I encounter with multi-national organizations is a data steward initiative that is focused primarily on the country where the corporate headquarters are located. The data architecture and the data resource data are based on perceptions of the corporate headquarter country and are distributed to the other countries. There is little input from people in those other countries. This approach leads to the same situation described above where people are not involved in developing the data resource and are continually encouraged to develop their own data.

The structure of data stewards in international organizations needs to be expanded to include representation from all aspects of the business in all countries. Local data stewards need to be designated to act as liaison from their country to the corporate data steward initiative to ensure that all parts of the business are represented and all concerns are addressed. The best approach is to designate *tactical data stewards* between the strategic data stewards and detail data stewards to manage the international aspects of the data resource. The specific arrangements are different with each organization, but the basic principle is to provide adequate input about the international aspects for development of the data resource.

Reasonable Management Procedures

Adequate data responsibility includes the establishment of reasonable procedures for managing the data resource. When the data stewards have been designated, they can begin developing procedures for management of the data resource. These procedures must be as rigorous as those for managing finances, the human resource, and real property, and they must include both the business and the technical aspect of the data resource.

> Reasonable management procedures
> must be rigorous and reasonable.

The procedures must also be reasonable, meaning they must be practical, understandable, and easy to follow. They must encourage people to become involved in developing a shared data resource rather than mandating their compliance. Reasonable procedures must provide an approach that is the easiest route for people to follow rather than a route of progressively unfolding standards that must be followed. The best guiding principle I have found is to *develop the procedures that you would like to see if you were on the receiving end of those procedures!* Establish procedures that would encourage you to become a team player.

One of the things that I learned in the public sector is how to make things happen in an environment where organizations are autonomous. Federal agencies, states, counties, and cities all have elected and appointed officials who are autonomous, and Indian tribes are sovereign nations. Unlike a private organization, there is no one place in the public sector to implement a mandate that applies to all public sector organizations that can be enforced. There is no way to enforce a mandate across all autonomous jurisdictions. The approach must be one that is simply the easiest route for people to follow.

The procedures must be readily visible and available to anyone in the organization who contributes to or uses the data resource. When the reasonable procedures are readily available, like readily available data resource data, they encourage people to become involved and to provide comments and input into those procedures. When people become involved, the data resource quality improves.

Centralized Control

Adequate data responsibility includes centralized control of the data resource architecture. When the data stewards are established and reasonable procedures have been developed, there begins to be a centralized control over the data resource architecture. The data resource architecture is developed along the lines of the ecological theme of *thinking globally and acting locally*. The basic principle is a single common data architecture for the organization with local implementation to meet business needs.

> The basic premise of centralized control
> is to think globally and act locally.

Many people perceive that centralized control of the data resource means absolute control over the entire data resource and how it is used to support the business. Someone in the organization, whether executive or database technician, makes decisions about everything pertaining to the data resource and issues those decision to the whole organization. There is minimal involvement from the people building and using the data resource.

Worse yet, many people perceive that central control means one central database for all data in the organization. This perception is sometimes referred to as the *database in the sky*. This is the perception that I most often face in an organization. People perceive their local data being moved to some corporate database that will impact their access to the data and the performance of their business activities. Incidentally, this is why the data deployment schema was added to the five-schema concept.

These are real perceptions about centralized control of the data resource architecture. There is also a false perception that is promoted by those who want an excuse not to have central control so they can do their own thing. There are many different approaches and hidden agendas to block the centralized control over the data resource architecture. In some organizations there is an active, though subtle, campaign to defeat any initiative to establish any form of centralized control over the data resource architecture. The only way to solve this situation is to establish strategic, tactical, and detail data stewards that represent all aspects of the business.

I worked with one executive who frequently made the comment that he would not yell "Charge!" until all the troops were pointed in the same direction, knew their target, and he was standing behind them. To do otherwise would be hazardous to their health and his. The majority of his time was spent aligning the troops, designating their targets, and gaining consensus. When the troops were aligned and he was behind them, he never hesitated to yell "Charge!" The results were always very successful.

There are many messages in this executive's philosophy, ranging from priorities to personnel management. The most important message is one of centralized control. He let everyone know the game plan for the organization. He planted seeds and encouraged feedback on the initiatives. He encouraged people to become involved and contribute their knowledge and skills. He was a team builder who did his homework, and the results were well worth the effort.

Adequate Data Responsibility Benefits

Initiatives to develop adequate data responsibility must integrate the business and the technology, as well as management and knowledge workers. Everyone must be encouraged to contribute their skills and knowledge to development of the data resource. The benefits of establishing adequate data responsibility are a shared data resource and success motivation for developing that shared data resource. Each of these benefits is explained below.

Shared Data Resource

The primary benefit of adequate data responsibility is a shared data resource. All the stakeholders of that data resource must be involved in its development and management. There must be strong business client involvement because the knowledge about the business, and about the data resource that supports the business, is often vested in the business community. To restate something I over-heard in one organization: "A data resource that is about the business, by the business, and for the business shall not perish from this organization."

> Formal data stewardship promotes a shared data resource.

There is a basic principle that *involvement leads to commitment, which leads to acceptance, which leads to success!* When people become actively involved in an initiative, they become committed to that initiative. When they are committed to an initiative, and actively participate in that initiative, they are likely to accept and support the results of that initiative. The acceptance and support of the results leads to a successful initiative. Any break in this chain compromises development of a high-quality data resource.

Best Practices

The good practices for developing an adequate data responsibility emphasize cooperative development and management of a shared data resource. The best practices are to designate data stewards, develop reasonable procedures, and then establish a centralized control over the data resource. It is interesting to note that the bad habits usually evolve in the reverse order. An organization attempts to gain centralized control through mandates, then to put procedures in place to carry out the mandates, and then to designate data stewards to enforce the procedures. The stage is set for failure right from the first mandate, and the failure is often carried out with a vengeance.

> Adequate data responsibility provides a cultural success motivation.

The sequence of good practices provides a success motivation to continue developing a shared data resource. This is the only approach that will gain early benefits and achieve ultimate success. It provides a cultural motivation that pulls people together into a team that works toward developing an integrated data resource within a common data architecture.

The basic principle is that *people do not mind changing* because that is the name of the game in a dynamic business environment. *People do mind being changed*; they mind it very much and will fight it to the end. Most people want to do a better job; they have just been burned too many times and do not want to be burned again. Most people are willing to follow a new approach if they have confidence in that approach. Providing adequate data responsibility provides that confidence.

Designate Data Stewards

The first step to establishing adequate data responsibility is to designate strategic and detail data stewards. Tactical data stewards may be designated in large international organizations. The data stewards can be designated on a priority basis according to the priorities for developing the data architecture. It is seldom necessary to designate all data stewards at the beginning of a data quality improvement initiative. The data stewards can contribute to identifying problems and impacts, and establishing priorities to prevent those problems and impacts. This step begins getting people involved in the development and management of a shared data resource.

Develop Reasonable Procedures

The second step is to start developing reasonable procedures for managing the data resource and improving data resource quality. The procedures are developed by the data stewards with input from business clients and information technology staff. This step builds on the involvement of the stakeholders through the designated data stewards. It gives all the stakeholders a sense of ownership in the data resource and builds on the concept of involvement leads to commitment, which leads to acceptance, which leads to success.

Establish Centralized Control

The third step is to use the designated data stewards and the reasonable procedures to establish a centralized control of the data resource architecture. In many situation, putting the first two steps in place almost automatically results in a centralized control of the data resource. It is an easy way to gain centralized control without establishing mandates and enforcing compliance to those mandates.

There is one caution about implementing centralized control over the data resource architecture. Centralized control does not mean one centralized database containing all the data. It means a centralized data architecture where the entire data resource is developed within one common data architecture and is then deployed and implemented to meet business needs. It follows the concept of a *global data architecture with local implementation*. The local business client may not see the difference, but there are is a tremendous difference to the organization at large.

Summary

The bad habits leading to inadequate data responsibility, the impacts of those bad habits, the good practices for adequate data responsibility, the benefits of those good practices, and the most beneficial best practices are summarized below. This list is also contained in Appendix A.

> Bad practices leading to inadequate data responsibility:
>> No centralized control of the data resource.
>> No management procedures for developing the data resource.
>> No data stewards responsible for the data resource.
>
> Impacts of inadequate data responsibility:
>> Limited data sharing across the business.
>> Disparate data creation is encouraged.
>
> Good practices for adequate data responsibility:
>> Establish data stewards.
>>> Strategic level.
>>> Detail level.
>>> Tactical level for large organizations.
>> Reasonable management procedures for the data resource.
>> Centralized control of the data resource.
>
> Benefits of adequate data responsibility:
>> Shared data resource that supports the business.
>
> Best practices for success motivation:
>> Designate data stewards.
>> Develop reasonable procedures.
>> Establish centralized control over the data resource.

The bad habits, good practices, and best practices for establishing adequate data responsibility can be used to evaluate the status of an organizations data resource. Fill in the horizontal bar (below) to show the degree to which the bad habits exist and the degree to which the good practices and the best practices have been implemented. You can provide definitions for the Poor, Fair, Moderate, Good, and Excellent headings to suit your organization, or you can use a numeric scale if it is more appropriate. You can also select the items that are important for your organization, but don't be too hasty at excluding items, because they may be valuable later. This list is also contained in Appendix B.

	P	F	M	G	E
Bad Habits					
No centralized control	☐	☐	☐	☐	☐
No management procedures	☐	☐	☐	☐	☐
No data stewards	☐	☐	☐	☐	☐
Good Practices					
Establish data stewards					
Strategic level	☐	☐	☐	☐	☐
Detail level	☐	☐	☐	☐	☐
Tactical level for large organizations	☐	☐	☐	☐	☐
Reasonable management procedures	☐	☐	☐	☐	☐
Centralized control	☐	☐	☐	☐	☐
Best Practices					
Designate data stewards	☐	☐	☐	☐	☐
Develop reasonable procedures	☐	☐	☐	☐	☐
Establish centralized control	☐	☐	☐	☐	☐

CHAPTER 10

Expanded Data Vision

> An expanded data resource vision
> can make a world of difference.

After adequate data responsibility, the ninth way to achieve data resource quality is through an expanded vision of the data resource. The scope of the data resource, the direction of data resource development, and the planning horizon for the data resource may be constrained in one or more ways. Generally, organizations suffer from a narrow scope, the wrong development direction, and short-term planning horizons for their data resource. Low data resource quality is usually the result of this narrow vision.

The scope of the data resource may be limited to business critical data, automated data, current operational data, or tabular data. The direction of data resource development may not match the business direction or the technology direction. The planning horizon may be too short or too long. Any of these restricted data visions may appear to be appropriate for today or the near future, but they will more than likely impact the business in the future. An organization needs to develop a wider scope for their data resource, a development direction that matches the business and the technology plans, and a planning horizon that is realistic.

This chapter presents the fourth set of non-architectural bad habits that lead to a restricted data vision. These bad habits can impact the organization in many different ways if allowed to continue. The bad habits, however, can be turned into good practices that provide an enhanced vision for the data resource. These good practices provide both near-term and long-term benefits to the organization.

This chapter explains what needs to be done to expand the data resource vision. It does not explain how the data resource vision is expanded. How the data resource vision is expanded varies from one organization to another and is usually unique to each organization. There are no generic how-to steps for expanding the data resource vision that applies to all organizations.

Restricted Data Vision

Vision is defined as intelligent foresight, the manner in which one sees or conceives something, or a mental image produced by the imagination. The *data resource vision* is an intelligent foresight about the data resource that includes the scope of the data resource, its development direction, and the planning horizon. A *restricted data resource vision* is the situation where the scope of the data resource is limited, the development direction is unreasonable, or the planning horizon is unrealistic. Each of these bad habits is explained below.

Limited Data Scope

The first bad habit leading to a restricted data resource vision is limiting the scope of the data resource. *Scope* pertains to the range of a person's perceptions, the breadth or opportunity to function, or the area covered by a given activity. The *data resource scope* is the portion of the total data resource available to an organization that is formally managed. The *actual data resource scope* is the actual portion of the data resource that is formally managed, and the *perceived data resource scope* is the portion of the data resource that is perceived to be formally managed. In most situations, the perceived portion of the data resource that is formally managed is far larger than the actual portion that is formally managed.

> The scope of the data resource is
> severely limited in most organizations.

There is a cognitive dissonance about the state of the data resource in many organizations. ***Cognitive dissonance*** is the disharmony that is created when an individual's personal reality does not fit the actual reality of a situation. When a person perceives that the state of the data resource is pretty good and receives information that the state of the data resource is quite bad, there is a tremendous disharmony created. That person usually reacts in some way, such as ignoring the situation, denying that the situation exists, laying blame for the situation, or setting about correcting the situation.

It was mentioned earlier that only about 15% of an organization's total data resource is ever modeled, and that portion may have been modeled several times by several different methods. This means that, at best, only 15% of the organization's total data resource is developed within any type of a formal data architecture. Realistically, about 15% of the total data that an organization has at its disposal from within the organization and from outside sources are included within the scope of any formal data resource management.

The scope of data resource management is often limited to automated data, current operational data, tabular data, business critical data, or any combination of these. Each of these limitations is explained below.

Automated Data Only

The data resource scope is often limited to automated data. The common perception is that only the data that are stored in electronic form need to be formally managed. Any data that are not automated or stored in electronic form are not considered important enough to be formally managed. In some organizations the non-automated data are not even considered part of the total data resource available to the organization.

> The scope of data resource management
> is often limited to automated data.

Although the quantity of data that is automated is increasing, there is still a considerable volume of data that are not stored in electronic form. A rough estimate is that less than half the total data resource available to an organization is stored in electronic form. The other half is non-automated data that are manually stored and retrieved. These non-automated data often contain valuable information about the business that could be used to analyze trends and patterns and to develop business strategies. They are part of the hidden data resource that is largely untapped.

Many people laugh when I say that about half of the organization's data resource is non-automated. As an exercise, I ask them to perform their business activities for a week using only data that they can obtain in electronic form from terminals, personal computers, printed reports, and so on. They are not allowed to use any non-electronic data to perform their business activities. It is quite interesting to see the responses. Usually by the second day many people are looking at non-automated data to carry out their business activities. By the end of the week there are very few people who could completely perform their business activities without looking at some form of non-automated data.

Current Data Only

The data resource scope is often limited to current operational data. Historical data are seldom included in formal management of the data resource. It was mentioned in the chapter on Precise Data Integrity Rules that there are seldom any data integrity rules for maintaining data that are no longer operationally useful. The operational data are usually discarded when their operational usefulness is over without any consideration for the future value of those data.

> The scope is often limited to current operational data.

Look carefully at what is happening with many data warehouse initiatives today. First, a data warehouse application is implemented and people are ready to load historical data for the analysis of trends and patterns. To their surprise, there are very few historical data available for the data warehouse. The historical data that do exist are usually disparate and may not be useful for analysis without extensive data transformation. Many organizations are just now starting to save operational data when their usefulness is over so that they can have historical data for future analysis.

Second, the data stored in the data warehouse are frequently considered outside the scope of formal data resource management. People are summarizing, sorting, extracting, and analyzing data, and storing the results in the data warehouse without any formal management or documentation. They are actively creating the next wave of disparate data while complaining about the existing disparity of operational data.

I was recently contacted by an organization that wanted help understanding and organizing the disparate data they had in their data warehouse. They had followed the traditional approach of identifying the single system of reference, extracting the data, and placing those data in the data warehouse; a process referred to as the *suck and squirt approach*. They analyzed those data and stored the results, periodically added new sets of data to the data warehouse, re-analyzed the data and stored those results, and so on, without any formal management or documentation. They now have an extensive set of disparate evaluational data that they do not understand.

Tabular Data Only

The data resource scope is often limited to tabular data. Tabular data are the traditional data in most organizations that are displayed in tabular form. Non-tabular data, such as spatial data, imaging data, textual data, voice data, video data, and so on, are usually excluded from formal data resource management. The reason most frequently given for their exclusion is that they are managed under a different architecture. What this statement really means is that they are stored according to a different physical architecture.

> The scope is often limited to only tabular data.

Non-tabular data are becoming very prominent in many organizations as technology evolves and costs decline. Many public sector organizations have large quantities of spatial data, and many private sector organizations have large quantities of image data. The technology for processing non-tabular data is going onto the desktop, and the quantities of non-tabular data are increasing as the technology evolves. The problem is that the non-tabular data are becoming as disparate as the tabular data. They are following the same disparate data cycle that tabular data followed, and very little is being done about the problem. Most people seem quite willing to let the disparity continue with non-tabular data while they complain about the disparity of tabular data.

Business Critical Data Only

The data resource scope is often limited to business critical data. Only the data critical to the business or data of organization-wide importance are included in any formal data resource management. The common perception is that if these business critical data are properly managed, the less critical departmental and personal data will take care of themselves. On close examination, this perception is really an excuse not to manage any data that are not business critical.

> The scope is often limited to
> business critical or enterprise-wide data.

There is one qualification about formally managing personal data. Some people are very sensitive about their personal data and do not want other people to know even what personal data they maintain. I encountered one situation where the sales staff had their own personal data about clients and potential clients. There was an attempt in the organization to identify, define, and manage these personal data as part of the formal data resource. The sensitivity was so high that their personal data would become available to other competing sales staff that there was a tremendous resistance to any formal data management. In this situation, the initiative to formally manage the personal data of the sales staff was dropped because it was not in the best interest of the organization.

Unreasonable Development Direction

The second bad habit leading to a restricted data resource vision is setting an unreasonable direction for development of the data resource. The *data resource direction* is the course of data resource development toward a particular goal or objective. There are two basic problems with an unreasonable data resource direction. Both of these problems may appear to be acceptable for today and the near term, but they will result in future impacts to the business.

> The unreasonable development direction
> is not compatible with the direction of business or technology.

Incompatible with Business Direction

Data resource development can be oriented in a direction that is not compatible with the business direction. The planned direction of data resource development is unreasonable with respect to the planned direction of the business. In other words, the direction of data resource development and the direction of the business are not in synch. For example, the business may be heading toward e-commerce and e-business and the data resource may be heading toward bulk transaction processing.

Incompatible with Database Technology Direction

Data resource development can be oriented in a direction that is not compatible with the database technology direction. The planned direction of data resource development is unreasonable with respect to the planned direction of database management system technology. In other words, the direction of data resource development and the direction of database technology are not in synch. For example, the technology is moving toward universal databases and complex data types while the data resource is heading toward traditional data types. The business directions include the concepts of universal databases and complex data types, while the data resource direction does not include these capabilities.

Unrealistic Planning Horizon

The third bad habit leading to a restricted data vision is setting an unrealistic planning horizon for the data resource. The **data resource horizon** is the distance into the future that a person is interested in planning for data resource development. An unrealistic data resource horizon can be too nearsighted, too far-sighted, or overly optimistic. Each of these situations is explained below.

Nearsighted Horizon

The data resource horizon may be very nearsighted. Many organizations have a very short-term horizon for their data resource management. The data resource development is focused on short-term objectives to the detriment of long-term goals. The organization is doing what is best for the near-term without any consideration for the future. It was mentioned in the chapter on Reasonable Data Orientation that the only reason for developing data models was to cut the code to generate a database. This is a very nearsighted approach to data resource management.

> The data resource horizon
> can be too nearsighted and meaningless.

The horizon for a data resource vision can also be unreasonably short. The vision can be perceived as too easy to achieve or too close to what currently exists. There is nothing new or nothing to be solved with the vision because it does not look far enough into the future. It is not challenging or interesting, and is essentially meaningless to most people.

A nearsighted data horizon often results in a lack of data integration within a common enterprise-wide data architecture. The databases are developed independently with the objective of quick delivery, which leads to data disparity. The lack of data integration is a major cause of the disparate data resource.

Farsighted Horizon

The data resource horizon may be too farsighted. The vision is too far over the horizon to be of interest to most people. It is unreasonably far into the future or is too difficult to accomplish and is perceived to be unachievable by most people. The horizon is often perceived as esoteric and meaningless for solving the current problems.

> The data resource horizon
> can be too farsighted and beyond interest.

I once presented the concept of a pocket computer with a thousand megahertz of speed, terabytes of data storage, bioprobes, satellite uplink, and projection screen on the person's eyeglasses. A person could think of the information they needed and it would be obtained either from their in-pocket computer or from the network and projected for them. Some of this technology may be coming in the near future and some may not ever be available, but the vision was so unrealistic for the current business needs that the group laughed.

Another situation is an organization that wanted to install a data dictionary and document their primary business data during the next five years. With the flurry of business activities that were in progress for the next six months to a year, there was absolutely no interest in a five-year vision. The five-year vision was perceived to be accomplished in the fifth year, not in the next six months. A few people commented that it was a nice vision but was not appropriate right now. It would have been better to have set the horizon to one or two years and tie that vision to support of the current business situation. That would probably have gained more acceptance.

I encounter a number of similar situations where the horizon for the data resource vision is too farsighted. It is beyond the interest of most people in the organization. They may well understand the vision, but it is beyond their current interest and is considered not useful or realistic for current business problems. Little attention is paid to the vision in favor of shorter-term accomplishment. One major disadvantage of a farsighted vision is that people revert to a near-sighted vision that is more realistic.

Overly Optimistic Horizon

The data resource horizon may be overly optimistic. The vision may be quite valid and realistic, but the horizon is overly optimistic. In spite of the good intentions, the vision just cannot be achieved within the designated horizon. This situation forces people to revert to the near-term accomplishment.

> The data resource horizon can be valid but overly optimistic.

I was contacted by one organization that had established a very nice vision and plan for developing an integrated data resource. The plan, however, stated that they would organize and integrate 75% of their data resource in the first year and the remainder of their data the following year. Unless this organization has a very small quantity of disparate data, or a large unused human resource, this is an unrealistic data horizon. The other possibility is that the scope was only current operational data for business critical functions. In this situation the horizon would be valid, but the scope should have been stated and the vision should have provided for a wider scope in the future.

I was contacted by a multi-national organization several years ago that wanted me to teach half their data administration staff one week, the other half the following week, put a data resource management plan in place the third week, and do any mid-course correction the fourth week. This was their one-month plan to organize their disparate data and develop a high-quality data resource. The vision may have been realistic, but the horizon was totally unrealistic and had little chance of ever being implemented.

Restricted Data Vision Impacts

When the data resource scope, development direction, and planning horizon are restricted in any way, there are impacts on the organization. These impacts can be short-term or they can occur at some point in the future. Each of these situations is explained below.

Short-Term Impact

The impacts of a restricted data vision may occur in the near term. The most prominent short-term impact results from a limited scope where only business critical, current operational, non-tabular, automated data are formally managed. Limiting the scope of data resource management in this manner can bring immediate impacts as the organization moves into a data warehouse environment or attempts to integrate tabular and non-tabular data. It becomes immediately obvious that the disparate nature of the data will not support the initiative.

> Most short-term impacts are due to a limited data resource scope.

An unreasonable development direction and an unrealistic planning horizon usually do not result in short-term impacts to the business. One exception is the lack of data integration that often occurs with a nearsighted planning horizon. When everyone is doing their own data development with no attempt at integration within a common architecture, the impact of the resulting disparate data can be immediate. Developing a data warehouse or implementing an enterprise resource planning (ERP) application with disparate data can bring immediate impacts to the business.

Future Impact

The impact of a restricted data vision is more likely to occur in the future than in the short-term. In most situations, the impact may be unknown until it actually happens and it is too late to take preventive action. People are usually so overly concerned about the short-term deliverables that they fail to notice any impending impact from a restricted data vision. This progressive concern about the short-term masks the evolution of a long-term impact.

> The impact of a restricted
> data vision is likely to occur in the future.

The impact of a restricted data vision usually evolves slowly until it surfaces and hits the business. It is similar to the *boiled frog syndrome*. If a frog is placed in boiling water, it will immediately react and jump out. If, however, the frog is put in cool water and the water is slowly heated, the frog will likely be boiled. The difference is in the rate of change. In the first situation the rate of change is great and the frog responds immediately. In the second situation the rate of change is gradual and is seldom noticed until it is too late to take corrective action.

Expanded Data Vision

The data vision must be expanded to develop a comparate data resource that can be shared across business activities. The vision must be enlarged and improved so that it more appropriately supports the current and future business information demand. The expanded data vision must include a wider data scope, a more reasonable development direction, a more realistic planning horizon, and cooperative establishment of the vision. Each of these good practices is explained below.

Wider Data Scope

An *expanded data resource vision* must have a wider data resource scope that ultimately includes all of the data that are available to the organization. It needs to include data that are not business critical or of organization-wide importance, non-tabular data, historical data, and non-automated data. Each of these wider scopes is explained below.

Non-Critical Data

A wider data resource scope must include all the data that are available to the organization. The scope must not be limited to business critical data or data of enterprise-wide importance. Ultimately, all data that the organization creates or acquires from internal or external sources to meet the business information demand must be included in formal data resource management. All of these data, at some point in time and at some level of usefulness, will be important to the organization.

> All data used by the organization
> must be included in the data resource scope.

There may be a prioritization and phasing for including data within the scope of formal data resource management. The prioritization may begin with business critical data, current operational data, or any other data where the lack of formal management and current disparity are impacting the business. Regardless of what the priorities are, the ultimate scope for formal data resource management must include all data that are at the organization's disposal.

Non-Tabular Data

A wider data resource scope must include both tabular and non-tabular data. All non-tabular data types, such as spatial, imaging, video, textual, voice, and so on, must be included within the data resource scope. They must all be managed within a single common data architecture for the organization. Their inclusion may be done on a prioritized or phased basis as mentioned above, but they must eventually be included.

> Non-tabular data must be included in the data resource scope.

The different types of data form a data type hierarchy that includes data megatypes, base data types, and distinct data types. A ***data megatype*** is a major grouping of data based on their overall structure and physical management, such as spatial data, image data, textual data, and so on. Data megatypes fall into two broad groups for tabular data and non-tabular data. ***Tabular data*** are the traditional data maintained in traditional databases and displayed in tabular form. ***Non-tabular data*** are any data that are not generally maintained in traditional databases or typically displayed in tabular form, such as spatial, textual, voice, image (photo, digitized, remote sensed, and so on), and video data. These two broad groups are sometimes referred to as *structured data* and *unstructured data*. These terms are not appropriate because both tabular and non-tabular data may be either structured or unstructured with respect to the common data architecture.

A **base data type** is a specific form of data within a data megatype, such as date, text, integer, and so on for tabular data. It is commonly known today as a *data type*. A **distinct data type** is a data unit or style within a base data type, such as meters, yards, inches, and so on for measurements. It has no equivalent in current database management systems.

This data type hierarchy provides a structure for managing all types of data in the future. As universal databases, complex data types, and user-defined data types emerge, they can be readily classified and managed within the data type hierarchy. The data type hierarchy applies to all tiers in the five-tier five-schema concept. The data in any tier can belong to any of the data megatypes, base data types, or distinct data types. The data type hierarchy concept allows organizations to be proactive about preventing data disparity as the technology evolves.

Historical Data

A wider data resource scope must include historical as well as current operational data. Historical data are often referred to as *temporal data* or *time relational data*.[1] The increasing interest in data warehousing and ultimately data mining applications require that historical data be retained and that they be formally managed within a common data architecture. People need to thoroughly understand historical data and the changes that have occurred in the data resource over the years in order to properly use those historical data to analyze the business.

> Historical data must be included in the data resource scope.

There is a general trend from disparate operational data, to cross-system reporting, to data warehousing, to data mining. Many of these terms are misused and abused today, and it is often difficult to determine what a person really means when they use these terms. The definitions below help people understand the trends and how they relate to the formal management of historical data.

Operational data are subject-oriented, integrated, time-current, volatile data in support of day-to-day transactions and operational decision-making.[2]

---

[1] A discussion of time relational data can be found in *Practical Data Design*.

[2] Operational data and evaluational data definitions are very similar to those promoted by Bill Inmon.

Operational processing is the day to day transactional processing using current operational data to perform the business activities. These operational data exist in the data space and are designed according to relational data modeling techniques.[3] *Cross-system reporting* is the collection of current operational data from a variety of different, often disparate, operational databases for the purpose of integrated reporting and operational decision-making. These data also exist in the data space and are not considered part of true data warehousing, even though a data warehouse application may be used to process the reports. The term *operational data stores* is often used to represent the collection of operational data across independent information systems that are used for operational decision making.

Evaluational data are subject-oriented, integrated, time-variant, non-volatile data in support of management decision-making. *Data warehousing* is the analysis of historical data to verify or disprove known or suspected trends or patterns in the business. These historical data and the results of the analytical processing are evaluational data, and they exist in the aggregation space. They are designed according to dimensional data modeling techniques. *Data warehousing* is used in many organizations today, but the term is often confused with the cross-system reporting described above.

Data mining is the analysis of historical data to identify unknown or unsuspected trends and patterns in the business. The data exist in the influence and variation space and are manipulated by predictive analysis that uses a variety of techniques, such as artificial intelligence and fuzzy logic. The data are designed by rotational data modeling techniques. Data mining is not as prominent as data warehousing even though the term is frequently used, but it does have promise when large quantities of comparate historical data are available.

Non-Automated Data

A wider data resource scope must include non-automated data as well as automated data. Any data maintained in manual form that are of importance to understanding the business must be included in formal data resource management. One excellent example was the existence of thousands of well logs produced by well drillers that showed the sub-surface lithology. The information contained in these well logs would be invaluable to groundwater hydrologists for

---

[3] A discussion of operational data modeling, dimensional data modeling, and rotational data modeling are beyond the scope of this book.

determining the size and extent of underground aquifers, a critical part of water resource management. Capturing this lithology, adding formal geologic names to the well driller's terminology, and storing the data for analysis provided detail that was previously unavailable.

> Non-automated data must be included in the data resource scope.

Including non-automated data within the scope of data resource management opens up a whole area of the hidden data resource. There is a tremendous wealth of information contained in both current and historical non-automated data that could be valuable for the business. In many situations the automation of non-automated historical data provides the data necessary for analysis of trends and patterns in the business.

Reasonable Development Direction

An expanded data resource vision must have a reasonable development direction. The business direction must be determined and the direction of data resource development must be established to support the business direction. The trend toward e-commerce and e-business is one good example. Business planning and data resource planning must be integrated and synchronized to ensure that the data resource supports both the current and future business information demand.

> Data resource development
> must support the business and follow technology.

The direction of database management system technology must also be considered in setting the direction for data resource development. Organizations can not readily control the direction that vendors take with their hardware and software products, but they can monitor the technology trends and pick a reasonable direction for the data resource. Universal databases and complex data types are one example. If there is a common data architecture in place and all data are formally managed within that architecture, then changes can be easily made as the business direction or the technology direction changes. As one data resource manager once told me "As long as the data are well architected, we can change from one business direction or technology direction to another with relative ease."

I was recently contacted by an organization about understanding the disparate data in their enterprise resource planning (ERP) application. They had purchased an ERP and loaded the data from the single system of reference with minimal transformation. The ERP was not supporting the business as expected because of the data disparity. This is one example illustrating how the business direction was toward integrated applications that crossed business units but the data resource was still maintained as islands of disparate data.

Realistic Planning Horizon

An expanded data resource vision must have a realistic planning horizon. The planning horizon that is challenging yet achievable must be established. It must stretch the imagination slightly but not be unrealistic. It must be understandable and achievable, but not too close and not too distant. A nearsighted planning horizon is perceived to be no challenge and little effort is expended. Likewise, a farsighted planning horizon is perceived to be impossible or unattainable and little effort is expended.

> A realistic planning horizon must create the "aha! syndrome."

One excellent approach is to prepare multiple visions to address multiple audiences, much the same as is done for data structures. Some people are more concerned about the near-term and others are more concerned about the future, and there is nothing wrong with developing a strategic vision, a tactical vision, and a detail vision to address specific audiences. Providing a long-range *strategic vision*, intermediate-term *tactical visions* to achieve that strategic vision, and short-term *detail visions* for those intermediate phases, draws more people into the process. It provides a set of visions for the data resource that addresses a variety of audiences.

One of the best data resource management plans that I developed was for water resources. It was labeled as a 5-year plan (tactical vision) but actually included a vision out to 10 years (strategic vision). Things that needed to be accomplished, and could be accomplished, immediately, were listed as early deliverables (detail vision). Subsequent deliverables were built on these early deliverables, and so on. The strategic vision for water resource data management explained what the ideal environment would be like when everything was accomplished.

This plan contained a set of visions that provided a horizon (immediate, 5-year, and 10-year) for nearly everyone who was interested in water resource data management. Even though people wanted their needs met at the earliest possible time, they could visualize and understand the sequence of development and how one phase built on the previous phase to achieve the ultimate goal in the most reasonable manner.

Cooperative Establishment

An expanded data resource vision must be established collectively by all the stakeholders of the data resource through the strategic, tactical, and detail data stewards, and it must be accepted by those stakeholders after it is established. Both of these objectives need to be met if formal data resource management is to be successful. When the vision is in place, procedures can be developed to implement the good practices, and the data resource can be brought under control as explained in the last chapter.

> The stakeholders must collectively set and accept the data vision.

The *normative planning process* works backward from the ultimate goal to the present instead of working forward from the present toward the ultimate goal. The strategic vision is established, and then intermediate phases with their tactical visions are defined to meet that ultimate vision. If any tactical vision is too confusing or beyond interest, that phase can be further broken down into sub-phases with their detail visions. This process provides a set of visions that are relevant to many different people.

The normative planning process can be applied to the good practices presented in this book. Instead of saying that the bad habits are wrong and how they should be corrected with good practices, start with a strategic vision of a comparate data resource and show how the good practices can be used to achieve that vision. Then describe how to implement the good practices and how they will achieve that vision. The bad habits will begin to quietly fade away, and the disparate data cycle will slow and eventually stop.

The water resource data management plan described above was developed by this process. People could visualize how the current phases lead into later phases and to the ultimate goal, or they could visualize the ultimate goal and see how each preceding phase contributed to achieving that goal. The plan provided a positive approach to managing data that is useful for multiple audiences and draws a wide variety of people into the process of formally managing water resource data.

> A good vision describes what is to be accomplished, not how it is accomplished.

One caution about developing the strategic vision for a compare data resource. The vision may be part of a plan, but it is not a plan and should not include all the details of a plan. An otherwise good vision can be compromised if it is diluted with too many details about how that vision is achieved, who is going to perform tasks, and when the tasks will be completed. A good vision should paint a vivid picture of the ideal situation and the major phases to achieve that situation. It might have some major objectives for each major phase, but it should not have all the detail of a formal plan.

Expanded Data Vision Benefits

There are many benefits to an expanded data resource vision. The most prominent benefits are improved short-term and long-term business support, and success motivation to continue development of a compare data resource. Each of these benefits is explained below.

Improved Business Support

The business is better supported through a partnership that integrates the business direction, the technology direction, and the direction of data resource development. Immediate benefits are provided for current business problems without compromising long-term objectives for a compare data resource. A high-quality data resource is developed that includes all the data available to an organization and meets the current and future business information demand.

> Expanding the data resource vision provides better support for the business.

A comprehensive data resource management plan includes a sequence of phases with their respective visions that provides a course of development toward a comparate data resource. This plan begins to get people involved in the process and builds enthusiasm. As the phases are accomplished, the confidence builds that the disparate data can be resolved and a sharable data resource can be developed.

Best Practices

The good practices for developing an expanded data resource vision emphasize a wider scope, a reasonable direction, and a realistic horizon. There is no single best practice for developing an expanded data resource vision, but providing both near-term and long-term benefits results in a tremendous success motivation for continued development of a comparate data resource. People begin to see how the architectural and the non-architectural good practices combine to develop a comparate data resource. They begin to understand that developing a comparate data resource is not a trivial task, nor is it an impossible task.

> Expanding the data resource vision
> provides a tremendous success motivation.

The stakeholders and data stewards must pick a reasonable direction and a realistic horizon for business support. They must develop a plan that has the full scope of the data resource in mind and lay out phases that are incrementally successful and self-perpetuating. A good friend of mine frequently used the phrase "To eat an elephant, you must first cut it into little pieces." Providing a plan that includes a wide data scope, a reasonable development direction, and realistic planning horizons draws people in and adds the motivation to continue attacking an almost insurmountable task.

Summary

The bad habits leading to a restricted data vision, the impacts of those bad habits, the good practices for an expanded data vision, the benefits of those good practices, and the most beneficial best practices are summarized below. The list is also contained in Appendix A.

Bad habits leading to a restricted data vision:
   Limited scope of the data resource.
      Automated data only.
      Current data only.
      Tabular data only.
      Business critical data only.
   Unreasonable development direction for the data resource.
      Incompatible with business direction.
      Incompatible with database technology direction.
   Unrealistic planning horizon for the data resource.
      Nearsighted planning horizon.
      Farsighted planning horizon.
      Overly optimistic planning horizon.

Impacts of a restricted data vision:
   Short-term impacts on the business.
   Future impacts on the business.

Good practices for an expanded data vision:
   A wider data resource scope.
      Non-critical data.
      Non-tabular data.
      Historical data.
      Non-automated data.
   Reasonable development direction for the data resource.
   Realistic planning horizon for the data resource.
   Cooperative establishment of the data resource vision.

Benefits of an expanded data vision:
   Improved support to the business.

Best practices for success motivation:
   Pick a reasonable direction and a realistic horizon for the vision.
   Develop a general plan that includes the full scope of the data resource.

The bad habits, good practices, and best practices for the data vision can be used to evaluate the status of an organization's data resource. Fill in the horizontal bar (below) to show the degree to which the bad habits exist and the degree to which the good practices and the best practices have been implemented. You can provide definitions for the Poor, Fair, Moderate, Good, and Excellent headings to suit your organization, or you can use a numeric scale if it is more appropriate. You can also select the items that are important for your organization, but don't be too hasty at excluding items, because they may be valuable later. This list is also contained in Appendix B.

	P	F	M	G	E
Bad Habits					
Limited scope of the data resource					
Automated data	☐	☐	☐	☐	☐
Current data	☐	☐	☐	☐	☐
Tabular data	☐	☐	☐	☐	☐
Business critical data	☐	☐	☐	☐	☐
Unreasonable development direction					
Incompatible with business direction	☐	☐	☐	☐	☐
Incompatible with database direction	☐	☐	☐	☐	☐
Unrealistic planning horizon					
Nearsighted planning horizon	☐	☐	☐	☐	☐
Farsighted planning horizon	☐	☐	☐	☐	☐
Overly optimistic planning horizon	☐	☐	☐	☐	☐
Good Practices					
A wider data resource scope					
Non-critical data	☐	☐	☐	☐	☐
Non-tabular data	☐	☐	☐	☐	☐
Historical data	☐	☐	☐	☐	☐
Non-automated data	☐	☐	☐	☐	☐
Reasonable development direction	☐	☐	☐	☐	☐
Realistic planning horizon	☐	☐	☐	☐	☐
Cooperative establishment	☐	☐	☐	☐	☐
Best Practices					
Reasonable direction/horizon	☐	☐	☐	☐	☐
General plan	☐	☐	☐	☐	☐

CHAPTER 11

Appropriate Data Recognition

> Data must be recognized as a
> critical resource of the organization.

After an expanded data vision, the tenth way to achieve data resource quality is through appropriate recognition of data as a critical resource of the organization and the current state of that critical resource. The organization at large must recognize the serious nature of data resource quality. Many individuals are aware of specific problems in their area of expertise, and executives are aware that there are general problems getting the information they need, but very few people recognize the overall lack of data resource quality.

In addition, people who are trying to establish initiatives to improve data resource quality by developing a comparate data resource are encountering obstacles. Many of these obstacles are unnecessary and are hindering the efforts to improve data resource quality. Many executives do not recognize the grave situation and are requiring extensive justification before proceeding. Line managers recognize their local situation, but do not recognize the necessity for an enterprise-wide data resource. Technicians recognize the physical situation, but cannot make changes without impacting the business.

Collectively, the organization knows the data resource is low quality. Many people are actually denying the low-quality situation because they do not want to face up to the reality, or they do not know how to solve the problem if they do face up to the reality. The attitude of many people is to ignore the problem and maybe it will go away, or buy an application that will resolve the problem. They do not recognize the reality of stopping the development of disparate data and then resolving the data disparity that currently exists.

This chapter presents the fifth set of non-architectural bad habits related to inappropriate data recognition. These bad habits are impacting the organization in a variety of ways and will continue to impact the organization as long as data disparity reigns supreme. These bad habits can be turned into good practices that provide appropriate recognition of the data resource and lead to support for developing a comparate data resource.

Inappropriate Data Recognition

The prominent bad habits that lead to inappropriate data recognition are a wrong target audience for a data quality initiative, an unnecessary justification for data quality improvement, an ongoing search for silver bullets, attempts to automate data understanding, and a belief that standards or generic data models will resolve the situation. Each of these bad habits is described below.

Wrong Target Audience

A data quality initiative is often started at the wrong level in the organizations. Although there is no one place to start a successful data resource quality initiative that is best for every organization, there are some wrong places to start the initiative. The basic problem is targeting the wrong audience or trying to convince the wrong people that there is a serious problem with data resource quality. Targeting the wrong audience is attempting to get attention where there is no attention to get. Typically, the initiative is either too high or too low in the organization. Each of these situations is explained below.

Too High in Organization

Many well-intentioned data resource quality initiatives are started too high in the organization. Prominent approaches today encourage, and even demand, that commitment for a data resource quality initiative must come from the top. The belief is that if you do not have top executive commitment, you will not get the resources and do not have a project. The reality is that many data resource quality initiatives that are started at the top just do not take and are not successful for a variety of reasons.

The initiative may originate
too high in the organization to be successful.

I met with one organization to discuss development of a comparate data resource. Their approach sounded good and the team was enthusiastic. After some discussion I asked what would be the first task that they wanted me to perform, and they responded that I should find a way to meet with the president, convince him that there was a problem with data quality, and that he should fund the initiative to improve data quality. The team perceived they could not move ahead without an executive blessing. This project will never get off the ground because they are seeking approval too high in the organization.

Executive recognition of a data resource quality improvement initiative is certainly a consideration, but it is not of primary importance if they are not aware of the data resource problems and the impacts of those problems. Many good data quality improvement initiatives have been successful without top executive recognition. Attempting to get top executive recognition for the solution to a problem that is not in their problem set is a wasted effort.

Too Low in Organization

Many well-intentioned initiatives start too low in the organization. The intent is good, great results are produced, and the project was successful, but the result was not visible enough to the organization at large for proper recognition. The initiative is often abandoned to the detriment of the organization. These small successes, using the good practices described later, can be carried up through the organization for visibility and could lead to a larger data resource quality initiative.

The initiative may originate
too low in the organization to be successful.

I worked with a public sector organization that wanted to integrate all the spatial data that was scattered throughout the organization. There were approximately 10,000 maps with different accuracy, various scales, on a variety of different media. The organization wanted to develop a spatial data resource with all their maps stored electronically in a geographic information system (GIS) and readily available to anyone in the organization. The initiative began with a new GIS manager that attempted to sell an organization-wide initiative for a spatial data resource. For whatever reason, the approach did not work, the manager left, and the initiative was abandoned.

The initiative, however, was picked up by one of the GIS technicians who joined with a cartographer and slowly began to inventory and develop an index of all the existing maps. These two people had informal meetings with technical staff throughout the organization and eventually inventoried and indexed all the existing maps in the organization. That task alone was a monumental success because people now at least know what maps existed and the quality of those maps. This informal team grew and slowly began to coordinate their efforts, digitize the most critical maps, upgrade the data, and discard the old maps. Ultimately this project was recognized and became a formal initiative in the organization.

Requiring Unnecessary Justification

A serious bad habit is to believe that an initiative to understand disparate data and create a comparate data resource requires extensive justification. Many organizations want to thoroughly justify the need for developing a high-quality data resource before they begin taking any action. They want to know why it is necessary to develop and maintain an organization-wide data resource. In many situations they really want to understand the problem and what needs to be done, but this is not a justification for creating a high-quality data resource.

> An unnecessary justification is often
> required to improve data resource quality.

Organizations certainly need to scope and prioritize the development of a comparate data resource and determine the resources to be allocated, just like the acquisition of real property or the training of employees. Organizations certainly need to determine the benefits of different options for developing the data resource or the sequence of development, just like facilities management or vehicle maintenance. But, they certainly do not have to justify the need for improving data resource quality before proceeding.

I was contacted by one organization that wanted me to help them resolve their disparate data situation. Their approach sounded appropriate and the team seemed quite capable and willing to tackle the problem. After some discussion, I asked what was the first thing that they expected me to accomplish. Their reply was to develop a comprehensive justification for improving data resource quality, contact executive management, and get them to accept the justification. I considered this a project that would not get off the ground because the team perceived that a full justification of the initiative was needed before they could proceed.

Search for Silver Bullets

There is a never-ending search for the silver bullet in many organizations. A *silver bullet* is an attempt to achieve some gain without any pain. The result of such an effort is usually a minimal gain with considerable pain. In many situations the end state of a silver bullet is worse than the initial state; the situation gets worse rather than better. The bottom line is that silver bullets just do not exist.

> There are no silver bullets!

There is a current and continuing trend in the information technology discipline today to buy a solution to a problem. Buying a solution to some problems, such as hardware capacity, is appropriate. Buying a solution to disparate data, however, is not appropriate. Many people believe they can buy a data cleansing application, install it, suck the data out of their old database, pass it through the application, squirt it into a new database, and all the disparate data problems are solved. I have yet to see this happen to any data in any public or private sector organization. There is no way, unfortunately, to automatically develop a comparate data resource from disparate data.

The situation is much like the homemaker who went to the store and saw a display for the new Zippo-Zappo that cut housework in half. This person immediately went to the counter and bought two of them. I often wonder if this cut the housework to three-quarters or eliminated it altogether, or what would happen if this person bought three or four.

Attempt to Automate Understanding

Another bad habit is a belief in the automated understanding of disparate data. People believe that by buying a large data repository or data dictionary, installing it, scanning the existing databases and programs, and loading the results, all the disparate data will be readily understood. Repositories and scanning are good, but only for an inventory of the data; they do not and cannot understand the data.

> Disparate data cannot be
> automatically understood by an application.

I met a data resource manager at a conference recently. He was ecstatic that he had just loaded seven gigabytes of data into their data repository from a variety of scanners. I asked how he did that and he replied that he had scanned all databases, all programs, all copy libraries, and so on, and loaded the results into the repository. I asked if he had seven gigabytes of understanding about the data resource. He responded that anyone could search by a data name, a program, and so on, and find the location of any piece of data. I again asked if he had seven gigabytes of understanding about the data resource. He said that they had entered all the existing data definitions and anyone could read those definitions. After several cycles of the same question, he admitted that they had minimal understanding of the data resource from the scanning. They simply had seven gigabytes of inventory and good search capability.

Applications can discover and document the existing disparate data, but the discovery needs verification or confirmation. The verification and confirmation leads to an understanding of the current disparate data and a comprehension of the current quality of the data resource. *Applications cannot understand or comprehend disparate data!* A belief in automated data understanding is an attempt to absolve a person from the responsibility of understanding the data resource because they can blame the situation on the application. Applications only search, scan, document, and support a person's understanding of the data resource. Automated understanding of disparate data is a mindset that must be changed.

Belief in Standards

Organizations often rely on standards to resolve their disparate data problem. Many different data standards have been developed by a variety of different organizations that believe they have the right to develop those standards. These data standards, however, are often physically oriented, have a narrow scope, are too general, are not part of any common data architecture, and are poorly documented. Many data standards have no entity-relation diagram, formal data names, or comprehensive data definitions. They are simply physical file formats. Different data standards have been developed for the same topic area resulting in a conflict between the standards.

> Belief in data standards is simply another silver bullet.

Even if data standards were formally developed within a common data architecture and consistent across the organizations developing those standards, they will not apply to every organization maintaining data in that topic area. Each organization does business slightly differently, and this difference is reflected in their data resource. The data standards could be a beginning for development of a data resource, but they can never represent the total data resource of an organization. Data standards are useful, however, for sharing data between organizations.

Data standards will not resolve the existing data disparity. At best they can only define the architecture for a comparate data resource. There is absolutely no way to write a data standard for resolving the data disparity that exists in every data resource of every organization. The resolution of existing disparate data is a very lengthy and involved process that requires considerable effort to understand the intricacies of the data. It is beyond the scope of any data standards.

Data standards themselves are becoming a problem. More data standards are being produced by more organizations, and they are creating more conflict and confusion than commonality. Data standards are becoming as disparate as business data and data resource data. Disparate data standards are rampant in the information technology discipline today and it may be many years before this situation can be corrected. One basic principle to remember about disparate data standards is that *when two or more data standards conflict, there is no data standard.* Any attempt to enforce these standards will only result in failure because there are more people finding ways to violate the standards than there are people developing and enforcing the standards, and they have the client-friendly tools to support them.

Data standards are becoming disparate.

The only solution is to develop data standards within the common data architecture. Data standards should be presented as a logical data model that can be physically implemented in a variety of operating environments. The logical data model should have a business orientation, and subject matter experts should be involved in their development. It should be developed within a common data architecture to provide consistency with other standards. It should be developed using the good practices described in this book. This is the only successful approach to developing and implementing data standards.

Generic Data Models

Another bad habit is a complete reliance on generic data models rather than developing a common data architecture. There are many generic data models available today, mainly for core private sector business functions. They can be a good start for developing the common data architecture and for developing commonality within an organization and between organizations. Organizations do differ, however, and those differences are not reflected in generic data models. The common data architecture will need to be enhanced to include the data specific to an organization that is not in the generic data models.

Generic data models are not
a substitute for a common data architecture.

There are many sources for generic data models, and generic data models are being produced on a regular basis. The generic data models from different sources may be disparate and it may be difficult to find the similarities and differences between these generic data models. An organization needs to carefully select the generic data models or the parts of generic data models they use so that the disparity is minimized.

Generic data models do provide a quick start for developing a common data architecture in a particular subject area. Generic data models, however, do not typically follow the formality of the common data architecture with respect to formal data names, comprehensive data definitions, proper data structure, and precise data integrity rules. When a common data architecture is developed from generic data models, the data names will need to be enhanced to follow the data naming taxonomy, data definitions will need to be enhanced to match the specifics of the organization, the data structure may need to be adjusted, and data integrity rules will need to be developed.

Inappropriate Data Recognition Impacts

The impacts of the inappropriate data recognition bad habits are business impacts and an encouragement to continued data disparity. Each of these impacts is explained below.

Business Impacts

The inappropriate data recognition bad habits impact the business by delaying any effort to understand the disparate data and create a comparate data resource. Targeting the wrong audience, requiring an extensive justification, searching for a silver bullet, attempting to automate data understanding, or a belief in data standards and generic data models only delays any effort to improve data resource quality. These delays allow the business impacts described in the previous chapters to continue unchecked.

> Inappropriate data recognition impacts the business
> by delaying a data resource quality improvement initiative.

Plausible deniability is the ability of an organization to deny the fact that their data resource is disparate and live with an illusion of high data quality. What an organization perceives about their data resource quality and the real data resource quality are often quite different. Organizations do not want to believe their data resource quality is bad and certainly do not want to admit it to anyone.

There is enough plausible deniability about the state of the data resource in most public and private sector organizations to last the rest of their organizational life.

Most people in the organization are aware, often painfully aware, of the state of the data resource. Most people are aware of what is happening with the data resource, but have other agendas or other problems to handle. There are many excuses for the current condition of the data resource and searches for quick fixes or automated understanding. Many approaches are very physical, very limited in scope, very process oriented, and very superficial. Development of a high-quality data resource in this environment just will not happen.

The result of a search for silver bullets and plausible deniability is a *self-defeating fallacy*. No matter how much you believe that something can happen, if it is not possible it will not happen. This is the flip side of the *self-fulfilling prophecy*, which says that if you really believe in something that can happen, and it is possible, it will happen. This self-defeating fallacy is perpetuating the business impacts from a disparate data resource.

Encourage Data Disparity

The inappropriate data recognition bad habits also encourage continued data disparity. While data resource quality initiatives are being delayed through the bad habits, people are continuing to produce large quantities of disparate data. The increased quantity of disparate data results in an increase in both the number and severity of the business impacts described earlier.

> Inappropriate data recognition
> encourages continued data disparity.

The situation is very similar to a cartoon I saw where there was a button on the wall with a lighted sign above saying *Push to Activate*. A person pushed the button and the lighted sign immediately changed to *Release to Detonate*. The person is now totally confused as to what to do and continues holding the button. Organizations have pushed the button to activate the data resource for isolated business support in the short term and are now afraid to release that button and try to develop a comparate data resource for fear that the business will detonate in the process.

Appropriate Data Recognition

Appropriate data recognition can be achieved by turning the bad habits into good practices, including targeting the vested interest, direct business involvement, tapping the knowledge base, starting within current budget, being incrementally cost-effective, adopting a proof positive approach, being opportunistic, building on lessons learned, taking a no-blame no-whitewash approach, and not requiring an unnecessary justification. Each of these good practices are explained below.

Target Vested Interest

The correct audience needs to be targeted for a data resource quality initiative. The most appropriate audience may be a president or director, a vice president or assistant director, a line manager, or some other person *who has a vested interest in the data resource!* The correct audience may vary from one organization to another, and there may be several audiences within the organization. The guideline is to select the audience with a vested interest in a high-quality data resource that is highest in the organization or that is associated with the most business critical data. This is the audience that provides the highest chance of success. Once an audience with a vested interest in the data resource is found, the initiative can be worked up or down the organizational structure from that point.

> Target the audience that has
> a vested interest in a quality data resource.

By far the most successful approaches I have seen are those that are initiated from somewhere in the middle of the organizational structure. This from-below or from-the-middle approach is far more successful than any top-down or bottom-up approach. As mentioned above, many initiatives that start with top executives or with technical staff will fail for a variety of reasons. Executives typically have other problems to handle and technical staff typically do not have the visibility. The best place to start is with the people who have a vested interest in improving data resource quality.

Let me make it very clear that I am not advocating any overt acts, any hidden agendas, or any subversive efforts of any kind in any organization. Nor am I encouraging people to take independent or unilateral action, or to violate estab-lished policies and procedures in their organization. I am saying that many of the successful data quality improvement initiatives that I have seen are initiatives that were initiated from below by targeting an audience with vested interest in data resource quality. Individuals took the initiative and used many of the good prac-tices described below to begin changing the mindset and developing a comparate data resource.

Direct Business Involvement

Another good practice is to ensure the direct involvement of knowledgeable business clients in a data resource quality initiative. The successful initiatives that I have seen involve a mix of business clients and technical staff. There is a definite pattern where a greater involvement by business clients leads to a greater chance for a successful initiative. The flip side is *the greater the limitation of business clients, the greater the chance for failure and continued data disparity!*

> Knowledgeable business clients
> must be involved in any data design effort.

I have been involved in situations where business clients were prevented from being involved in the design of a data resource. Any correspondence or communication was done in writing or indirectly outside the design sessions. I have also been involved in situations where business clients could attend design sessions but had to sit in the back of the room and be quiet. They could not actively participate in the design effort. Most of these design sessions were run by technical people who seem to have a fear of business client involvement or a fear that they cannot design the data resource to meet the business informa-tion needs. They need time to assimilate the comments and create a design that looks good.

I have been in situations where there were intermediaries between the busi-ness clients and the technical designers. Sometimes these intermediaries are busi-ness clients, but more often they are senior technical people who presumably know the business. There is always something lost in communication through these intermediaries, like the game of passing a phrase through a string of people and comparing the end phrase with the initial phrase.

In all of these situations the synergy of business knowledge and technical skills is lost. The result is a data resource that does not fully support the business information demand. By far the best approach is the direct involvement of knowledgeable business clients and the synergy that is created through a discussion of options and alternatives. The direct involvement of business clients leads to their commitment to developing a high-quality data resource, which leads to an acceptance of the resulting data resource, which leads to a successful data resource quality improvement initiative.

Tap the Knowledge Base

Find out who has the knowledge about the existing data resource that is necessary to help correct the disparate data situation and develop a comparate data resource. In several instances, knowledgeable business clients and technical staff were moved aside pending retirement. I brought those people into the process, their input was priceless, their self-esteem went up, and the initiative was successful. In a few situations these people stayed after retirement and continued contributing to the improvement of the data resource.

> Finding the really knowledgeable people
> is key to developing a high-quality data resource.

A person once asked me how I find out so much about an organization. My response was "I buy a lot of coffee." I had coffee with many different business clients and technical staff and basically said "I buy, you talk." I gain tremendous information about the organization and its problems. I learn about business problems and data resource support problems, and where to target the initiative, and where not to target the initiative. Most importantly, I identify the knowledgeable people in the organization and include them in the team. Their inclusion provides more synergy and leads to a successful initiative.

Start within Current Budget

Start a data resource quality initiative within current budget. Most initiatives that are started from-below and within current budget get recognition very quickly. I have seen executives in both the public and private sector raise their eyebrows at the fact that an initiative was done within current budget without an initial request for additional resources. Similarly, I have never seen or heard of a from-below initiative that was done within current budget that was cast aside by executives.

> The first data resource quality improvement
> initiative should be within current budget.

The best approach is to start small and grow as the recognition grows. One of the best initiatives I have been involved with started with a few knowledgeable people and an Access database. They built a few tables, screens, and reports and started inventorying the existing disparate data driven by critical business needs. As the understanding improved and the audience expanded, more tables, screens, and reports were developed and the scope was broadened. More and more people became interested in the initiative and its success finally reached the executives who committed additional resources for its continuation.

The Access database was well designed, based on a data resource data architecture, and followed the principle of *do as I do not do as I say*. Its design was done within an initial common data architecture for the organization and was readily available to the organization. The team intended that the data resource data would be the first formal design within an organization-wide data architecture and to show that a good data resource design could be done in house.

Ultimately the number of people involved and the volume of data were too large to manage in Access. The decision was made to acquire a larger data repository, and the Access database became the design specifications for acquiring and customizing the data repository. In addition, the Access database supported the initiative while the data repository was under development. When the data repository was implemented and customized, the data was easily moved from the Access database to the new data repository with no interruption in the initiative.

Sometimes a data resource quality initiative can be self-defeating. People start with the acquisition of a data repository application. Staff need to be acquired and trained, and the application needs to be installed and customized. There is a large up-front cost and a long lead time before any results are produced. No wonder executives want extensive justification, given the typical history of an information technology initiative.

Incrementally Cost Effective Approach

An excellent practice is to take an incrementally cost effective approach. The term *long-term benefit* has lost its meaning in many public and private sector organizations. The term *short-term benefit* is beginning to lose its meaning as well. A more acceptable term to many people is *incrementally cost-effective*, meaning: Give me a few resources and I'll lay a success on the table. Give me some more resources and I'll lay another success on the table.

> A successful data resource quality
> initiative must be incrementally cost effective.

Taking an incrementally cost-effective approach where the very first step is done within current budget is an excellent way to gain executive recognition. It sets a pattern of small commitments with small successes that eventually build to monumental successes for the organization. Once the cycle of starting within current budget, producing a success, making it known, gaining additional resources, producing another success, and so on, is established, it is self perpetuating.

Proof-Positive Perspective

Another good practice is to have a proof-positive perspective about a data resource quality initiative. One of the best ways to gain executive recognition is to get one or more successes within current budget and then go to management on a proof-positive basis for additional resources to continue. This approach is far better than asking for a resource commitment with trust me promises to deliver something sometime in the future. Don't laugh; I have seen many such proposals presented to executives.

> Executives should be approached on a proof-positive basis.

Proof-positive is a refreshing perspective for executives. One executive told me after a proof-positive presentation on a data resource quality initiative "It was like fresh air in an otherwise stuffy room." A proof-positive approach provides results and lessons learned, not plans and predictions. It provides actual successes, not projected benefits. Executives are more willing to commit resources with a proof-positive perspective that starts within current budget and is incrementally cost effective.

A proof-positive perspective does have a higher risk for the team. They must have a good vision for a comparate data resource and a working understanding of the business. They must be intuitive about how a high-quality data resource can support the business information demand. They must be fully versed in the concepts, principles, and techniques for understanding disparate data and developing a comparate data resource within a common data architecture. They must be clever at perceiving opportunities to be successful and seizing those opportunities. The rewards of success, however, far outweigh the risks.

Be Opportunistic

By all means, be opportunistic with a data resource quality initiative. It is one thing to thoroughly plan to the last detail how the disparate data will be resolved and how a comparate data resource will be built. It is another thing to seize opportunities as they arise. The business is dynamic and things change, often on very short notice. The people involved in a data resource quality initiative must be able to recognize and seize the opportunity to successfully support the business.

> A successful data resource quality
> improvement initiative must be opportunistic.

Far too much effort is spent finding the right pilot study, determining how the pilot study will be evaluated, and setting up the pilot study. Far too much time is spent developing detailed plans for resolving disparate data and creating a comparate data resource. The information technology discipline seems to be very good at paralysis by analysis. People need to have a general plan, but they must seize the opportunity to support a critical business need. That will get recognition far quicker than any detailed pilot study or plan.

The size of the opportunity is not important. A five-minute phone call or a major project can be opportunistic. A ten-minute presentation in a meeting or a week-long seminar can be opportunistic. Any opportunity to spread the message about developing a comparate data resource to support the business, however large or small, must be taken. Far too much time is spent finding the best opportunities and determining how to leverage current resources. Many good opportunities are lost in the process. You certainly need to leverage your efforts, but all the leverage in the world is no good without some successes along the way.

Building on Lessons Learned

Be sure to build on lessons learned. Every project has some failures and some successes. I have not yet encountered any project that was a total success or a total failure. Every project has some good and some bad lessons to be learned. Even a project that was a substantial failure has good lessons to be learned to help prevent a future failure. All of these lessons must be applied to the next opportunity so that the data resource quality initiative will be increasingly successful.

> Both successes and failures are valuable lessons learned.

Another aspect of lessons learned is that management must accept constructive failures and the lessons learned from those failures. When management comes down hard on project failures, it only makes people more cautious and more hesitant to take risks. The result is simply continued data disparity with meager efforts at creating a comparate data resource. After all, that is the safer approach.

No Blame–No Whitewash Attitude

Adopt a no blame–no whitewash attitude. One attitude I repeatedly encouraged teams to adopt is the no blame–no whitewash approach to understanding and resolving disparate data. There is no doubt that the current disparate data situation exists and that it must be resolved. Laying blame for the existence of disparate data only polarizes people, creates antagonism, alienates people, destroys synergy, and substantially defeats any initiative to resolve the situation. Any blame for the existing situation must be removed from a data resource quality initiative.

> An attitude of no blame and no whitewash must be established.

Similarly, whitewashing, covering up, or ignoring the disparate data situation will not make it go away. It will only get worse. It is like putting a heavy coat of paint over rotten wood. It looks great, but the rotten wood is still there, the building is still structurally unstable, it will continue to deteriorate, and will eventually collapse regardless of the quantity of paint applied. The best approach is to recognize the situation exists, recognize what causes the situation, and set about making corrections.

No Unnecessary Justification

Eliminate the requirement for a detailed justification of data resource quality improvement. You do not need an extensive justification to improve data resource quality; it should be a truism. If an organization needs an extensive justification for data resource quality improvement, the disparate data problem is not yet painful enough. If there is no alternative to an extensive justification, just wait for the pain to increase.

> Extensive justification is not
> required for improving data resource quality.

When was the last time that the organization fully justified the need for a chief financial officer and formal management of the financial resource of the organization, such as accounts payable, accounts receivable, general accounting principles, audits, and so on? When was the last time that the organization fully justified the need for a human resource manager and the need for formal management of the human resource of the organization, such as affirmative action, training, and so on? When was the last time that the organization fully justified the need for formal facilities and real property management?

I have asked these questions of a number of organizations and received blank stares or uncomfortable shrugs. Never once have I been told when these resource management functions were last justified or the results of the justification. No one seems to remember because they are truisms.

Then why are organizations demanding a detailed justification to formally manage the data resource? Are data not a critical resource of the organization the same as finances, people, and property? Is the data resource adequately supporting the information needs of the organization without any need for improvement? Is there a more viable option to having a high-quality data resource?

Certainly priorities need to be established, resources need to be allocated, and benefits need to be listed the same as they are for financial management, human resource management, and property management. It is the data resource management and data resource quality improvement function that does not need to be justified. Formal data resource management should be a truism the same as the financial management, human resource management, and property management functions.

The best approach to identifying the pain of a disparate data resource is to use the four basic problems with disparate data to review the organization's data resource and determine how they are impacting the business—like the public organization that cannot get summary reports to management in less than six months; the multi-national retailer that is not sure if it converted all its monetary values to U.S. dollars, or if it has converted more than once; or the international manufacturer/retailer that is adding thousands of new customers a month because it lost track of its customer numbers. I could go on and on with examples of problems, but if you have problems with your data resource, you will know it and you need to start a data resource quality improvement initiative immediately.

Appropriate Data Recognition Benefits

The two major benefits of appropriate data recognition are continued business support and continued success motivation. Each of these benefits is explained below.

Continued Business Support

Following the ten good practices for appropriate data recognition directly supports the good practices described in the previous chapters. They provide a cultural support to the other good practices to ensure that they produce a high-quality data resource that adequately supports the business information demand. The result is what you would want to see if you owned the organization, or were a citizen or customer of the organization.

> Appropriate data recognition improves business support.

One public sector organization did a review of the benefits for improved data resource quality. They started with a two-fold reduction in data redundancy and estimated the benefits to information technology and the business clients. The resulting savings and cost avoidance in computer time, disk space, technical staff time, business client time, and so on, was $25 million in one year, or $50 million a biennium. This is a resource that could be spent on other more important value-added tasks. The surprising thing is that there was no reduction in staff as a result of these savings. The people would be oriented toward more important tasks. Morale and enthusiasm went up, and there was a corresponding increase in productivity.

Best Practices

The good practices for developing an appropriate data recognition emphasize cultural issues and success motivation. There is nothing like a little success to spur people on to additional successes. Implementing the good practices for appropriate data recognition with the good practices described in previous chapters ensures a successful data resource quality improvement initiative.

> Appropriate data recognition
> provides a cultural success motivation.

Plan on targeting the correct audience, include knowledgeable people, produce successes on an incrementally cost-effective basis, and take the results to management with a proof positive attitude. Find the low-hanging fruit that benefits the organization with minimal expenditure. Be opportunistic with evolving business needs, learn from every project, and apply that learning to the next project. Leverage every opportunity to successfully support the business.

Previous chapters listed the good practices that could be used to gain the maximum advantage in the shortest time. It is not possible to list the good practices for appropriate data recognition that are most important because they are all important to the success of a data quality improvement initiative. Slighting any of these good practices could impact the success of the initiative. They must all be included in any data resource quality initiative regardless of its size, scope, or duration. The good news is that all of these good practices are relatively easy to implement.

Summary

The bad habits leading to inappropriate data recognition, the impacts of those bad habits, the good practices for appropriate data recognition, the benefits of those good practices, and the most beneficial best practices are summarized below. This list is also contained in Appendix A.

Bad habits leading to inappropriate data recognition:
  Wrong target audience.
    Too high in the organization.
    Too low in the organization.
  Requiring an unnecessary justification for a data resource quality improvement initiative.
  Search for silver bullets to resolve the situation.
  Attempt to automate data understanding.
  Belief that standards will resolve the situation.
  Belief that generic data models are the common data architecture.

Impacts of inappropriate data recognition:
  Business impacts continue.
  Encourage data disparity to continue.

Good practices for appropriate data recognition:
  Target the vested interest in data resource quality.
  Direct business client involvement.
  Tap the existing knowledge about the data resource.
  Start within the current level budget.
  Incrementally cost-effective approach.
  Proof-positive attitude.
  Be opportunistic.
  Build on lessons learned.
  No blame–no whitewash attitude.
  No unnecessary justification for data resource quality improvement.

Benefits of appropriate data recognition:
  Continued business support.

Best practices for success motivation:
  Apply all the good practices to any data resource quality initiative.

The bad habits, good practices, and best practices for appropriate recognition of the data resource can be used to evaluate the status of an organization's data resource. Fill in the horizontal bar (below) to show the degree to which the bad habits exist and the degree to which the good practices and the best practices have been implemented. You can provide definitions for the Poor, Fair, Moderate,

Good, and Excellent headings to suit your organization, or you can use a numeric scale if it is more appropriate. You can also select the items that are important for your organization, but don't be too hasty at excluding items, because they may be valuable later. This list is also contained in Appendix B.

	P	F	M	G	E
Bad Habits					
Wrong target audience					
Too high in the organization	☐	☐	☐	☐	☐
Too low in the organization	☐	☐	☐	☐	☐
Requiring an unnecessary justification	☐	☐	☐	☐	☐
Search for silver bullets	☐	☐	☐	☐	☐
Attempt to automate data understanding	☐	☐	☐	☐	☐
Belief in standards	☐	☐	☐	☐	☐
Belief in generic data models	☐	☐	☐	☐	☐
Good Practices					
Target the vested interest	☐	☐	☐	☐	☐
Direct business involvement	☐	☐	☐	☐	☐
Tap the knowledge base	☐	☐	☐	☐	☐
Start within current budget	☐	☐	☐	☐	☐
Incrementally cost effective approach	☐	☐	☐	☐	☐
Proof positive attitude	☐	☐	☐	☐	☐
Be opportunistic	☐	☐	☐	☐	☐
Build on lessons learned	☐	☐	☐	☐	☐
No blame–no whitewash attitude	☐	☐	☐	☐	☐
No unnecessary justification	☐	☐	☐	☐	☐
Best Practices					
Apply all good practices	☐	☐	☐	☐	☐

CHAPTER 12

Data Resource Quality Direction

> A new direction for data resource
> quality must be established.

The state of data resource quality in most public and private sector organizations is low. The data are disparate and that disparity is increasing rapidly in spite of attempts to control the disparity. The ten sets of bad habits, individually and collectively, that are prominent in most organizations are totally unacceptable for designing, developing, and managing a high-quality data resource to meet the current and future business information demand.

Organizations must set a new direction and establish a strong and lasting initiative for improving their data resource quality in the new millenium. A comparate data resource that is built within a common data architecture and is based on sound concepts, principles, and techniques is the only way to ensure a quality data resource that meets the business information demand. The ten sets of good practices correct the bad habits and provide a way to stop the disparity and improve data resource quality.

The first phase in this new direction is to slow and ultimately stop the spiraling disparate data cycle and begin altering the natural drift of the data resource away from disparity.

269

The desired level of quality must be built into a new compare data resource and must be consistently maintained. Any data entering the compare data resource must meet rigid quality criteria before they are allowed to enter.

Stopping the disparate data cycle is a proactive phase that prevents the creation of new disparate data, but it does not resolve the existing disparate data. It only begins the process of gaining control of the data resource. It provides organizations the opportunity to stop a situation that is increasingly impacting the business and allows them to be proactive in developing a high-quality data resource.

The second phase in this new direction, which is beyond the scope of this book, is to resolve the existing disparate data.[1] Once the disparate data cycle is stopped and a compare data resource is established, the existing disparate data can be transformed into compare data. Resolving existing disparate data is a reactive phase that will not need to be done until the proactive phase has been implemented. Attempting to clean up the existing disparate data without first stopping the disparate data cycle is fruitless.

These two phases together provide a high-quality data resource that is stable across both business change and technology change. This stability is the ultimate data resource quality that provides the foundation to become a learning intelligent organization. It helps organizations proceed with resolving disparity in business activities and information systems. It reduces one level of complexity that organizations face, and both supports and encourages an improvement in business activities and application integration.

This chapter sets a new direction for data resource quality by breaking the disparate data cycle, altering the natural drift of the data resource, and starting the development of a high-quality compare data resource that supports the current and future business information demand. It emphasizes the need to manage the data resource with the same intensity that other resources in the organization are managed. The chapter provides a quick review of the bad habits and good practices, an explanation of a data resource value chain for the good practices, and a new course for data resource quality based on that value chain.

---

[1] Details can be found in *The Data Warehouse Challenge: Taming Data Chaos*. The author is preparing a book on the formal transformation of disparate data within the common data architecture.

A Quick Review

A brief review of the ten sets of bad habits, the ten sets of good practices, and the things that did not get on the list are summarized below. Appendix A contains a complete listing of the ten sets of bad habits, their impacts on the business, the ten sets of good practices, their benefits to the business, and the best practices to implement first to leverage the data resource quality initiative. Appendix B contains the bad habits, good practices, and best practices that can be used to evaluate your data resource. Either of these Appendices may be used to make your case for implementing a data resource quality initiative.

The Bad Habits

The ten sets of bad habits that result in a low-quality disparate data resource are divided into two groups. The first group pertains to the architecture of the data resource and include informal data names, vague data definitions, improper data structure, imprecise data integrity rules, and limited data documentation. The second group pertains to non-architectural issues related to the management and availability of the data resource, including unreasonable data orientation, unacceptable data availability, inadequate data responsibility, restricted data vision, and inappropriate data recognition.

> The ten sets of bad habits lead to a disparate data resource.

Any of these bad habits contribute to the spiraling disparate data situation. The worst habits, however, are those that limit the ready identification and thorough understanding of the data. Any of the bad habits related to informally naming data, vaguely defining data, or limited data documentation are the fastest route to burgeoning data disparity. They will destroy a person's confidence in the data resource quicker than any of the other bad habits and will encourage people to create their own data.

Impacts of the Bad Habits

The impacts of the architectural bad habits are that data cannot be readily identified, there is limited data understanding, the disparate data cycle is continually

reinforced, and data disparity rapidly increases. There is limited business understanding, inappropriate use of the data, inappropriate business actions, poor perception of services and products by citizens and customer, and an increasing loss
of business client and technical staff productivity.

> The bad habits increasingly impact the organization.

The impacts of the non-architectural bad habits are a loss of business focus,
a cultural encouragement for continued data disparity, limited data sharing,
increasing hardware and software performance problems, increasing loss of productivity, and increasing frequency and severity of both short-term and long-
term impacts on the business and on people. These impacts are contrary to the
current situation of decreased resources and increased demands that exist in
most organizations today.

The Good Practices

The ten sets of good practices resolve the bad habits and lead to a high-quality
comparate data resource. The first group of good practices resolves the architectural bad habits and includes formal data names, comprehensive data definitions,
proper data structure, precise data integrity rules, and robust data documentation.
The second group of good practices resolves the non-architectural bad habits and
includes a reasonable data orientation, an acceptable data availability, sufficient
data responsibility, an expanded data vision, and appropriate data recognition.

> The ten sets of good practices resolve the bad habits.

These good practices are the flip side of the bad habits that ruin data
resource quality. They are the ten best ways to achieve data resource quality.
Collectively, they produce a high-quality data resource that meets the current
and future business information demand, supports the business intelligence
value chain, and assists the knowledge workers in an intelligent learning organization: the i-organization.

Benefits of the Good Practices

The benefits of the architectural good practices are readily identifiable and understandable data, an improved business understanding, a progressive slowing of the disparate data cycle, and productivity improvement for both business client and technical staff. There is increased awareness of data resource data, the data resource contains higher quality data, and the success motivation encourages people to continue with data resource quality improvement.

> The good practices prevent the impacts to the business from low-quality data.

The benefits of the non-architectural good practices are a shared data resource, a more fully utilized data resource, improved business support, and the promotion of a comparate data resource. There is continued productivity improvement and a cultural boost to the success motivation.

One comment needs to be made about the role of the data resource in business decisions. Many people say that a high-quality data resource leads to better information, which leads to better business decisions. This is not true. Better business decisions result from improvements in the decision-making process, not from higher-quality data and better information. *A higher-quality data resource produces better information, which leads to more informed decisions!*

Best Practices to Implement First

All of the good practices cannot all be implemented at one time; the task is just too large. A few of the good practices can be used to quick-start a data resource quality initiative and make the most progress toward limiting the spiraling data disparity. These best practices provide the maximum gain with the minimum effort and produce short-term successes that motivate people to continue with the initiative.

> Correct the worst habits first and the rest will fall into place.

The architectural best practices are to formally name, abbreviate, define, and structure data subjects, data characteristics, and coded data values for the business critical data supporting operational processing. The best approach is to move down through the top three tiers of the five-tier concept, develop one data structure for all data, and provide formal training for business clients and technical staff. The major data errors impacting business must be identified, and data rules to resolve those errors must be defined and implemented in a proactive data error reduction program. A model for data resource data must be developed within the common data architecture, the data resource must be thoroughly documented, and that documentation must be made readily available to all audiences.

The non-architectural best practices are to take a business subject orientation, involve both business knowledge and technical skills, and identify and attack the greatest impacts on the business. The data resource must be protected from alteration, destruction, and improper disclosure. Regular backups and quick recovery must be provided. Strategic and detail data stewards must be established, a vision with a reasonable direction and realistic horizon must be prepared, reasonable procedures and a general plan must be prepared, and all the good practices for appropriate data recognition must be followed. Although this list of non-architectural best practices appears long, the good practices are relatively easy to implement compared to the architectural best practices.

What Didn't Get on the List

A number of items did not get into the ten sets of bad habits because they are relatively unimportant. Many people use excuses like human resource limitations, limited training, skill shortage, working conditions, poor project planning and management, lack of funding, lack of executive interest, lack of business client interest, non-existent standards, no policies or procedures, no techniques available, no support tools, and so on, for not starting a data resource quality initiative. Most of these excuses are begging the issue and are bordering on abdication of responsibility to manage a critical resource.

> The things that did not get on the list provide ancillary support.

None of these items are serious enough to be included in the ten sets of bad habits that actively contribute to disparate data. They are pseudo-reasons for not implementing a data resource quality initiative. They are often the scapegoat for the existing low-quality data resource. A few of them are actually board-room tactics to gain approval to resolve a situation that should never have occurred. The important thing is to get the good practices in place to resolve the serious bad habits and these secondary issues will be resolved in the process.

Data Resource Value Chain

The ten sets of good practices form a *data resource value chain* that improves data resource quality and ultimately results in an ideal comparate data resource that fully supports the current and future business information demand. The value chain consists of an architectural and a non-architectural component corresponding to the architectural and non-architectural sets of bad habits and good practices.

Data Architecture Value Chain

The five sets of architectural good practices form a *data architecture value chain*, as shown in Figure 12.1. This value chain is part of the data resource component of the business intelligence value chain described in the first chapter. Each of the good practices in the data architecture value chain supports the other components, and each can be the weakest link in the chain if not properly developed.

Formal data names are necessary to uniquely identify all data in the data resource. Comprehensive data definitions are necessary for thoroughly understanding the content and meaning of the data. A proper data structure is necessary for adequately representing the business through the data resource. Precise data integrity rules are necessary for ensuring high-quality data values. Robust data documentation is necessary for organization-wide awareness of the data resource.

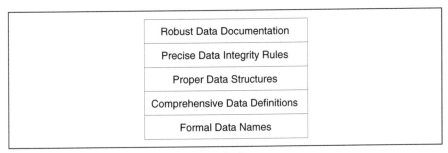

Figure 12.1   Data architecture value chain.

Data Management Value Chain

The five non-architectural good practices form a ***data management value chain***, as shown in Figure 12.2. This value chain is also part of the data resource component of the business intelligence value chain. Each of these good practices are managerial or cultural in nature and provide direct support to the architectural good practices. Each can also be the weakest link in the chain if not properly developed.

A reasonable data orientation is necessary for properly orienting development of the data resource architecture. Acceptable data availability is necessary to ensure the proper sharing and utilization of the data resource. Adequate data responsibility is necessary to ensure active stakeholder involvement in managing the data resource. An expanded data vision is necessary to ensure that management of the data resource is integrated with management of the business. Appropriate data recognition is necessary to gain long-term executive commitment to a high-quality data resource.

Data Resource Framework

These two value chains are combined into a ***data resource framework*** that includes an architectural component and two non-architectural components for data management and data availability, as shown in Figure 12.3.[2] The data resource framework provides a complete set of components for the overall design, implementation, management, and use of a high-quality data resource. It has been developed and modified over many years based on sound principles and constructive feedback.

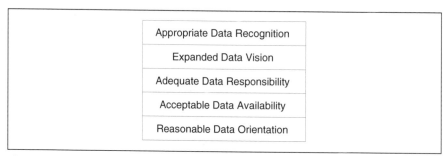

Figure 12.2   The data management value chain.

---

[2] The data resource framework is explained in detail in *Data Sharing Using a Common Data Architecture* and in *The Data Warehouse Challenge: Taming Data Chaos*. Both books are by the author and are listed in the Bibliography.

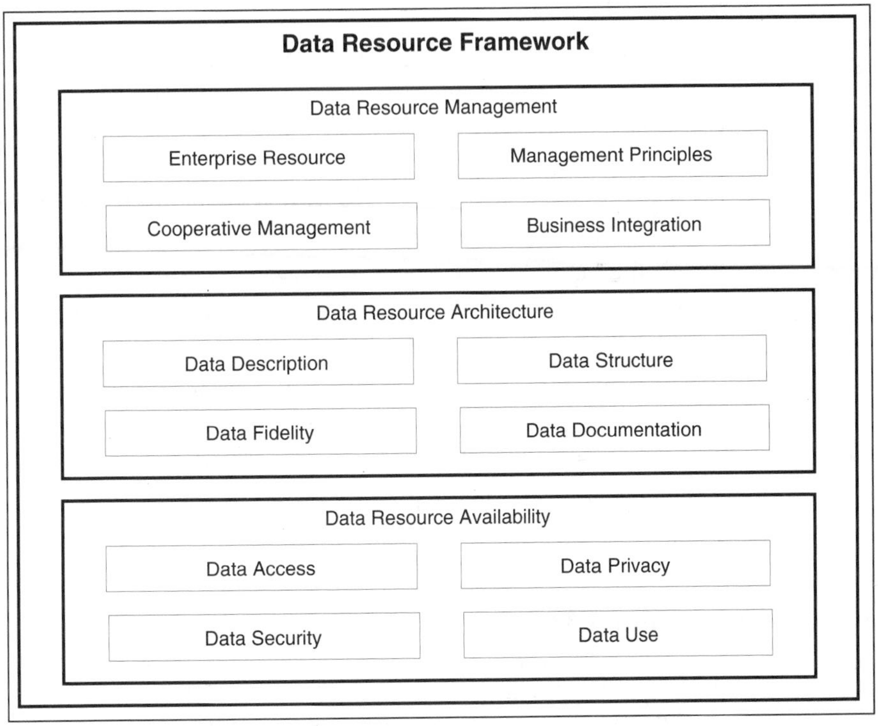

Figure 12.3   Data resource framework.

The data resource framework
is the foundation for the data resource value chain.

Data management includes managing data as a resource of the organization, managing data by the same principles by which other resources are managed, ensuring that all stakeholders have responsibility for cooperatively managing the data resource, and integrating management of the data resource with business planning. Most of these items were covered in the non-architectural good practices.

Data architecture includes the formal names and comprehensive definitions of data (data description), the proper structure of data, improved data fidelity, and robust data resource documentation. Data fidelity includes data integrity, data accuracy, and data completeness. These items were covered in the architectural good practices.

Data availability includes ensuring that the data are readily accessible, ensuring a person's and organization's right to privacy and confidentiality, providing security through adequate backup and recovery of the data resource, and the appropriate and ethical use of the data resource. These items were covered in the non-architectural good practices.

The data resource framework can be used as an outline for a policy and procedure manual for the management of an organization-wide data resource. I have taken this approach in several organizations with tremendous success. People identify their problems within the framework, they develop their standards or guidelines within the framework, and they begin development of a common data architecture using the framework. The ten sets of good practices provide the initial substance to the framework and organization specifics add the detail to implementing the good practices. The data resource framework is an excellent way to focus all the problems and initiatives within one integrated construct.

Setting a New Course for Quality

The data resource framework is used to set the course for improving data resource quality. That course approaches the ideal of a comparate data resource and desired data resource quality although an organization may never achieve the ideal. They will get progressively closer with each project in a data resource quality initiative, but may never achieve a completely comparate data resource. It is up to each individual organization to apply the good practices as it deems necessary to improve data resource quality enough to meet its business objectives. Each organization must determine the degree to which they want to improve their data resource quality.

I am frequently asked how long it takes to get a comparate data resource in place. This is a difficult question to answer precisely because it depends on the degree of disparity and the specific needs of the organization. The indications, from past experience with both public and private sector organizations, are that it takes about ten years to implement a comparate data resource that substantially meets the organization's needs. Significant benefits are certainly achieved much earlier than that, but it takes about ten years to substantially complete development of a comparate data resource.

Setting a new course involves an awakening for both business management and information technology management, a shift in emphasis from technology to information, the avoidance of the quick-fix hype, an understanding of what will happen with a status quo attitude, the realization that no blessing is required for implementing quality improvement, an awareness that the principles and techniques already exist, and an acceptance of the cost of quality improvement. Each of these topics is explained below.

An Awakening

The disparate data situation evolved very slowly over many years, as described in the first chapter. It resulted from many different causes through many different scenarios. Basically, data resource quality was sacrificed for business function and short-term objectives. This approach resulted in a continued increase in data disparity until the shock of business impacts hit the organization. Even after the shock hit, organizations continued to allow data disparity to run rampant until it reached the current situation of spiraling data disparity.

Many organizations, in trying to find the elusive silver bullet, evolved into plausible deniability with many excuses and denial that the situation exists, and are now stuck in a self-defeating fallacy situation. The disparate data cycle is spiraling out of sight. I made the statement in an earlier book that the situation would get worse before it got better. The situation is getting far worse through spiraling data disparity and cumulative business impacts.

I believe that the information technology discipline is entering an age of awakening. Both executive management and information technology management realize that there is disparity throughout information technology and that disparity is increasing rapidly. Both are becoming increasingly aware of the other's situation. Both realize that neither is wholly to blame and that each inherited the current situation. They must work together in a true business—information technology partnership to resolve the situation because blame just will not lead anywhere.

> The information technology
> discipline is approaching an awakening.

This age of awakening will lead an organization into a foundation of frameworks and architectures. Organizations will begin to cut out the fat but leave the bone; in other words they will eliminate the disparity and keep the architecture.

A theme of architectures leading to quality leading to improved productivity will become the stability across dynamic business change. James Gleick's book *Faster: The Acceleration of Just About Everything* explains how nearly everything is changing at an ever-increasing rate. A high-quality data resource built within a common data architecture may be the only degree of stability that an organization has against an ever-increasing rate of change.

I made a statement in an earlier book that when the pain of crossing organizational boundaries and sharing becomes greater than the pain of not meeting the business information demand, then people will share data. I now state that *when the pain of not having a high-quality data resource within a common data architecture exceeds the pain of not meeting business information needs, organizations will begin developing a comparate data resource!* One manager I talked with wanted to know how to start an initiative to rapidly increase the pain of not meeting business information needs. This book provides the bad habits that can be used to raise awareness of the disparate data situation and increase the pain through an understanding of the business impacts.

Information versus Technology

The information technology discipline to date has concentrated its efforts largely on the technology aspect rather than on the information aspect of the discipline. It has focused on the technology aspect too long; almost like kids with a new toy. It has been overly concerned about what new technology can do rather than what it can do for the business. It has been oriented toward the short-term use of new technology rather than the long-term benefits of good information.

> It is time to concentrate on the *I*
> of Information Technology, not the *T*.

The discipline needs to concentrate more on the information aspect of information technology than on the technology aspect. It needs to concentrate on providing information to meet the current and future business information demand rather than playing with new technology. It needs to concentrate on long-term support to the business rather than short-term fascination with new technology.

John Zachman repeatedly emphasizes the information aspect rather than the technology aspect of information technology. Once the orientation is primarily toward the information aspect, the emphasis can be placed on building a high-quality data resource within a common data architecture to support the information aspect. This is the foundation for the business intelligence value chain.

Quick-Fix Hype

Watch out for quick-fix products and methods. There are many out there and they are often oriented toward making money for the promoter. There are many false promises about success from automated solutions, but the successes are usually very narrow in scope. There are also many good products, but they are seldom integrated to provide a consistent comparate data resource across all data megatypes. The lack of an integrated approach impacts the effectiveness of most products.

> Automated fixes will not stop or correct data disparity.

I ran across a product recently that claimed to resolve the disparity in data resource data that were captured and maintained by several other products. It is quite ironic that there are tools that create disparity in data resource data because of their lack of data integration within a common data architecture, and then there are tools that resolve that data disparity. Products are actually creating disparity with the data resource data in the name of correcting the disparity in the real data. The discipline seems to be unable to integrate its approach to solving data disparity.

Incidentally, I asked this vendor about the disparity across different data megatypes. He did not have a clue to what I was talking about, but did claim that their product was the best on the market. I explained the data megatypes, such as spatial, textual, imaging, and so on, to him. Their product did not cover those data megatypes; only tabular data. So, even their product perpetuated the disparity of data resource data with respect to all the data megatypes. The sad fact is that as of today I have not found a single product that routinely maintains integrated data resource data across all data megatypes.

Quick fixes, or even long-term fixes, to the disparate data problem ignore the fact that disparate data are still being created. The creation of disparate data needs to be attacked before the existing disparate data can be resolved. The source of the problem needs to be attacked, lest the resolution of disparate data go on forever. Then again, maybe that is the intent of the quick-fix solutions. After all, if there are no more disparate data, there is no more need for quick fix solutions to disparate data.

Just within the last few months I received my first contact to help an organization resolve disparate data within their data warehouse. They had done the traditional suck and squirt approach to building the data warehouse. They had *sliced and diced* their data and stored the results with no documentation of the analysis performed. Now they have a large volume of evaluational data in their data warehouse and have very little understanding about what those data represent. This lack of understanding casts doubt on the results obtained from the analysis of evaluational data.

> The *suck and squirt approach* is a major step toward disaster.

The **suck and squirt approach** is what I named the method of finding the record of reference or system of reference, sucking the data out of that reference, performing some minor or superficial cleansing, and squirting the data into the data warehouse. Analysis is performed on the data, new data are added from the system of reference on a regular basis, and additional analysis is performed. The result is ever-increasing quantities of disparate evaluational data.

One major flaw of the suck and squirt approach is using a single record of reference or system of reference as the data source. In all the work I have done with public and private sector organizations, I have not yet found a single record of reference or system of reference in any organization for any subject area. It has always been a case of the best name in one system, the best address in another system, the best profile in a third system, and so on. The best data for any subject area are scattered across all the disparate databases in an organization.

> ERPs can never substitute for a common data architecture.

Enterprise resource planning (ERP) applications are in a similar situation. Not only do they usually follow the suck and squirt approach, they are often touted as the common data architecture for an organization. An ERP is not, cannot, and will never be the common data architecture for an organization. It is simply another application that must fit within the enterprise-wide common data architecture the same as any other application. A discussion of ERPs is beyond the scope of this book, but Appendix D lists the reasons why an ERP can never be the common data architecture for an organization.

Just recently I received my first contact from an organization regarding their implementation of an ERP. After all the effort and expense of implementing an ERP, it contained disparate data and was not supporting the business as intended. The organization had presumed that the ERP was going to be the enterprise-wide common data architecture, as claimed by the vendor, and used a traditional suck and squirt approach from a record of reference with minimal data transformation. They had sincerely believed that when they turned the switch on their ERP that their disparate data problems would be solved.

Quick-fix products cannot create a common data architecture or resolve disparate data. They never have and they never will because they cannot understand data. They cannot make decisions about what is disparate data and what is comparate data. They cannot decide what data are necessary to adequately support the business information demand. Only people can understand data and develop a common data architecture to meet the business information demand. Products can help people by scanning, inventorying, storing, indexing, searching, retrieving, and so on; but they cannot understand data. When people make the decisions, the products can support those decisions.

> Support products must be a cooperative effort.

The development of products that support a comparate data resource must be a cooperative effort between vendors and organization management. On one hand, organizations can only purchase products that are available. If the products they need are not available, they must either develop their own or do without. The flip side is that vendors only build products that can be sold or that they perceive can be sold. They typically will not build products for which there is no perceived market. So, it is a cooperative effort for organizations to demand the products they need to support the development of a comparate data resource and for vendors to build those products. Both must face reality and sidestep the current hype about quick-fix solutions to the disparate data situation.

What Happens with a Status Quo

Many people ask me what will happen if they ignore implementation of a data resource quality initiative and accept the status quo? Let's face reality—*there is no status quo for data resource quality!* The data resource will not stay the same as it is today if you ignore a data resource quality initiative. The spiraling disparate data cycle and the natural drift of the data resource will move the data resource toward ever-increasing disparity. The data resource will get worse, and it will get worse faster than it has in the past. There will be less support for the business and increased impacts on the business.

> There is no status quo for data resource quality.

I was in the fire service for a number of years and took many courses on how to fight both wildfires and structure fires. These courses were oriented toward understanding fire dynamics and approaching each fire objectively and scientifically. The emphasis was on how to attack the heart of the fire, extinguish it quickly, and prevent as much personal injury and property damage as possible. Some people were only interested in driving fire trucks and squirting water; they did not need to know anything about fire dynamics to be able to squirt water on flames. After all, that is what firefighting is all about. The result of this approach is that they fought a fire all the way to the ground.

There are only two alternatives for managing a data resource: let the natural drift of the data resource toward increased disparity continue or launch a data resource quality initiative to alter that natural drift toward a comparate data resource. There is no third alternative. There is no middle ground. You either watch it *burn to the ground* or you take action to understand the dynamics and resolve the disparity with minimal impact on the business.

> A status quo leads to
> organization failure by information deprivation.

The result of a data resource quality status quo is organizational failure by information deprivation! The business information demand will not be met and the organization will slowly fail and ultimately die without proper information. The spiraling data disparity will increase both the number and severity of the business impacts, and the impacts will accumulate and eventually cascade from one to another. The cascade will become so rapid that one impact cannot be resolved before another one hits. There will be no time to recover.

The organization will fail by not becoming an intelligent learning organization. It will become sluggish and non-responsive to changing business needs. It will become reactive to business impacts rather than proactive to the changing business environment. There are many different scenarios, but the general pattern is the same. The organization ultimately collapses under the weight of the impacts of disparate data.

The term *data rich and information poor* has been used many times, but it is not an accurate term. Organizations are certainly information poor when they have large quantities of disparate data and cannot meet the business information demand, but they are not data rich. Large volumes of data alone do not make an organization rich in data. Those data must readily support the business information demand for an organization to be data rich. An organization is only data rich when it has a comparate data resource that fully supports the business information demand. The comparate data resource is one situation where less is more; where less data become a more valuable resource.

> A status quo leads to a spiraling loss of productivity.

One major impact of a data resource quality status quo is a spiraling loss of productivity. Disparate data start a ***lost productivity cycle*** that, once started, is very hard to stop. More and more time is spent reactively resolving problems leaving less and less time to be proactive and prevent those problems. The situation is much like the dull axe syndrome where the woodsman is chopping down trees. The more he chops, the duller the axe gets; the duller the axe gets, the harder he chops. A fellow woodsman asked him why he didn't stop and sharpen his axe. He replied that he couldn't because he was already behind schedule and didn't want to fall any further behind.

The lost productivity cycle is hard to break, but it is not impossible to break. The best practices can be used to slow the disparate data cycle and start a comparate data cycle. The comparate data cycle starts a success motivation cycle that slows the lost productivity cycle and starts a productivity improvement cycle.

The disparate data situation is like being stuck in a rut. It is easier to stay in the rut than it is to risk getting out of the rut. But, the problem is that the rut is getting deeper and narrower and it is getting harder and harder to get out of the rut. People are convincing themselves that the situation will get better, the rut will eventually disappear, and they will be home free. This type of group-think only gets people in deeper and makes it increasingly difficult to recover.

I have seen the results of group-think. I have seen it in progress in many organizations. I have been in meetings and work sessions where it is happening. I have heard a multitude of excuses and reasons why the problem is not as bad as many people seem to think, why the problem will go away in time, and why the situation can be resolved with a purchased application. *The reality is that disparate data will not go away if you ignore the problem; the problem will only get worse!*

Principles and Techniques Available

Let's face another reality about a data resource quality initiative. The concepts, principles, and techniques for stopping the development of disparate data, developing a comparate data resource, and resolving the existing disparate data are readily available today.[3] They have been tested and proven successful on many data resource quality initiatives. They are very practical and are based on sound theory; they are not hypothetical, esoteric, or academic.

> The techniques to build
> a comparate data resource are available and proven.

One excuse I frequently hear is that there are no techniques available to stop the development of disparate data, develop a comparate data resource, and resolve existing disparate data. People say the discipline just has not matured enough to be able to handle these problems, With this attitude, the discipline will never be able to handle the problem.

The concepts, principles, and techniques are provided in this book and in previous books. They can be put into practice in any way that best suits the organization. No two organizations take exactly the same approach to developing a

---

[3] Refer to the Bibliography for the books I published in 1990, 1994, and 1996.

comparate data resource and resolving disparate data. In fact, there is no single approach that works best for every organization. The concepts, principles, and techniques are used to build a phased approach that solves the problems and provides successes unique to the organization.

No Blessing Required

Let's face a third reality about a data resource quality initiative. *There is no approval required to begin doing things right!* There is no justification necessary to begin a data resource quality initiative. There is no reason whatsoever to delay a quality improvement initiative. People just need to take action and start improving data quality.

> No approval is required to improve data resource quality.

If anything, there should be permission and approval to continue creating disparate data that continue to impact the business. There should be an extensive justification to spend resources unnecessarily to create disparate data and the business impacts of those disparate data. Approval should be required to mess things up, not do things right. It often baffles me why organizations routinely allow people to ruin data resource quality and then require approval or justification to fix the quality problem.

The good practices described in this book are relatively easy to implement. They can bring early benefits to the organization and begin building a success motivation cycle. They are not rocket science; they are everyday common sense things that most people can do with minimum effort. There is nothing magical or mythical about the good practices. They are very simple and straightforward.

Many people promote the establishment of benchmarks and lengthy studies to prove the concepts and determine how to continue. These are only delaying tactics that are unnecessary for beginning a data resource quality initiative. They are time-consuming and only delay action to stop the development of disparate data. Watch out for these approaches, because the situation will only get worse while these studies are taking place.

You may certainly want to start a data resource quality initiative with a pilot study that produces some success and provide lessons learned about the organization and its business information need. Select a problem that is small and can produce early successes. Begin using the good practices to show what can be accomplished and how the problems can be resolved. Then build on those successes with larger projects.

The Cost of Quality

Let's face a fourth reality about a data resource quality initiative. Developing a high-quality comparate data resource from the existing disparate data is not free. Many people promote the concept that quality is free. If quality is built into a comparate data resource from the beginning, then quality is free. There is no cost incurred to remove or correct disparate data and there is no cost from impacts to the business. But the cost to correct the existing disparate data is not free.

> Correcting existing low-quality data is not free.

The good news is that the cost to develop a comparate data resource and resolve the existing disparate data is far less expensive than letting the disparate data continue to impact the business. It is far less expensive than business failure by information deprivation. Take a hard look at financial management, human resource management, and real property management.

Approaching a comparate data resource approaches free quality. But there are costs to change the current mindset and resolve disparate data that are far from free. Those costs are increasing every day that disparate data are produced. Those costs, however, are less than the cost of continued data disparity. The quicker you take action, the less the cost for developing a comparate data resource.

I hear excuses like not being funded, not being properly staffed to do it right, and so on. These are weak excuses and are part of the group-think syndrome where a group of people convince themselves that there is no problem and they are doing the right thing. *It is less expensive to do things right than it is to do things wrong and make corrections later!* So why do people continue to do things wrong? The difference is that it is perceived to be less expensive to do things wrong and not make corrections than it is to do things right. If you ignore the cost of correction, it is less expensive to do things quick and move on to other projects.

At least that is the way it appears on the surface, and we have certainly been flying on the surface for a long time. When you look at the costs incurred from the impacts on the business, things take on a different perspective. Now it is not only the correction cost but also the business impact cost that enter the equation. It is far less costly to do it right in the beginning and avoid both the cost of correction and the cost of business impacts. The difference is the impacts of disparate data on the business.

> Data resource quality has an internal and an external aspect.

There are two aspects to data resource quality. The first aspect is the *internal data resource quality* related to how well the data resource meets the current and future business information demand. The second aspect is the *external data resource quality* related to how citizens or customers perceive the data quality based on the services or products they receive.

Use the good practices described in this book to initiate a data resource quality initiative that meets both the internal and external aspects of data resource quality. Take the initiative to launch an initiative to improve data resource quality. Take some action to break the status quo and begin improving data resource quality. I haven't seen a statue yet that was erected to someone who maintained the status quo.

Developing a comparate data resource is a continuous effort to achieve the desired quality and to keep the desired quality. It is an ongoing process to ensure that a high-quality data resource is always available to meet the business information demand. It is a costly process to start, but the rewards are well worth the resources. The only alternative is to continue touting the benefits of plausible deniability and the self-defeating fallacy.

Summary

I have a few last words of wisdom for those interested in stopping the creation of disparate data, developing a comparate data resource, and resolving existing data disparity. Follow these words of wisdom and success will be the reward.

> Do not delay the implementation of a data resource quality initiative. The current situation will only get worse, the business impacts will only increase in number and severity, and the situation will be far more difficult to correct.

Remember that as use of the data resource goes up the quality goes up, and as the use goes down the quality goes down. Develop a shared data resource that increases use of the data resource and improves the quality of that data resource.

There are no silver bullets that can be purchased and implemented to automatically stop the development of disparate data and resolve existing data disparity. There is no way to automatically understand disparate data. Stop looking for a quick fix.

The concepts, principles, and techniques for improving data resource quality are available today and have been proven successful. There is no reason to delay the implementation of a data resource quality initiative for a lack of good techniques or to begin a benchmark or proof of concept project.

No permission or blessing is required to start a data resource quality initiative or to continue that initiative. The need for improved data resource quality is a truism and an initiative to improve quality needs no justification.

Include the business clients in any data resource quality initiative. Go to the business, encourage interested people to become involved, open the door to their contributions, and share the benefits with them. Remember that information technology is a staff function in support of the business.

When a data resource quality initiative has been properly launched, the success of that initiative will motivate people to continue the initiative. Once started, a data resource quality initiative is self-perpetuating.

Seize the opportunity, take the initiative, use the good practices described in this book, and start developing a high-quality data resource that will support the current and future business information demand of an intelligent learning organization.

Summary of the Ten Ways

The Bad Habits and Good Practices

The bad habits leading to a low-quality data resource, the impacts of those bad habits, the good practices for a high-quality data resource, the benefits of the good practices, and the best practices to begin implementing a data resource quality initiative are summarized below for each of the ten best ways to achieve data resource quality.

Formal Data Names

Bad habits leading to informal data names:

Meaningless data names—difficult to identify and initially understand the data.

Non-unique data names—many synonyms and homonyms across the data resource.

Structureless data names—no formal structure or sequence to the words in the name.

Incorrect data names—no match to the definition or the structure.

Informal data name abbreviations—random, informal, and inconsistent.

Unnamed data resource components.

Impacts of informal data names:

The data cannot be readily identified.

The disparate data cycle is reinforced and disparate data increased.

Lost productivity finding data, remembering abbreviations, and creating additional data.

Good practices for formal data names:

Data naming taxonomy must be established.

Supporting data name vocabulary must be established.

Primary data names must be developed based on acceptable business terms.

Standard data names can be useful if developed within the data naming taxonomy.

Data name word abbreviations must be developed.

Data name abbreviation algorithm must be developed.

Benefits of formal data names:

The data are readily identified.

The disparate data cycle begins to be limited.

Productivity begins to improve for business clients and information technology staff.

Best practices for success motivation:

Identify business critical data that cause major problems.

Formally name data subjects, data characteristics, and coded data values.

Formally abbreviate data subject and data characteristic names.

Comprehensive Data Definitions

Bad habits leading to vague data definitions:

Non-existent data definitions—never existed, lost, or misplaced.

Unavailable data definitions—exist but are not readily available.

Short data definitions—short, truncated phrases.

Meaningless data definitions—useless for understanding the data.

Outdated data definitions—never enhanced after development.

Incorrect data definitions—do not correctly represent the business.

Unrelated data definitions—not related to the content and meaning of the data.

Impacts of vague data definitions:

Inhibited data understanding.

Inappropriate use of the data.

Perpetuation of the disparate data cycle and hidden data.

Continued loss of productivity.

Good practices for comprehensive data definitions:

Meaningful data definitions prepared based on business meaning.

Thorough data definitions prepared with no length limitations.

Enhanced data definitions that remain current with the business.

Fundamental data definitions created to be inherited by specific data definitions.

Benefits of comprehensive data definition:

Improved data understanding.

Continued slowing of the disparate data cycle.

Improved productivity of business clients and information technology staff.

Best practices for success motivation:

Data subjects, data characteristics, and coded data values are defined first.

Business clients must be directly involved in data definitions.

Proper Data Structure

Bad habits leading to an improper data structure:

Detail overload—excessive detail on the entity-relation diagram.

Useless semantics.

Data cardinalities.

Data attributes.

Primary key notations.

Wrong audience focus.

Wrong level of detail for the audience.

Poor presentation format.

All audiences not covered.

Inadequate business representation.

Incomplete business detail.

Incomplete business coverage.

Redundant business coverage.

Poor data structuring techniques.

Data normalization and denormalization.

Primary key designations.

Data definition inclusion.

Incorrect data structure.

Impacts of an improper data structure:

Poor business understanding.

Poor performance of the hardware and system software.

Continued data disparity.

Lower productivity of both business clients and information technology staff.

Good practices for a proper data structure:
  Data structure components.
    Entity-relation diagram.
    Data attribute structure.
  Proper detail to each audience.
    Five-schema concept.
    Three-tier concept.
    Combined three-tier and five-schema.
  Formal design techniques.
    Data normalization.
    Data denormalization.
    Primary keys and foreign keys.
    Semantic statements.
    Data cardinalities.
    Integrated data structure.

Benefits of a proper data structure:
  Improved business representation and understanding.
  Reduced data disparity.
  Improved productivity for business clients and information technology
    staff.

Best practices for success motivation:
  Focus on core business functions first.
  Use the three tiers—move down through the strategic, tactical, and
    detail tiers.
  Target the audience with the appropriate level of detail.
  Provide formal training for key business clients and information
    technology staff.

Precise Data Integrity Rules

Bad habits leading to imprecise data integrity rules:
  Ignoring a high data error rate.
  Incomplete data integrity rules.
  Delayed data error identification and correction.
  Default data values frequently used.
  Nonspecific data domains.

Nonspecific data optionality.
Undefined data derivations.
Uncontrolled data deletion.

Impacts of imprecise data integrity rules:
   Bad perception about the service and products offered by the
      organization.
   Inappropriate business actions for both citizens and
      customers.
   Lost productivity for business clients, information technology
      staff, and hardware.

Good practices for precise data integrity rules:
   Data rule concept.
   Data integrity rule names.
   Data integrity rule notation.
   Data integrity rule types.
   Formal names for data integrity rules.
   Specific notations for data integrity rules.
   Six types of data integrity rules.
      Data value rule.
      Conditional data value rule.
      Data structure rule.
      Conditional data structure rule.
      Data derivation rule.
      Data retention rule.
   Fundamental data integrity rules.
   Data integrity rule enforcement.
      One set of rules.
      Apply to all data in the data resource.
      Apply close to data capture.
      Violation actions defined.
      Default data values specified.
   Proactive data quality management.
      Rapid identification of data errors.
      Apply to entire data resource.
      Document default values that are inserted.

Benefits of precise data integrity rules:

    Higher data quality.

    Limited data disparity.

    Improved productivity.

Best practices for success motivation:

    Focus on core business functions first.

    Focus on errors with the largest impact on the business.

    Proactive approach to identify data errors with the largest business impact.

Robust Data Documentation

Bad habits leading to limited data documentation:

    Data documentation not complete.

    Data documentation not current with the business.

    Data documentation not understandable to all audiences.

    Data documentation is redundant.

    Data documentation not readily available.

    Data documentation existence largely unknown to the organization.

Impacts of limited data documentation:

    Limited awareness about the data documentation.

    Disparate data cycle continues.

    Lost productivity continues.

Good practices for robust data documentation:

    Data resource data concept replaces 'metadata.'

    Data resource data aspects for business and technical data.

    Complete data documentation.

    Current data documentation.

    Understandable data documentation.

    Non-redundant data documentation.

    Readily available data documentation.

    Data documentation known to exist.

    Ancillary data documentation.

        Data subject thesaurus.

        Data characteristic thesaurus.

        Business term glossary.

Benefits of robust data documentation:

There is increased awareness of data resource data.

Halted the disparate data cycle.

Improved productivity.

Best practices for success motivation:

Document current activities.

Documentation readily available.

Provide documentation support.

Data resource data architecture.

Reasonable Data Orientation

Bad habits leading to an unreasonable data orientation:

Physical database orientation.

Multiple fact, multiple value data item orientation.

Process orientation toward use of the data.

Operational orientation with no consideration for historical data.

Independent database development orientation.

Inappropriate business orientation.

Impacts of an unreasonable data orientation:

Loss of business focus.

Continuation of data disparity.

Unnecessary performance problems.

Loss of productivity.

Good practices for a reasonable data orientation:

Business subject orientation based on business objects and
events.

Business client orientation.

Five-tier concept for the data resource.

Data normalization to include the five tiers.

Single fact data attribute orientation.

Single data architecture orientation.

Benefits of a reasonable data orientation:

Improved business support.

Promotion of a comparate data resource.

Improved productivity for business and information technology staff.

Best practices for success motivation:
   Take a business subject orientation.
   Involve business knowledge in design.
   Include technical skills in design.

Acceptable Data Availability

Bad practices leading to unacceptable data availability:
   Data are not readily accessible.
   Inadequate protection of the data.
   Inadequate recovery of the data.
   Unprotected right to privacy and confidentiality.
   Inappropriate use of the data.

Impacts of unacceptable data availability:
   Data sharing is limited.
   Data disparity is encouraged.
   Impact on the business.
   Impact on people.

Good practices for acceptable data availability:
   Adequate accessibility to data to support business activities.
   Adequate protection of the data resource.
   Adequate data recovery for continued busies support.
   Protect privacy and confidentiality of individuals and organizations.
   Appropriate use of the data.

Benefits of acceptable data availability:
   Better use of the business and technical staff.
   Shared data resource across business activities.
   Fewer impacts on the business and on people.

Best practices for success motivation:
   Target greatest impacts on the business.
   Backup and recovery of data critical to the business.
   Adequate protection from alteration, destruction, or improper disclosure.

Adequate Data Responsibility

Bad practices leading to inadequate data responsibility:
   No centralized control of the data resource.

No management procedures for developing the
    data resource.
No data stewards responsible for the data resource.

Impacts of inadequate data responsibility:
    Limited data sharing across the business.
    Disparate data creation is encouraged.

Good practices for adequate data responsibility:
    Establish data stewards.
        Strategic level.
        Detail level.
        Tactical level for large organizations.
    Reasonable management procedures for the data resource.
    Centralized control of the data resource.

Benefits of adequate data responsibility:
    Shared data resource that supports the business.

Best practices for success motivation:
    Designate data stewards.
    Develop reasonable procedures.
    Establish centralized control over the data resource.

Expanded Data Vision

Bad habits leading to a restricted data vision:
    Limited scope of the data resource.
        Automated data only.
        Current data only.
        Tabular data only.
        Business critical data only.
    Unreasonable development direction for the data resource.
        Incompatible with business direction.
        Incompatible with database technology direction.
    Unrealistic planning horizon for the data resource.
        Nearsighted planning horizon.
        Farsighted planning horizon.
        Overly optimistic planning horizon.

Impacts of a restricted data vision:
>   Short-term impacts on the business.
>   Future impacts on the business.

Good practices for an expanded data vision:
>   A wider data resource scope.
>> Non-critical data.
>> Non-tabular data.
>> Historical data.
>> Non-automated data.
>   Reasonable development direction for the data resource.
>   Realistic planning horizon for the data resource.
>   Cooperative establishment of the data resource vision.

Benefits of an expanded data vision:
>   Improved support to the business.

Best practices for success motivation:
>   Pick a reasonable direction and a realistic horizon for the vision.
>   Develop a general plan that includes the full scope of the data resource.

Appropriate Data Recognition

Bad habits leading to inappropriate data recognition:
>   Wrong target audience
>> Too high in the organization.
>> Too low in the organization.
>   Requiring an unnecessary justification for a data quality improvement initiative.
>   Search for silver bullets to resolve the situation.
>   Attempt to automate data understanding.
>   Belief that standards will resolve the situation.
>   Belief that generic data models are the common data architecture.

Impacts of inappropriate data recognition:
>   Business impacts continue.
>   Encourage data disparity to continue.

Good practices for appropriate data recognition:
>   Target the vested interest in data resource quality.
>   Direct business client involvement.

Tap the existing knowledge about the data resource.

Start within the current level budget.

Incrementally cost-effective approach.

Proof-positive attitude.

Be opportunistic.

Build on lessons learned.

No blame—no whitewash attitude.

No unnecessary justification for data resource quality improvement.

Benefits of appropriate data recognition:
Continued business support.

Best practices for success motivation:
Apply all the good practices to any data resource quality initiative.

Summary of Best Practices

The best practices of the ten ways to achieve data resource quality are listed below for quick reference. If you want to make a quick start toward improving data resource quality that produces early successes, these are the things that you need to consider. They will gain recognition and encourage people to continue developing a high-quality data resource.

Formal data name best practices:
Identify business critical data that cause major problems.
Formally name data subjects, data characteristics, and coded data values.
Formally abbreviate data subject and data characteristic names.

Comprehensive data definition best practices:
Data subjects, data characteristics, and coded data values are
defined first.
Business clients must be directly involved in data definitions.

Proper data structure best practices:
Focus on core business functions first.
Use the three tiers—move down through the strategic, tactical, and
detail tiers.
Target the audience with the appropriate level of detail.
Provide formal training for key business clients and information
technology staff.

Precise data integrity rule best practices:

    Focus on core business functions first.

    Focus on errors with the largest impact on the business.

    Proactive approach to identify data errors with the largest business impact.

Robust data documentation best practices:

    Document current activities.

    Documentation readily available.

    Provide documentation support.

    Data resource data architecture.

Reasonable data orientation best practices:

    Take a business subject orientation.

    Involve business knowledge in design.

    Include technical skills in design.

Acceptable data availability best practices:

    Target greatest impacts on the business.

    Backup and recovery of data critical to the business.

    Adequate protection from alteration, destruction, or improper disclosure.

Adequate data responsibility best practices:

    Designate data stewards.

    Develop reasonable procedures.

    Establish centralized control over the data resource.

Expanded data vision best practices:

    Pick a reasonable direction and a realistic horizon for the vision.

    Develop a general plan that includes the full scope of the data resource.

Appropriate data recognition best practices:

    Apply all the good practices to any data resource quality initiative.

Summary of Evaluation Criteria

The bad habits, good practices, and best practices for the ten ways to achieve data resource quality are listed below. You can use these criteria to evaluate the current data resource quality and the improvements in data resource quality resulting from the elimination of bad habits and implementation of good practices.

Fill in the horizontal bar to show the degree to which the bad habits exist and the degree to which the good practices and the best practices have been implemented. You can provide definitions for the Poor, Fair, Moderate, Good, and Excellent headings to suit your organization, or you can use a numeric scale if it is more appropriate. You can also select the items that are important for your organization, but don't be too hasty at excluding items because they may be valuable later.

	P	F	M	G	E
Formal Data Names					
Bad Habits					
Meaningless data names	☐	☐	☐	☐	☐
Non-unique data names	☐	☐	☐	☐	☐
Structureless data names	☐	☐	☐	☐	☐
Incorrect data names	☐	☐	☐	☐	☐
Informal data name abbreviations	☐	☐	☐	☐	☐
Unnamed data resource components	☐	☐	☐	☐	☐
Good Practices					
Data naming taxonomy	☐	☐	☐	☐	☐
Data naming vocabulary	☐	☐	☐	☐	☐
Primary data name	☐	☐	☐	☐	☐
Standard data names	☐	☐	☐	☐	☐
Data name word abbreviations	☐	☐	☐	☐	☐
Data name abbreviation algorithm	☐	☐	☐	☐	☐

	P	F	M	G	E
Best Practices					
Business critical data identified	☐	☐	☐	☐	☐
Data subjects named	☐	☐	☐	☐	☐
Data characteristics named	☐	☐	☐	☐	☐
Data codes named	☐	☐	☐	☐	☐
Data subject names abbreviated	☐	☐	☐	☐	☐
Data characteristic names abbreviated	☐	☐	☐	☐	☐

Comprehensive Data Definitions

	P	F	M	G	E
Bad Habits					
Non-existent data definitions	☐	☐	☐	☐	☐
Unavailable data definitions	☐	☐	☐	☐	☐
Short data definitions	☐	☐	☐	☐	☐
Meaningless data definitions	☐	☐	☐	☐	☐
Outdated data definitions	☐	☐	☐	☐	☐
Incorrect data definitions	☐	☐	☐	☐	☐
Unrelated data definitions	☐	☐	☐	☐	☐
Good Practices					
Meaningful data definitions	☐	☐	☐	☐	☐
Thorough data definitions	☐	☐	☐	☐	☐
Current data definitions	☐	☐	☐	☐	☐
Fundamental data definitions	☐	☐	☐	☐	☐
Best Practices					
Data subject definitions	☐	☐	☐	☐	☐
Data characteristic definitions	☐	☐	☐	☐	☐
Data code definitions	☐	☐	☐	☐	☐
Business client involvement	☐	☐	☐	☐	☐

Proper Data Structure

	P	F	M	G	E
Bad Habits					
Detail overload					
Useless semantics	☐	☐	☐	☐	☐
Data cardinalities	☐	☐	☐	☐	☐
Data attributes	☐	☐	☐	☐	☐
Primary key notations	☐	☐	☐	☐	☐

	P	F	M	G	E
Wrong audience focus					
Wrong level of detail for audience	☐	☐	☐	☐	☐
Poor presentation format	☐	☐	☐	☐	☐
All audiences not covered	☐	☐	☐	☐	☐
Inadequate business representation					
Incomplete business detail	☐	☐	☐	☐	☐
Incomplete business coverage	☐	☐	☐	☐	☐
Redundant business coverage	☐	☐	☐	☐	☐
Poor data structure techniques					
Data normalization and denormalization	☐	☐	☐	☐	☐
Primary key designations	☐	☐	☐	☐	☐
Data definition inclusion	☐	☐	☐	☐	☐
Incorrect data structure	☐	☐	☐	☐	☐
Good Practices					
Understand the concepts					
Entity-relation diagrams	☐	☐	☐	☐	☐
Data attribute structure	☐	☐	☐	☐	☐
Identify the audience					
Five-schema concept	☐	☐	☐	☐	☐
Three-tier concept	☐	☐	☐	☐	☐
Combined three-tier five-schema concept	☐	☐	☐	☐	☐
Use proper techniques					
Data normalization	☐	☐	☐	☐	☐
Data denormalization	☐	☐	☐	☐	☐
Primary keys and foreign keys	☐	☐	☐	☐	☐
Semantic statements	☐	☐	☐	☐	☐
Data cardinalities	☐	☐	☐	☐	☐
Integrated data structure	☐	☐	☐	☐	☐
Best Practices					
Core business functions	☐	☐	☐	☐	☐
Use the three tiers	☐	☐	☐	☐	☐
Target the audience	☐	☐	☐	☐	☐
Formal training	☐	☐	☐	☐	☐

	P	F	M	G	E
Precise Data Integrity Rules					
Bad Habits					
Ignoring a high data error rate	☐	☐	☐	☐	☐
Incomplete data integrity rules	☐	☐	☐	☐	☐
Delayed data error identification	☐	☐	☐	☐	☐
Default data values	☐	☐	☐	☐	☐
Nonspecific data domains	☐	☐	☐	☐	☐
Nonspecific data optionality	☐	☐	☐	☐	☐
Undefined data derivations	☐	☐	☐	☐	☐
Uncontrolled data deletion	☐	☐	☐	☐	☐
Good Practices					
Data rule concept	☐	☐	☐	☐	☐
Data integrity rule names	☐	☐	☐	☐	☐
Data integrity rule notation	☐	☐	☐	☐	☐
Data integrity rule types					
Data value rule	☐	☐	☐	☐	☐
Conditional data value rule	☐	☐	☐	☐	☐
Data structure rule	☐	☐	☐	☐	☐
Conditional data structure rule	☐	☐	☐	☐	☐
Data derivation rule	☐	☐	☐	☐	☐
Data retention rule	☐	☐	☐	☐	☐
Fundamental data integrity rules	☐	☐	☐	☐	☐
Data integrity rule enforcement					
One set of rules	☐	☐	☐	☐	☐
Apply to all data	☐	☐	☐	☐	☐
Apply close to data capture	☐	☐	☐	☐	☐
Violation actions defined	☐	☐	☐	☐	☐
Default values specified	☐	☐	☐	☐	☐
Proactive data quality management					
Rapid identification of data error	☐	☐	☐	☐	☐
Apply to entire data resource	☐	☐	☐	☐	☐
Document default values that are inserted	☐	☐	☐	☐	☐
Best Practices					
Focus on core business functions	☐	☐	☐	☐	☐

	P	F	M	G	E
Focus on largest impact	☐	☐	☐	☐	☐
Proactive approach	☐	☐	☐	☐	☐

Robust Data Documentation

Bad Habits

	P	F	M	G	E
Data documentation not complete	☐	☐	☐	☐	☐
Data documentation not current	☐	☐	☐	☐	☐
Data documentation not understandable	☐	☐	☐	☐	☐
Data documentation redundant	☐	☐	☐	☐	☐
Data documentation not readily available	☐	☐	☐	☐	☐
Data documentation existence unknown	☐	☐	☐	☐	☐

Good Practices

	P	F	M	G	E
Data resource data concept	☐	☐	☐	☐	☐
Data resource data aspects	☐	☐	☐	☐	☐
Complete data documentation	☐	☐	☐	☐	☐
Current data documentation	☐	☐	☐	☐	☐
Understandable data documentation	☐	☐	☐	☐	☐
Non-redundant data documentation	☐	☐	☐	☐	☐
Readily available data documentation	☐	☐	☐	☐	☐
Data documentation known to exist	☐	☐	☐	☐	☐
Ancillary data documentation					
Data subject thesaurus	☐	☐	☐	☐	☐
Data characteristic thesaurus	☐	☐	☐	☐	☐
Business term glossary	☐	☐	☐	☐	☐

Best Practices

	P	F	M	G	E
Document current activities	☐	☐	☐	☐	☐
Documentation readily available	☐	☐	☐	☐	☐
Provide documentation support	☐	☐	☐	☐	☐
Data resource data architecture	☐	☐	☐	☐	☐

Reasonable Data Orientation

Bad Habits

	P	F	M	G	E
Physical orientation	☐	☐	☐	☐	☐
Multiple fact orientation	☐	☐	☐	☐	☐
Process orientation	☐	☐	☐	☐	☐

	P	F	M	G	E
Operational orientation	☐	☐	☐	☐	☐
Independent orientation	☐	☐	☐	☐	☐
Inappropriate business orientation	☐	☐	☐	☐	☐

Good Practices

	P	F	M	G	E
Business subject orientation	☐	☐	☐	☐	☐
Business client orientation	☐	☐	☐	☐	☐
Five-tier concept	☐	☐	☐	☐	☐
Data normalization expansion	☐	☐	☐	☐	☐
Single fact data attribute	☐	☐	☐	☐	☐
Single data architecture	☐	☐	☐	☐	☐

Best Practices

	P	F	M	G	E
Take a business subject orientation	☐	☐	☐	☐	☐
Involve business knowledge	☐	☐	☐	☐	☐
Include technical skills	☐	☐	☐	☐	☐

Acceptable Data Availability

Bad Habits

	P	F	M	G	E
Data not readily accessible	☐	☐	☐	☐	☐
Inadequate data protection	☐	☐	☐	☐	☐
Inadequate data recovery	☐	☐	☐	☐	☐
Unprotected privacy and confidentiality	☐	☐	☐	☐	☐
Inappropriate data use	☐	☐	☐	☐	☐

Good Practices

	P	F	M	G	E
Adequate data accessibility	☐	☐	☐	☐	☐
Adequate data protection	☐	☐	☐	☐	☐
Adequate data recovery	☐	☐	☐	☐	☐
Protect privacy and confidentiality	☐	☐	☐	☐	☐
Appropriate data use	☐	☐	☐	☐	☐

Best Practices

	P	F	M	G	E
Target greatest impacts	☐	☐	☐	☐	☐
Backup and recovery	☐	☐	☐	☐	☐
Adequate protection	☐	☐	☐	☐	☐

	P	F	M	G	E
Adequate Data Responsibility					
Bad Habits					
No centralized control	☐	☐	☐	☐	☐
No management procedures	☐	☐	☐	☐	☐
No data stewards	☐	☐	☐	☐	☐
Good Practices					
Establish data stewards					
Strategic level	☐	☐	☐	☐	☐
Detail level	☐	☐	☐	☐	☐
Tactical level for large organizations.	☐	☐	☐	☐	☐
Reasonable management procedures	☐	☐	☐	☐	☐
Centralized control	☐	☐	☐	☐	☐
Best Practices					
Designate data stewards	☐	☐	☐	☐	☐
Develop reasonable procedures	☐	☐	☐	☐	☐
Establish centralized control	☐	☐	☐	☐	☐
Expanded Data Vision					
Bad Habits					
Limited scope of the data resource					
Automated data	☐	☐	☐	☐	☐
Current data	☐	☐	☐	☐	☐
Tabular data	☐	☐	☐	☐	☐
Business critical data	☐	☐	☐	☐	☐
Unreasonable development direction					
Incompatible with business direction	☐	☐	☐	☐	☐
Incompatible with database direction	☐	☐	☐	☐	☐
Unrealistic planning horizon					
Nearsighted planning horizon	☐	☐	☐	☐	☐
Farsighted planning horizon	☐	☐	☐	☐	☐
Overly optimistic planning horizon	☐	☐	☐	☐	☐
Good Practices					
A wider data resource scope					
Non-critical data	☐	☐	☐	☐	☐

	P	F	M	G	E
Non-tabular data	☐	☐	☐	☐	☐
Historical data	☐	☐	☐	☐	☐
Non-automated data.	☐	☐	☐	☐	☐
Reasonable development direction	☐	☐	☐	☐	☐
Realistic planning horizon	☐	☐	☐	☐	☐
Cooperative establishment	☐	☐	☐	☐	☐

Best Practices

Reasonable direction/horizon	☐	☐	☐	☐	☐
General plan	☐	☐	☐	☐	☐

Appropriate Data Recognition

Bad Habits

Wrong target audience

Too high in the organization.	☐	☐	☐	☐	☐
Too low in the organization.	☐	☐	☐	☐	☐
Requiring an unnecessary justification	☐	☐	☐	☐	☐
Search for silver bullets	☐	☐	☐	☐	☐
Attempt to automate data understanding	☐	☐	☐	☐	☐
Belief that standards	☐	☐	☐	☐	☐
Belief in generic data models	☐	☐	☐	☐	☐

Good Practices

Target the vested interest	☐	☐	☐	☐	☐
Direct business involvement	☐	☐	☐	☐	☐
Tap the knowledge base	☐	☐	☐	☐	☐
Start within current budget	☐	☐	☐	☐	☐
Incrementally cost effective approach	☐	☐	☐	☐	☐
Proof-positive attitude	☐	☐	☐	☐	☐
Be opportunistic	☐	☐	☐	☐	☐
Build on lessons learned.	☐	☐	☐	☐	☐
No blame—no whitewash attitude	☐	☐	☐	☐	☐
No unnecessary justification	☐	☐	☐	☐	☐

Best Practices

Apply all good practices	☐	☐	☐	☐	☐

Data Structure Examples

Entity-Relation Diagram

An example of strategic-, tactical-, and detail-level entity-relation diagrams are shown below. These examples are relatively simple, but they show the progression from the strategic level, through the tactical level, to the detail level. The example shown is from the development of a land appraisal system for a county.

Strategic Level

The strategic level was developed primarily with the elected County Assessor who was concerned about adequately representing 1) the districts that each tax parcel belong to, 2) the groups that each tax parcel belong to, 3) the features of each tax parcel, and 4) the geographic areas for each parcel. When this diagram was presented, along with the basic data definitions, the Assessor was quite happy and said that these data would answer the problems faced by the Assessor's Office.

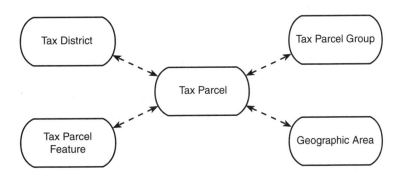

Note that there are many-to-many data relations and that there are no detailed data entities. The data entities represent the business objects that are of interest to the County Assessor. Any further detail would have confused the issue.

Tactical Level

When the strategic diagram was presented to the Chief Appraisers, there was considerable concern about the detail. First, they were concerned about the assignment of the tax districts, the tax parcel groups, the tax parcel features, and the geographic areas to each tax parcel. The addition of the four assignment data entities, their definitions, and a few major data attributes with their data definitions, resolved the many-to-many data relations and the concern.

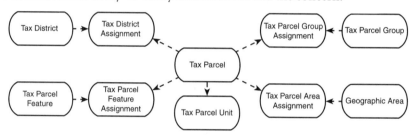

Second, a tax parcel could contain many individual units, such as a family residence, an area that is farmed, and a home for elderly parents. Each of these units had to be documented and taxed separately within a single tax parcel. The addition of a tax parcel unit, its definition, and a few major data attributes with their data definitions resolved this concern. The resulting data structure was satisfactory to the Chief Appraisers.

Detail Level

When the tactical diagram was presented to the residential and commercial appraisers, there was concern about handling the vast quantity of code tables that are used to document all the tax districts, tax parcel groups, tax parcel features, and geographic areas. There were literally hundreds of code tables, and more are continuously being added.

This concern was resolved with the addition of four data entities for the types of code tables, their data definitions, all the data attributes and their data definitions. For example, Tax District Type could be 'Fire District,' 'Cemetery District,' 'Library District,' and so on. Tax District represented specific fire districts, cemetery districts, library districts, and so on. Tax District Assignment assigned one fire district, one cemetery district, one library district, and so on, to each tax parcel. This resolved the concerns for the individual appraisers.

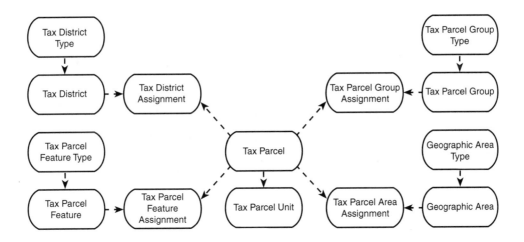

Notice that these diagrams meet the two basic objectives for entity-relation diagrams. They are technically correct and culturally acceptable for the business clients. The arrangement of the data entities and relations is easy to understand and readily draws business clients into the process. They are also structurally stable and business flexible, allowing the appraisal staff to add new code tables or new values to existing code tables without any structural changes to the data architecture.

Data Attribute Structure

The data attribute structure for a few of the data entities that appear in the diagrams are shown below. Note that a data attribute structure would actually be prepared for every data entity. They show how the data attributes and their roles in a data entity are documented. Like the entity-relation diagrams above, the data attribute structure is technically correct and culturally acceptable. It draws business clients into the process of developing data architecture that truly represents the business.

Tax District Type

Primary Key   Tax District Type. Code

Alternate Key   Tax District Type. Name

Data Attribute List
  Tax District Type. Begin Date
  Tax District Type. Code
  Tax District Type. Definition

Tax District Type. End Date
Tax District Type. Name

Tax District

Primary Key	Tax District. Number	
Alternate Key	Tax District. Name	
Foreign Key	Tax District Type	Tax District Type. Code

Data Attribute List
  Tax District. Abolished Date
  Tax District. Common Name
  Tax District. Established Date
  Tax District. Land Area, Square Miles
  Tax District. Legal Name
  Tax District. Number
  Tax District. Population
  Tax District Type. Code

Tax District Assignment

Primary Key	Tax District. Number	
	Tax Parcel. Identifier	
Foreign Key	Tax District	Tax District. Number
Foreign Key	Tax Parcel	Tax Parcel. Identifier

Data Attribute List
  Tax Parcel. Identifier
  Tax District. Number
  Tax District Assignment. Begin Date
  Tax District Assignment. End Date

Tax Parcel

Primary Key	Tax Parcel. Identifier

Data Attribute List
  Tax Parcel. Current Valuation
  Tax Parcel. Highest Elevation, Feet
  Tax Parcel. Identifier
  Tax Parcel. Land Size, Acres
  Tax Parcel. Lowest Elevation, Feet

Purchasing a Data Architecture

A common perception of many vendors and organizations is that a purchased application, such as an enterprise resource planning (ERP) application, defines the common data architecture for an organization. The belief is that use of a separate data architecture for an ERP that is developed within a common data architecture is just not needed. This belief is not well-founded, for the reasons listed below, and may result in more data disparity and data access difficulty than currently exists.

A common data architecture is the context within which all data are identified and understood, including in-house applications, purchased applications, data warehouses and data marts, ERPs, and whatever may replace these products. It encompasses all the data in an organization, including existing disparate data and the comparate data resource, and manual and automated data. The common data architecture is an insurance policy for data resource quality while an organization moves into formal management of their data resource.

ERP Just Another Application

An ERP is just another application, although a relatively large one, that usually does not conform to any enterprise-wide data architecture or a common data architecture. There is usually a discrepancy between an ERP and the existing applications, or the ERP and the enterprise data architecture. An ERP must be used within a common data architecture to ensure consistency of the data resource and the proper transformation of data between an ERP and other applications.

Mismatch with Business Needs

An ERP usually results in a mismatch between its capabilities and the organization's data needs. An ERP may contain data that are not useful to the organization, and an organization may have data needs that are not included in the ERP. Using an ERP within a common data architecture ensures that unused data attributes are not used inappropriately, and that needed data attributes are properly defined and used.

Understanding Existing Disparate Data

An ERP does not provide the capability to understand all the existing sources and variations of existing disparate data. Only the common data architecture provides the capability to inventory and cross-reference existing data, and only people can understand existing disparate data and their degree of redundancy and variability.

Determining the Best Data Source

Disparate data have an average redundancy of 10 in many organizations, resulting in a dilemma about where to get the most accurate and current value for loading an ERP. The common data architecture, through the identification and cross-referencing of all existing data sources, provides the base to determine the best source for data for loading an ERP with the highest-quality data available to the organization.

Determining the Desired Data Form

Disparate data have many variations in form, often reaching a factor of 20 for some facts, resulting in a dilemma about what variation is best for an ERP. The common data architecture, through the identification and cross-referencing of all existing data forms, provides the base to determine the official form for data to load an ERP. In addition, data translation schemes are developed within the common data architecture to uniformly and consistently translate data from non-official forms to official forms.

Transforming Disparate Data

An ERP does not contain data transformation schemes for getting disparate data into the ERP in an efficient and effective manner. The common data architecture provides the proper data transformation schemes that ensure disparate data are properly transformed between all applications, including ERPs.

Product Logical Data Model

Many ERPs are not well documented with a proper logical data model. Most have, at best, a physical data model with minimal definitions for the data entities (tables) and data attributes (columns). By cross-referencing an ERP to the common data architecture, the logical data structure can be understood within a common context and specific definitions from the common data architecture can be applied to each data entity and data attribute in the ERP.

Specific Data Attribute Use

Most ERPs, even if well documented with a formal logical data model, do not define how each data attribute will be specifically used for an organization. Usually nonspecific fields, such as *customer name* and *problem priority* are provided. ERPs may even contain generic fields, like *attribute 1*, *attribute 2*, and *attribute 3*. Formally understanding every data attribute in an ERP within the common data architecture provides the base to determine specifically how each data attribute will be used, such as the customer's legal name and problem priorities of *1, 2,* and *3*.

Data Quality

Most ERPs do not have specific, precise data integrity rules for maintaining high-quality data. The development of data integrity rules is often left up to the organization implementing the ERP and is seldom accomplished to any degree. The common data architecture provides the capability to understand existing data integrity rules and define precise data integrity rules that ensure high-quality data in an ERP and maintain data quality across multiple ERPs.

Product Scope

A single ERP does not cover all the processes within an organization, often resulting in multiple ERPs to encompass all processes. Multiple ERPs require coordination and integration to ensure that they are used consistently to meet the organization's business information demand. The coordination and integration can be a monumental task that is beyond the capability of an ERP. The common data architecture provides a commonality across multiple ERPs that cannot be provided by any single ERP.

Site Implementation

Without proper coordination, an ERP could be implemented and used differently at different sites within the organization. It cannot ensure commonality across different sites. The common data architecture provides the capability to uniformly implement an ERP at all sites where possible while still meeting the unique needs at each site. It also provides the capability to handle the globalization of data in a multi-national organization.

Other In-House Applications

An ERP must co-exist with existing in-house applications, either because all existing applications cannot be replaced overnight or because some applications will never be replaced by ERP. The common data architecture provides the coordination and integration between existing in-house applications and ERPs that cannot be provided by any single ERP.

Product Evolution

The industry is in a period of rapidly evolving ERPs. ERPs evolve through successive versions that include new features and new data attributes. The changes in each version are usually generic to allow applicability to many organizations. The specific use of new data attributes must be defined the same as the specific use of the attributes in the original ERP were defined.

Product Replacement

ERPs, like any purchased application, often serve their usefulness and are replaced, may be abandoned by the vendor, or may be merged with other ERPs. All of these situations occur in the industry today. The common data architecture provides the capability to understand these situations and smoothly transit from one ERP to another.

Product Trends

ERPs are only the beginning of new enterprise application integration (EAI) and application clustering trends. As with most trends in the information technology discipline, it is not known specifically where these trends will lead and what will be the ultimate status of ERPs. The common data architecture provides the stability across evolving product trends.

Evaluational Data Evolution

ERPs may well evolve into packaged data marts or data warehouses for processing evaluational data. The common data architecture provides the capability to integrate operational data and evaluational data and to ensure that operational data are properly transformed into evaluational data. It also provides the capability to document evaluational data that results from the analysis of operational data.

The terms listed below are the terms defined and used in this book. This is not a complete glossary of all the terms related to a data architecture or to data resource management. They are just the terms relevant to the bad habits, good practices, and best practices related to data resource quality. Other books by the author can be consulted for a more complete glossary of terms.

Actual data resource scope: The actual portion of the data resource that is formally managed. See Data resource scope, Perceived data resource scope.

Alias data name: Any data name, other than the primary data name, for a fact or group of facts in the data resource. It may be formal or informal, abbreviated or unabbreviated, long or short. See Data name, Formal data name, Primary data name.

Analytical data normalization: Data normalization for data in the analytical tier that brings data into normal form for analytical processing. See Analytical tier, Data normalization, Operational data normalization, Predictive data normalization.

Analytical tier: The fourth tier of the five-tier concept, oriented toward verifying or disproving known or suspected trends and patterns. It supports true data warehousing and is considered to be in the aggregation space. See Analytical data normalization, Five-tier concept, Operational tier, Predictive tier.

Architectural bad habits: Bad habits that pertain to the architecture of the data resource, including informal data names, vague data definitions, improper data structure, imprecise data integrity rules, and limited data documentation. See Bad habits, Non-architectural bad habits.

Architectural good practices: The good practices related to the data architecture, including formal data names, comprehensive data definitions, proper data structure, precise data integrity rules, and robust data documentation. See Good practices, Non-architectural good practices.

Bad habit: With respect to data resource quality, something that is being done to ruin data resource quality. See

Architectural bad habits, Good practice, Habit, Non-architectural bad habits.

Base data type: A specific form of data within a data megatype, such as date, text, integer, and so on, for tabular data. It is commonly known as a data type today. See Data megatypes, Distinct data types.

Best practice: A good practice that leads to early benefits and successes. See Bad habit, Good practice, Practice.

Brute-force physical approach: The development of a physical data structure oriented toward database construction and implementation without the benefit of a logical data structure. There is little or no consideration for the business support provided by the data. The emphasis is on the physical schema at the exclusion of the other data schema.

Business data domain: The data values that are allowed with respect to the business and the conditions under which those data values are allowed. It represents what is reasonable for the business and provides more accurate data. See Data domain, Database data domain, Mathematical data domain.

Business data optionality: A specific statement about the presence of a data value, including the conditions under which that data value will be present. The choices are required, prevented, or optional, and they provide more accurate data. See Data optionality, Database data optionality.

Business event: A happening in the real world that is related to the business,

such as a sale, purchase, fire, or flood. See Business event happening, Business object.

Business event happening: The actual happening of a business event, such as a specific sale, purchase, fire, or flood. See Business event.

Business feature: A trait or characteristic of a business event or business object, such as name, size, color, or date. See Business event, Business object.

Business information demand: An organization's continuously increasing, constantly changing need for current, accurate, integrated information, often on short notice or very short notice, to support its business activities. It is a very dynamic demand for information to support the business.

Business intelligence value chain: A chain where value is added from the data resource, through each step to the support of business goals. Any level in the business intelligence value chain has no better quality than its supporting level.

Business key: A primary key based on data attributes meaningful to the business. See Foreign key, Physical Key, Primary key, Surrogate key.

Business object: A person, place, thing, or concept in the real world, such as a customer, river, city, or account. See Business event, Business object existence.

Business object existence: The actual existence of a business object, such as a specific person, river, vehicle, or account. See Business object.

Business schema: A schema representing the business transactions that occur in the real world. See Conceptual Schema, Data view schema, Deployment schema, External Schema, Internal schema, Logical schema, Physical schema.

Business term glossary: A list of terms and abbreviations used in the business and a definition of each of those terms and abbreviations. A business term glossary does not include all the data definitions or the references between business terms and the data resource. It does not contain all of the common words used in preparing formal data names or the abbreviations of words used in formal data names. It does contain a definition of business terms and abbreviations and cross-references between business terms.

Butcher-paper diagram: A slang term for a data-entity diagram that is very long, has many data relations running in cardinal directions, and is very difficult to interpret and understand. See Entity-relation diagram.

Cardinality: See Data cardinality.

Class word: A word that has a common meaning wherever it is used in a data attribute name. Some organizations use a very restricted set of class words that are closely aligned with the data types available in a database management system and some organizations use a less restricted set of class. See Common word.

Coded data value: Data values that have been encoded or shortened in some manner. See Data value.

Cognitive dissonance: The disharmony that is created when an individual's personal reality does not fit the actual reality of a situation. When a person perceives that the state of the data resource is pretty good and receives information that the state of the data resource is quite bad, there is a tremendous disharmony created. That person usually reacts in some way, such as ignoring the situation, denying that the situation exists, laying blame for the situation, or setting about correcting the situation. See Actual data resource scope, Perceived data resource scope.

Common data architecture: A formal, comprehensive data architecture that provides a common context within which all data are understood and integrated. It transcends all data in the data resource. See Data architecture, Integrated data architecture.

Common word: A word that has consistent meaning whenever it is used in a data name. See Class word, Data naming vocabulary.

Comparate: The opposite of disparate. See Disparate.

Comparate data: Data that are alike in kind, quality, and character and are without defect. They are concordant, homogeneous, nearly flawless, nearly perfect, high-quality data. See Comparate data resource, Disparate data.

Comparate data cycle: A self-perpetuating cycle where the use of comparate data is continually reinforced because people understand and trust the data. See Comparate data, Disparate data cycle.

Comparate data resource: A data resource that is composed of comparate data that adequately support the current and future business information demand. The data are easily identified and understood, readily accessed and shared, and utilized to their fullest potential. A comparate data resource is an integrated, subject-oriented data resource. See Comparate data, Disparate data resource.

Comprehensive data definition: A formal data definition that provides a complete, meaningful, easily read, readily understood definition that thoroughly explains the content and meaning of the data. See Vague data definition.

Conceptual schema: A schema that is the common denominator between the internal schema and the external schema. It was added to the two-schema concept to create the three-schema concept. See Business schema, Data view schema, Deployment schema, External schema, Internal schema, Logical schema, Physical schema, Three-schema concept, Two-schema concept.

Conditional data structure rule: A data rule that specifies the data cardinality for a data relation when conditions or exceptions apply. See Conditional data value rule, Data derivation rule, Data retention rule, Data rule, Data structure rule, Data value rule.

Conditional data value rule: A data rule that specifies the domain of allowable values for a data attribute when there are conditions or exceptions that apply. It specifies both the conditions for optionality and the conditions for a relationship between data values in different data attributes. See Conditional data structure rule, Data derivation rule, Data retention rule, Data rule, Data structure rule, Data value rule.

Cross-system reporting: The collection of current operational data from a variety of different, often disparate, operational databases for the purpose of integrated reporting and operational decision-making. These data exist in the data space and are not considered part of true data warehousing even though a data warehouse application may be used to process the reports. See Data mining, Data warehousing, Operational processing.

Data: The individual raw facts that are out of context, have no meaning, and are difficult to understand. The term is used to represent the individual facts that are contained in a data resource. In this context, the term is considered plural the same as facts would be plural. See Data in context, Data resource, Information.

Data accuracy: A component of data fidelity that measures how well the data values represent the real world at a point in time. See Data completeness, Data fidelity, Data integrity.

Data architecture (1): A component of the data resource framework that includes the formal names and comprehensive definitions of data (data description), the proper structure of data, improved data fidelity, and robust data resource documentation. Data fidelity includes data integrity, data accuracy, and data completeness. See Data availability, Data management, Data resource framework.

Data architecture (2): The science and method of designing and constructing an integrated data resource that is business driven, based on real-world objects and events as perceived by the organization, and implemented into appropriate operating environments. It is the overall structure of a data resource that provides a consistent foundation across organizational boundaries to provide easily identifiable, readily available, high-quality data to support the business information demand. See Common data architecture, Integrated data architecture.

Data architecture value chain: The part of the data resource value chain that includes the five sets of architectural good practices. See Data management value chain, Data resource value chain.

Data attribute: Represents a variant of a fact about a data entity. It represents a data characteristic variation in a logical data structure. A data entity is described by a set of data attributes. See Data characteristic variation, Data entity.

Data attribute retention rule: A data retention rule that specifies how long the data values are retained and what is to be done with those data values when their usefulness is over. The rule applies to specific data values rather than to the entire data occurrence. See Data occurrence retention rule, Data retention rule.

Data attribute structure: A list that shows the data attributes contained within a data entity and the roles played by those data attributes. See Data item structure, Entity-relation diagram, File-relation diagram.

Data availability (1): The process of ensuring that the data are available to meet the business information demand while properly protecting and securing those data.

Data availability (2): A component of the Data Resource Framework ensuring that the data are available to meet the business information demand while properly protecting and securing those data. The data must be readily available to support business activities, but they must be protected enough to ensure proper access and recoverability in the event of a human or natural disaster. See Data architecture, Data management, Data resource framework.

Data cardinality: The number of data occurrences allowed on either side of a data relation. See Data relation, General data cardinality, Specific data cardinality.

Data characteristic: An individual characteristic that describes a data subject. It represents a single or combined fact about a data subject. Each data subject is described by a set of data characteristics. See Data characteristic variation.

Data characteristic substitution: The situation where any data characteristic variation can be used for a data characteristic, such as (Date) means any form of the date. See Data characteristic.

Data characteristic thesaurus: A list of synonyms and related terms that help people find the data characteristics that support their business information needs. It is usually less useful than the data subject thesaurus, but can provide considerable benefit as the volume of comparate data grows. See Date subject thesaurus.

Data characteristic variation: A variation in the content or meaning of a data characteristic. It represents a variant of a fact about a data subject. Each data characteristic usually has multiple data characteristic variations in a disparate data resource. See data characteristic.

Data column: See Data item.

Data completeness: A component of data fidelity that measures how well the scope of the data resource meets the scope of the business information demand. See Data accuracy, Data fidelity, Data integrity.

Data denormalization: The process to adjust the normalized data structure for optimum performance in a specific operating environment without compromising the normalized data structure. See Data normalization.

Data derivation rule: A data rule that specifies the contributors, the algorithm, and the conditions for deriving a data value. It also specifies the conditions for rederiving those data values if necessary. See Conditional data structure rule, Conditional data value rule,

Data retention rule, Data rule, Data structure rule, Data value rule.

Data dilemma: The situation where the ability to meet the business information demand is being compromised by the continued development of large quantities of disparate data. See Disparate data shock.

Data domain: A set of allowable values for a data attribute. See Business data domain, Database data domain, Mathematical data domain.

Data entity: A person, place, thing, event, or concept about which an organization collects and manages data. It represents a data subject in a logical data model. See Data subject.

Data error: A data value that provides incorrect or false knowledge about the business, or about business objects and events that are important to the business. See Explicit data error, Implicit data error.

Data fidelity: One of the three components the data architecture component dealing with the quality of the data architecture. It consists of data integrity, data accuracy, and data completeness. See Data accuracy, Data completeness, Data integrity, Data resource framework.

Data file: A physical file of data that exists in a database management system, such as a computer file, or outside a database management system, such as a manual file. Also referred to as a data table in a relational database management system.

Data globalization: A situation where a multi-national organization must manage different languages, measurement units, time zones, monetary units, local laws and customs, holidays, and so on. All the cultural, political, and geographical considerations must be included in management of the data resource. See Tactical data steward.

Data heritage: The source of data and its original meaning at the time of capture. See Data lineage, Data tracking.

Data hierarchy aggregation: Identifies the level of aggregation of a hierarchy, such as the product hierarchy in a data warehouse.

Data in context: Facts that have meaning and can be readily understood. They are more than raw facts, but they are not yet information. See Data, Information.

Data instance: A set of data values for the facts in a data occurrence that are valid at a point in time or for a period of time. There are usually many data instances for each data occurrence, particularly when historical data are maintained. See Data occurrence.

Data integrity: A component of data fidelity that measures how well the data are maintained in the data resource after they are captured or created. It indicates the degree to which the data are unimpaired and complete according to a set of data integrity rules. See Data fidelity, Data integrity rule, Imprecise data integrity, Integrity, Precise data integrity.

Data integrity rule: A formal specification of the criteria that needs to be met to ensure that the data resource provides the correct information about the business. Low data integrity results from the poor specification or poor enforcement of data integrity rules. See Data integrity, Imprecise data integrity rule, Precise data integrity rule.

Data integrity violation: The situation that occurs when a data integrity rule is violated. See Data integrity rule, Data integrity violation action, Data integrity violation notification.

Data integrity violation action: The action taken with the data that fail the rule. The typical data actions are to override the error with meaningful data, to suspend the data pending further correction, to apply a default data value, to accept the data, or to delete the data. See Data integrity violation, Data integrity violation notification.

Data integrity violation notification: The action taken to notify someone that a data integrity rule has been violated so that further preventive action can be taken. The typical notifications are to notify someone immediately, log the failure and the data action taken for later review, or to ignore the failure and the data action taken. See Data integrity violation, Data integrity violation action.

Data item: An individual field in a data record. Also referred to as a data column in a relational database management system.

Data item structure: A list that shows the data items in a data file and the roles played by those data items. It is the physical version of a data attribute structure for implementation. See Data attribute structure, Entity-relation diagram, File-relation diagram.

Data lineage: The pathway from the data origin to its current location and alterations made to the data along that pathway. See Data heritage, Data tracking.

Data management: The component of the data resource framework that includes managing data as a resource of the organization, managing data by the same principles by which other resources are managed, ensuring that all stakeholders have responsibility for cooperatively managing the data resource, and integrating management of the data resource with business planning. See Data architecture, Data availability, Data resource framework.

Data management value chain: The part of the data resource value chain that includes the five sets of non-architectural good practices. See Data architecture value chain, Data management value chain.

Data megatype: A major grouping of data based on their overall structure and physical management, such as spatial data, image data, textual data, and so on. See Base data types, Distinct data types, Non-tabular data, Tabular data.

Data mining: The analysis of historical data to identify unknown or unsuspected trends and patterns in the business. It is referred to as predictive processing and the data modeling that supports it is referred to as rotational data modeling. It exists in the influence and variation space, and uses different forms of analysis, such as artificial intelligence and fuzzy logic. See Cross-system reporting, Data warehousing, Operational processing.

Data name: A label for a fact or set of facts contained in the data resource or displayed on screens, reports, or other documents. See Data naming convention, Data naming taxonomy, Data naming vocabulary, Formal data name, Informal data name.

Data name abbreviation algorithm: A formal procedure for abbreviating the primary data name using an established set of data name word abbreviations. See Data name word abbreviation.

Data name homonym: Different facts in the data resource that are labeled with the same data name. See Data name, Data name synonym, Informal data name.

Data name synonym: The same fact that is labeled with more than one data name in different parts of the data resource. See Data name, Data name homonym, Informal data name.

Data name word abbreviation: A formal abbreviation for each word used in a data name. The abbreviation must be unique for the root word and for all manifestations of that root word, and it must not create another word. See Data name abbreviation algorithm.

Data naming convention: A traditional method to name data that was replaced by the formal data naming taxonomy. See Data naming taxonomy.

Data naming taxonomy: A method to provide a primary name for all existing and new data, and all components in the data resource within the common data architecture. It also provides a way to uniquely designate other features in the data resource. See Data naming convention, Data naming vocabulary.

Data naming vocabulary: The collection of all sets of common words that supports the data naming taxonomy by providing consistency to the words used in the data name. Some of the common words are organization dependent and other common words are consistent across organizations. See Common word, Data naming taxonomy.

Data normalization: The process that brings data into normal form that minimizes redundancies and keeps anomalies from entering the data resource. It provides a subject-oriented data resource that is based on business objects and events. See Analytical normalization, Data denormalization, Operational data normalization, Partial key dependencies, Predictive data normalization.

Data occurrence: A logical record that represents one existence of a business object or one existence of a business event happening in the real world. See Business event, Business object, Data instance.

Data occurrence group: A set of data occurrences that were selected based on some criteria, such as employees that are certified as pilots. See Data occurrence.

Data occurrence retention rule: A data retention rule that specifies how long the data occurrence is retained and what is done with that data occurrence when its usefulness is over. The rule applies to all data values in that data occurrence. See Data attribute retention rule, Data retention rule.

Data occurrence role: A role played by a specific data occurrence, such as a maintenance vendor or a lease vendor. See Data occurrence.

Data optionality: Shows whether a data value is required or is optional. In many situations these labels are not specific. See Business data optionality, Database data optionality.

Data owner: Not used in the common data architecture. See Data steward.

Data physicalization: The rampant changes to the data independent of any logical data structure.

Data quality: The quality, or accuracy, of the data values. It is only one small part of the overall data resource quality. See Data resource quality.

Data record: A physical grouping of data items that are stored in or retrieved from a data file. Also referred to as a data row in a relational database management system.

Data redundancy: The unknown and unmanaged duplication of data. See Data replication.

Data relation: An association between data occurrences in different data subject or within the same data subject. See Entity-relation diagram.

Data replication: The consistent copying of data from one official source to multiple secondary sources. The data are in synch and all represent the same version of truth about the data resource. See Redundant data.

Data resource: Represents a collection of data, or facts, within a specific scope. It is singular, such as the customer data resource, the environmental data resource, or the enterprise data resource.

Data resource data: Any data that document the data resource. It replaces the term metadata. See Metadata, Semantic data resource data, Technical data resource data.

Data resource direction: The course of data resource development toward a particular goal or objective. See Data resource scope, Data resource vision.

Data resource drift: The natural, steady drift of a data resource toward disparity if its development is not properly managed and controlled. See Disparate data resource.

Data resource framework: A framework that contains three major components for the management, architecture, and availability of data. It directly supports the data resource value chain. See Data architecture, Data availability, Data management, Data resource value chain.

Data resource hazard: The existence of low-quality data just sitting in the data resource. The greater the volume of disparate data and the lower the quality of those data, the greater the hazard. See Data resource risk, Hazard.

Data resource horizon: The distance into the future that a person is interested in planning for data resource development. An unrealistic data resource horizon can be too nearsighted, too farsighted, or overly optimistic. See Data resource scope, Data resource vision.

Data resource quality: A measure of how well the organization's data resource supports the current and future business information demand of the organization. Ideally, the data resource should fully support all the current and future information needs of the organization to be considered a high-quality data resource. The degree to which the data resource supports the business information demand is the level of data resource quality. See Business information demand, Information quality.

Data resource risk: The chance that the disparate data will be used and adversely impact the business. If the disparate data just sit there and are never used, there is no impact to the business. See Data resource hazard, Risk.

Data resource scope: The portion of the total data resource available to an organization that is formally managed. See Actual data resource scope, Data megatypes, Data resource horizon, Data resource vision, Perceived data resource scope, Scope.

Data resource value chain: A value chain that improves data resource quality and ultimately results in a compare data resource that fully meets the current and future business information demand. See Data architecture value chain, Data management value chain.

Data resource vision: An intelligent foresight for the data resource that includes the scope of the data resource, its development direction, and the planning horizon. See Data resource horizon, Data resource scope, Expanded data resource vision, Restricted data resource vision, Vision

Data retention rule: A data rule that specifies how long data values are retained in a particular database and what is done with data values when their usefulness in that database is over. The usefulness is with respect to where the data values are located, and the retention is with respect to the organization at large. See Conditional data structure rule, Conditional data value rule, Data attribute retention rule, Data derivation rule, Data occurrence retention rule, Data rule, Data structure rule, Data value rule.

Data row: See Data record.

Data rule: A subset of business rules that deal with the data column of the Zachman Framework. It specifies the criteria for maintaining the quality of the data

architecture. See Conditional data structure rule, Conditional data value rule, Data derivation rule, Data retention rule, Data structure rule, Data value rule.

Data site: Any location where data are stored, such as a database, a server, or a filing cabinet.

Data steward: A person who watches over the data and is responsible for the welfare of the data resource and its support of the business, particularly when the risks are high. See Detail data steward, Steward, Strategic data steward, Tactical data steward.

Data structure: A representation of the arrangement, relationship, and contents of data subjects, data entities, and data files in the common data architecture. See Improper data structure, Integrated data structure, Proper data structure.

Data structure rule: A data rule that specifies the data cardinality for a data relation when there are no conditions or exceptions that apply. See Conditional data structure rule, Conditional data value rule, Data derivation rule, Data retention rule, Data rule, Data value rule.

Data subject: A person, place, thing, concept, or event that is of interest to the organization and about which data are captured and maintained. Data subjects are defined from business objects and business events, and a compare data resource is built on data subjects. See Business event, Business object, Compare data resource.

Data subject thesaurus: A list of synonyms and related business terms that help people find the data subjects that support their business information needs. It is a list of business terms and alias data subject names that point to the formal data subject name. Any business term that could be used in the organization is listed with a reference to the data subject or data entities that may be related to that term. See Data characteristic thesaurus.

Data table: See Data file.

Data tracking: The data source, method of capture, storage location, movement between data sites, and processing for a set of data. See Data heritage, Data lineage.

Data value: Any value, such as a date, a name, or a description. See Data value rule, Default data value.

Data value rule: A data rule that specifies the domain of allowable values for a data attribute that applies for all situations. There are no conditions or exceptions placed on the allowable values. See Conditional data structure rule, Conditional data value rule, Data derivation rule, Data retention rule, Data rule, Data structure rule.

Data version: Identifies the specific version of data, such as a date or a timeframe.

Data view schema: The structure of the data as normalized into data entities. It was the original external schema. See Business schema, Conceptual schema, Deployment schema, External schema, Internal schema, Logical schema, Physical schema.

Data warehousing: The analysis of historical data to verify or disprove known or suspected trends or patterns in the business. These historical data and the results of the analysis are referred to as evaluational data. It is referred to as analytical processing and the data modeling that supports it is referred to as dimensional modeling. It exists in the aggregation space and uses traditional statistical analysis. See Cross-system reporting, Data mining, Operational processing.

Database data domain: The values allowed with respect to the database management system. They are usually general data types, such as text, integer, or date. See Business data domain, Data domain, Mathematical data domain.

Database data optionality: A general statement about the requirements of a data value with respect to a database management system. The choices are usually required or optional because the database management system cannot handle specific conditions. See Business data optionality, Data optionality.

Default data value: A data value that is automatically entered when no other data value is readily available.

Deployment schema: A schema showing the distribution of data on a network. It is one of the schema added to the three-schema concept to create the five-schema concept. See Business schema,

Conceptual schema, Data view schema, External schema, Five-schema concept, Logical schema, Physical schema, Three-schema concept.

Detail data steward: A person who is knowledgeable about the data by reason of their intimate familiarity with the data. That person is usually a knowledge worker who has been directly involved with the data for a considerable period of time. The detail data steward is responsible for developing the data architecture and the data resource data. Such persons have no decision-making authority for setting directions for the data resource or committing resources to data resource development. See Data steward, Strategic data steward, Tactical data steward.

Detail tier: The lowest tier in the three-tier concept that is appropriate for data analysts and database technicians. See Strategic tier, Tactical tier, Three-tier concept.

Disparate: Fundamentally distinct or different in kind; entirely dissimilar. See Compare.

Disparate data: Data that are essentially not alike, or are distinctly different in kind, quality, or character. They are unequal and cannot be readily integrated. They are low-quality, defective, discordant, ambiguous, heterogeneous data. See Compare data, Disparate data resource, Massively disparate data.

Disparate data cycle: A self-perpetuating cycle where disparate data are continuing to be produced at an ever-increasing rate because people either do not know about existing data or do not want to use existing data. See Compare data cycle, Disparate data, Disparate data spiral.

Disparate data resource: A data resource that is substantially composed of disparate data that are dis-integrated and not subject oriented. It is in a state of disarray, it does not, and it cannot, adequately support the business information demand. See Compare data resource, Disparate data.

Disparate data shock: The sudden realization that a data dilemma exists in the organization and it is severely impacting an organization's ability to be responsive to changes in the business environment. It is the panic that an organization has about the poor state of its data resource. See Data dilemma.

Disparate data spiral: The spiraling increase in data disparity from current technologies into new technologies. Both the volumes of disparate data and the complexity of that disparity are increasing. See Disparate data cycle.

Distinct data type: A data unit or style within a base data type, such as meters, yards, inches, and so on, for measurements. It has no equivalent in current database management systems. See Base data types, Data megatypes.

Domain: See Data domain.

Enterprise data resource: See Compare data resource.

Entity-relation diagram: A diagram showing only data entities and the data relations between those data entities. See Data attribute structure, Data item structure, Data relation, File-relation diagram.

Evaluational data: Subject-oriented, integrated, time-variant, non-volatile data in support of management decision-making. They are usually historical, are derived from operational data, and contain many levels of summarization above the operational data. See Operational data.

Expanded data resource vision: A data resource vision that has a wider data resource scope that ultimately includes the total data resource that is available to the organization. It needs to include data that are not business critical or of enterprise-wide importance, non-tabular data, historical data, and non-automated data. See Data resource scope, Data resource vision, Restricted data resource vision.

Explicit data error: A data error that is readily visible and known. It is routinely identified and made apparent through data edits. See Data error, Implicit data error.

External data resource quality: Data quality related to how citizens or customers perceive the data quality based on the services or products they receive. See Data resource quality, Internal data resource quality.

External schema: A schema representing the way data were used by applications. See Business schema, Conceptual schema, Data view schema, Deployment schema, Internal schema, Logical schema, Physical schema.

File-relation diagram: A diagram that shows the data files and the data relations between them as they are to be implemented. See Data relation, Entity-relation diagram, Data attribute structure, Data item structure.

Five-schema concept: A concept in the detail tier that consists of a business schema, a data view schema, a logical schema, a deployment schema, and a physical schema. It was developed from the three-schema concept. See Business schema, Data view schema, Deployment schema, Logical schema, Physical schema, Three-tier concept.

Five-tier concept: An expansion of the three-tier concept that includes two additional tiers for analytical data and predictive data. See Analytical tier, Operational tier, Predictive tier, Three-tier concept.

Foreign key: The primary key of a parent data entity that is contained in a subordinate data entity to identify its parent data occurrence. See Business key, Physical key, Primary key.

Formal: Having an outward form or structure, being in accord with accepted conventions, consistent and methodical, or being done in a regular form. See Formal data name.

Formal data name: A data name that readily and uniquely identifies a fact or group of facts in the data resource. It is developed within a formal data naming taxonomy and is abbreviated, when necessary, with a formal set of abbreviations and an abbreviation algorithm. See Alias data name, Data naming taxonomy, Data naming vocabulary, Informal data name.

Formal data name abbreviation: The formal shortening of a primary data name to meet a length restriction according to formal data name word abbreviations and a formal data name abbreviation algorithm. See Data name abbreviation algorithm, Data name word abbreviation, Informal data name abbreviation.

Fundamental data: Data that are not stored in databases and are not used in applications, but support the definition of specific data. See Fundamental data definition, Specific data.

Fundamental data definition: The data definitions for fundamental data. See Fundamental data.

Fundamental data integrity rule: A data integrity rule that can apply to many specific data values. The data integrity rule is defined once and is applied to many different situations. See Data integrity rule, Specific data integrity rule.

General data cardinality: The data cardinality indicated by semantic statements or the data relation between data entities. See Data cardinality, Data relation, Semantic statement, Specific data cardinality.

Good practice: With respect to data resource quality, describes something that should be done to achieve a high-quality data resource. See Bad habit, Best practice, Practice.

Habit: A recurrent, often unconscious pattern of behavior that is acquired through frequent repetition. It can be something that is routinely done that shouldn't be done or something that is routinely not done that should be done. See Bad habit.

Hazard: A possible source of danger or a circumstance that creates a dangerous situation. See Data resource hazard, Data resource risk, Risk.

Hidden data resource: The large quantities of data that are maintained by the organization that are largely unknown, unavailable, and unused because people are either not aware that the data exist or do not understand the data.

Implicit data error: A data error that is hidden and is only known through real-time discovery. It is not routinely identified through data edits and is not readily apparent. See Data error, Explicit data error.

Imprecise: Means not precise, not clearly expressed, indefinite, inaccurate, incorrect, or not conforming to proper form. See Imprecise data integrity rule, Precise.

Imprecise data integrity rule: Data integrity rule that does not provide adequate criteria to ensure high-quality data values and results in data errors. See Data integrity rule, Precise data integrity rule.

Improper: Not suited to the circumstances or needs. See Improper data structure.

Improper data structure: A data structure that does not provide an adequate representation of the data supporting the business for the intended audience. See Data structure, Proper data structure.

Inadequate: Insufficient, or not adequate to fulfill a need or meet a requirement. See Inadequate data responsibility.

Inadequate data responsibility: The situation where the responsibility as defined does not fulfill the need for properly managing a shared data resource. The responsibility is casual, lax, inconsistent, uncoordinated, and not suitable for the current environment of a shared resource. Any responsibilities that do exist are usually developed independently, are incomplete, and are largely unknown to the organization at large. Simply put, there are no formal responsibilities for the management of a critical resource. See Adequate data responsibility.

Informal: Casual, not in accord with prescribed form, unofficial, or inappropriate for the use intended. See Informal data name.

Informal data name: Data names that are casual and inappropriate for their intended use to readily and uniquely identify each fact or group of facts in the data resource. There is no formality, no structure, no nomenclature, and no taxonomy to informal data names. See Formal data name, Data naming taxonomy, Data naming vocabulary.

Informal data name abbreviation: The situation where there is no formality to the data name abbreviations. See Formal data name abbreviations.

Information: A set of data in context with relevance to one or more people at a point in time or for a period of time. Information is more than data in context; it must have relevance and a time frame. See Data, Data in context.

Information quality: A measure of the ability to get the right data, to the right people, in the right place, at the right time, in the right form, at the right cost, so they can make the right decisions and take the right actions. See Data resource quality.

Instance: See Data instance.

Integrated data resource: A data resource where the data are integrated within a single, organization-wide, common data architecture. See Common data architecture, Comparate data resource, Subject oriented data resource.

Integrity: The state of being unimpaired, the condition of being whole or complete, or the steadfast adherence to strict rules. See Data integrity, Data integrity rule, Imprecise data integrity, Precise data integrity.

Internal data resource quality: Data quality related to how well the data resource meets the current and future business information demand. See Data resource quality, External data resource quality.

Internal schema: A schema that represents the way data are stored in a data file. See Business schema, Conceptual schema, Data view schema, Deployment schema,

External schema, Logical schema, Physical schema.

Limited data documentation: Limited data documentation includes any documentation about the data resource that is sparse, incomplete, out of date, incorrect, inaccessible, unknown, poorly presented, poorly understood, and so on. Documentation has typically been an after-the-fact task that needed to be done to complete a project. See Robust data documentation.

Logical schema: The structure of the data by data entities as optimized from the data view schema. It was the original conceptual schema. See Business schema, Conceptual schema, Data view schema, Deployment schema, External schema, Internal schema, Physical schema.

Lost productivity cycle: A cycle where more and more time is spent reactively resolving problems leaving less and less time to be proactive and prevent problems.

Massively disparate data: The existence of large quantities of disparate data within a large organization or across many organizations involved in similar business activities. See Disparate data.

Mathematical data domain: The data values that are possible mathematically in a data attribute. It is usually the maximum range of data values allowed. See Business data domain, Data domain, Database data domain.

Metadata: Commonly defined as data about the data, but more recently it refers to documentation about the data.

Data resource data is becoming a more useful term. See Data resource data.

Multiple fact data attribute: A data attribute that contains more than one fact. See Data attribute, Multiple value data attribute, Single fact data attribute.

Multiple value data attribute: A data attribute that contains multiple values of the same fact or of different facts. See Data attribute, Multiple fact data attribute, Single fact data attribute.

Non-architectural bad habits: Bad habits that pertain to the availability and management of the data resource, including an unreasonable data orientation, unacceptable data availability, inadequate data responsibility, restricted data vision, and inappropriate data recognition. See Architectural bad habits, Bad habits.

Non-architectural good practices: The good practices that pertain to the availability and management of the data resource, including reasonable data orientation, acceptable data availability, adequate data responsibility, expanded data vision, and appropriate data recognition. See Architectural good practices, Good practices.

Non-tabular data: Any data that are not generally maintained in traditional databases or typically displayed in tabular form, such as spatial, textual, voice, image, and video data. See Tabular data.

Occurrence: See Data occurrence.

Operational data: Subject-oriented, integrated, time-current, volatile data in support of day-to-day operations and operational decision-making. They are detailed, largely primitive data necessary to keep the organization operating. See Evaluational data.

Operational data normalization: Data normalization for the operational tier that brings data into normal form for operational processing. See Data normalization, Operational tier.

Operational processing: The day-to-day transactional processing using current operational data to perform the business activities. The operational data exist in the data space and the data modeling that supports the operational data is referred to as relational modeling. See Cross-system reporting, Data mining, Data warehousing.

Operational tier: The third tier of the three-tier concept oriented toward the data necessary to maintain the day-to-day business operations. Mathematically, it is considered to be in the data space. See Analytical tier, Five-tier concept, Predictive tier, Three-tier concept.

Optionality: See Data optionality.

Perceived data resource scope: The portion of the data resource that is perceived to be formally managed. See Data resource scope, Actual data resource scope.

Physical key: A primary key generated by database technicians or the database management system. It is usually meaningless to the business. See Business key, Foreign key, Primary key.

Physical–logical data structure: A data structure that is really a physical data structure but is claimed to be a logical data structure. See Physical-physical data structure.

Physical–physical data structure: A physical data structure that is truly a physical data structure representing implementation of the data. See Physical-logical data structure.

Physical schema: The structure of the data as denormalized and physically implemented. It was the original internal schema. See Business schema, Conceptual schema, Data view schema, Deployment schema, External schema, Internal schema, Logical schema.

Plausible deniability: The ability of an organization to deny the fact that their data resource is disparate and live with an illusion of high data quality. What an organization believes about their data resource quality and the real data resource quality are often quite different. Organizations do not want to believe their data resource quality is bad and certainly do not want to admit it to anyone.

Practice: To perform something habitually, customarily, or repeatedly. See Best practice, Good practice.

Precise: Clearly expressed, definite, accurate, correct, and conforming to proper form. See Imprecise, Precise data integrity rule.

Precise data integrity rule: A data integrity rule that precisely specifies the criteria for high-quality data values and reduces or eliminates data errors. The consistent application and enforcement of those rules ensure high-quality data values. See Data integrity rule, Imprecise data integrity rule.

Predictive data normalization: Data normalization for the predictive tier that brings data into formal form for predictive processing. See Analytical data normalization, Data normalization, Operational data normalization, Predictive tier.

Predictive tier: The fifth tier of the five-tier concept, oriented toward discovering unknown or unsuspected trends and patterns. It supports true data mining and is considered to be a combination of the variation and influence spaces. See Analytical tier, Five-tier concept, Operational tier.

Primary data name: The formal data name that is fully spelled out, real world, unabbreviated, untruncated, business name of the data that has no special characters or length limitations. See Alias data name, Data name.

Primary key: One or more data attributes that uniquely identify each data occurrence in a data subject. See Business key, Foreign key, Physical key.

Primary productivity loss: This productivity loss related to the understanding and use of a disparate data resource. See Secondary productivity loss, Tertiary productivity loss.

Proper data structure: A data structure that provides a suitable representation of the business and the data resource supporting that business, and that is relevant

to the intended audience. See Data structure, Improper data structure.

Redundant data: Data that are inconsistently developed from multiple sources or by different methods. They are not in synch and represent conflicting versions of truth about the data resource. See Data replication.

Restricted data resource vision: A data resource vision where the scope of the data resource is limited, the development direction is unreasonable, or the planning horizon is unrealistic. See Data resource vision, Expanded data resource vision.

Risk: The possibility of suffering harm or loss from some event; a chance that something will happen. See Data resource risk, Hazard.

Robust data documentation: Documentation about a data resource that is complete, current, understandable, non-redundant, readily available, and known to exist. See Limited data documentation.

Schema: A data structure. See Business schema, Conceptual schema, Data view schema, Deployment schema, External schema, Internal schema, Logical schema, Physical schema.

Scope: The range of a person's perceptions, the breadth or opportunity to function, or the area covered by a given activity. See Data resource scope.

Secondary productivity loss: The productivity loss that includes unnecessary business activities, such as legal appeals, suits, returned merchandise, protests, vandalism, and other actions against the organization that take resources to resolve. See Primary productivity loss, Tertiary productivity loss.

Self-defeating fallacy: The situation where no matter how much you believe that something can happen, if it is not possible it will not happen. It is the flip side of the self-fulfilling prophecy. See Self-fulfilling prophecy.

Self-fulfilling prophecy: The situation where if you really believe in something that can happen, and it is possible, it will happen. See Self-defeating fallacy.

Semantic data resource data: The data resource data that help people understand the data resource and use that data resource to support their business activities. They are the data that people need to fully utilize the data resource. They include things like primary data names, data definitions, logical data structure, and so on. See Data resource data, Technical data resource data.

Semantic statement: A statement that verbally describes the relationship between data entities. See data relation.

Silver bullet: An attempt to achieve some gain without any pain. The result of trying to achieve any gain without some pain is usually a minimal gain with considerable pain. In many situations the end state of a silver bullet is worse than the initial state; the situation got worse rather than better. Silver bullets just do not exist.

Single fact data attribute: A data attribute that represents single facts and single values of those facts with respect to the business needs. See Data attribute, Multiple fact data attribute, Multiple value data attribute.

Specific data: Data that are stored in databases and are used in applications. The definitions of specific data may inherit fundamental data definitions. See Fundamental data, Fundamental data definitions.

Specific data cardinality: A notation on the data relation, usually one on either end of the data relation, showing the specific data cardinality. See Data cardinality, Data relation, General data cardinality.

Specific data integrity rule: A data integrity rule that is defined specifically for one situation. See Data integrity rule, Fundamental data integrity rule.

Steward: The word comes from the old English term *sty ward*; a person who was the ward of the sty. Such people watched over the stock and were responsible for the welfare of the stock, particularly during the night when the risks to the welfare of the stock were high. See Data steward.

Strategic data steward: A person who has legal and financial responsibility for a major segment of the data resource. That person has decision-making authority for setting directions and committing resources for that segment of the data resource. The strategic data steward is usually an executive or upper level manager and usually has responsibility along organizational lines, such as the director of human resources is the strategic data steward for human resource data. See Data steward, Detail data steward, Tactical data steward.

Strategic tier: The top tier in the three-tier concept that is appropriate for executives and managers. See Detail tier, Tactical tier, Three-tier concept.

Structurally stable–business flexible: The concept that a logical data architecture can remain relatively stable across business changes and technology changes.

Suck and squirt approach: A slang term referring to the method of finding the record of reference or system of reference, *sucking* the data out of that reference, performing some minor or superficial *cleansing*, and *squirting* the data into a data warehouse or enterprise resource planning application.

Subject oriented data resource: A data resource that is built from data subjects that represent a business object or business event in the real world where most public and private sector organizations operate. See Business event, Business object, Compare data resource, Data subject, Integrated data resource.

Tabular data: Any data that are maintained in traditional databases and displayed in tabular form. See Non-tabular data.

Tactical data steward: A data steward who manages the international aspects of the data resource. The specific arrangements are different with each organization, but the basic principle is to provide an international aspect to development of the data resource. See Data globalization, Data steward, Detail data steward, Strategic data steward.

Tactical tier: The second tier in the three-tier concept that is appropriate for line managers and business clients. See Detail tier, Strategic tier, Three-tier concept.

Technical data resource data: The data resource data that technicians need to build, manage and maintain databases. They include things like physical data names and structures, data types and formats, file specifications and sizes, blocking factors, access methods, and so on. See Data resource data, Semantic data resource data.

Technically correct and culturally acceptable: A technique for developing entity-relation diagrams that are technically correct and are easy to understand by business clients. See Entity-relation diagram.

Tertiary productivity loss: The productivity loss that includes lost customers and sales in the private sector and the avoidance of regulations in the public sector. See Primary productivity loss, Secondary productivity loss.

Thesaurus: A list of synonyms and related terms that help people find a specific term that meets their needs. See Data characteristic thesaurus, Data subject thesaurus.

Three-schema concept: The concept that followed the two-schema concept and preceded the five-schema concept. It consisted of an internal schema, external schema, and conceptual schema. See Conceptual schema, External schema, Five-schema concept, Internal schema, Two-schema concept.

Three-tier concept: A concept of three tiers formed from the original conceptual schema. It consists of a strategic tier, a tactical tier, and a detail tier. See Conceptual schema, Detail tier, Five-tier concept, Strategic tier, Tactical tier.

Two-schema concept: A concept where there was an internal schema and an external schema. See External schema, Five-schema concept, Internal schema, Three-schema concept.

Vague data definition: Any data definition that does not thoroughly explain, in simple understandable terms, the real content and meaning of the data with respect to the business. Vague data definitions can be anything from a non-existent data definition to meaningless data definitions. See Comprehensive data definition.

Vision: Intelligent foresight, the manner in which one sees or conceives something, or a mental image produced by the imagination. See Data resource direction, Data resource vision, Expanded data resource vision, Restricted data resource vision.

Bibliography

Brackett, Michael H. *Developing Data Structured Information Systems.* Topeka, KS: Ken Orr and Associates, Inc., 1983.

———. "What's Our Current Situation?" *Software News,* October, 1983.

———. *Developing Data Structured Databases.* Englewood Cliffs, NJ: Prentice Hall, 1987.

———. *Practical Data Design.* Englewood Cliffs, NJ: Prentice Hall, 1990.

———. *Data Sharing Using a Common Data Architecture.* New York: John Wiley & Sons, Inc., 1994.

———. *The Data Warehouse Challenge: Taming Data Chaos.* New York: John Wiley & Sons, Inc., 1996.

———. "Integrating Spatial Data." *GeoInfo Systems,* September 1998.

———. "Transforming Disparate Data." *DM Review,* October 1998.

———. "Business Intelligence Value Chain." *DM Review,* March 1999.

———. "Data Resource Quality for the Intelligent Organization." *e-Strategy International,* June 2000.

Covey, Steven R. *The 7 Habits of Highly Effective People.* New York: Simon and Schuster, 1989.

Gleick, James. *Faster—The Acceleration of Just About Everything.* New York: Pantheon Books, 1999.

English, Larry P. *Improving Data Warehouse and Business Information Quality.* New York: John Wiley & Sons, Inc., 1999.

Hay, David C. *Data Model Patterns: Conventions of Thought.* New York: Dorset House Publishing, 1996.

Inmon, W.H., Zachman, John. A, and Geiger, Johathan G. *Data Stores, Data Warehousing, and the Zachman Framework.* New York: McGraw-Hill, 1997.

Pagels, Heinz. *The Cosmic Code*. New York: Bantam Books, 1983.

———. *Perfect Symmetry*. New York: Bantam Books, 1986.

———. *The Dreams of Reason*. New York: Simon and Schuster, 1988.

Spewak, Steven H., and Hill, Steven C. *Enterprise Architecture Planning*. Boston, MA: QED Publishing Group, 1993.

Zachman, J. A. (1987). "A Framework for Information Systems Architecture," *IBM Systems Journal* 26, no. 3: 276–292.

Index

Note: A page entry in bold font denotes that the term's definition is on that page. A page entry with an *f* indicates that the topic is discussed on that and following pages.

Acceptable data availability, 196
  adequate data accessibility, 197
  adequate data protection, 197–98, 203
  adequate data recovery, 198, 203
  appropriate data use, 199–200
  benefits, 200–03
  best practices, 202–04
  data management and, 276
  good practices, 197–200, 204–05
  impacts minimized, 201–02
  privacy protection, 199
  shared data resource, 201
  See also Data availability; Unacceptable data availability
Actual data resource scope, **226**
Adequate data responsibility, 207–08, 212
  benefits, 219–22
  best practices, 220–21, 223
  centralized control, 218–19, 221–22
  data management and, 276
  detail steward, 214–16
  data steward, 212–17, 221
  good practices, 212–19, 222, 223
  shared data resource, 220
  stewardship balance, 215–16
  strategic steward, 213–16
  tactical steward, 217
  See also Data steward; Inadequate data responsibility
Alias data name, **41**
Analytical data normalization, **180**
  See also Data normalization
Analytical tier, **177**–79
  See also Five-tier concept
Appropriate data recognition, 257
  best practices, 266–68
  business client involvement, 258–59
  business support, 265–66
  cost-effective, 256
  data management and, 276
  good practices, 257–65, 268
  justification, 264–65
  knowledge base, 259
  opportunistic approach, 262–63
  proof-positive perspective, 261–62
  within current budget, 259–61
  See also Inappropriate data recognition